Poems by John Keats

John Keats

KENNEBEC
CHIVERS

This Large Print edition is published by Kennebec Large Print, Waterville, Maine, USA and by AudioGO Ltd, Bath, England.
Kennebec Large Print, a part of Gale, Cengage Learning.
The text of this Large Print edition is unabridged.
Other aspects of the book may vary from the original edition.
Set in 16 pt. Plantin.

LIBRARY OF CONGRESS CATALOGING-IN-PUBLICATION DATA

Keats, John, 1795–1821.
  [Poems. Selections]
  Poems / by John Keats. — Large print ed.
    p. cm. — (Kennebec large print perennial favorites collection)
  Originally published: Boston : Ginn & Co., 1896.
  ISBN-13: 978-1-4104-3297-1 (pbk.)
  ISBN-10: 1-4104-3297-1 (pbk.)
  1. Large type books. I. Title.
PR4830.E96 2010
821'.7—dc22   2010039297

BRITISH LIBRARY CATALOGUING-IN-PUBLICATION DATA AVAILABLE

Originally published in the 19th century and is now in Public Domain in the United States and the United Kingdom.

U.K. Hardcover: 978 1 408 49389 2 (Chivers Large Print)
U.K. Softcover: 978 1 408 49390 8 (Camden Large Print)

Printed and bound in Great Britain by the MPG Books Group
1 2 3 4 5 6 7 14 13 12 11 10

CONTENTS

7

9

11

■ ■ ■ ■

POEMS
1817

■ ■ ■ ■

'What more felicity can fall to creature,
Than to enjoy delight with liberty.'
— SPENSER, *Fate of the Butterfly*

DEDICATION

To Leigh Hunt, Esq.

Glory and loveliness have pass'd away;
  For if we wander out in early morn,
  No wreathed incense do we see upborne
Into the east, to meet the smiling day:
No crowd of nymphs soft-voiced and young
   and gay,
  In woven baskets bringing ears of corn,
  Roses, and pinks, and violets, to adorn
The shrine of Flora in her early May.
But there are left delights as high as these.
  And I shall ever bless my destiny,
That in a time when under pleasant trees
  Pan is no longer sought, I feel a free,
A leafy luxury, seeing I could please,
  With these poor offerings, a man like thee.

'I stood tip-toe upon a little hill'

'Places of nestling green for poets made.'
                 — *Story of Rimini*

I stood tip-toe upon a little hill,
The air was cooling, and so very still,
That the sweet buds which with a modest
    pride
Pull droopingly, in slanting curve aside,
Their scantly leaved, and finely tapering
    stems,
Had not yet lost their starry diadems
Caught from the early sobbing of the morn.
The clouds were pure and white as flocks
    new shorn,
And fresh from the clear brook; sweetly they
    slept
On the blue fields of heaven, and then there
    crept
A little noiseless noise among the leaves,
Born of the very sigh that silence heaves:
For not the faintest motion could be seen
Of all the shades that slanted o'er the green.
There was wide wand'ring for the greediest
    eye,
To peer about upon variety;
Far round the horizon's crystal air to skim,
And trace the dwindled edgings of its brim;
To picture out the quaint, and curious bend-
    ing
Of the fresh woodland alley never ending;
Or by the bowery clefts, and leafy shelves,
Guess where the jaunty streams refresh them-
    selves.
I gazed awhile, and felt as light and free
As though the fanning wings of Mercury

Had play'd upon my heels: I was light-
    hearted,
And many pleasures to my vision started;
So I straightway began to pluck a posey
Of luxuries bright, milky, soft, and rosy.

A bush of May-flowers with the bees about
    them;
Ah, sure no tasteful nook would be without
    them;
And let a lush laburnum oversweep them,
And let long grass grow round the roots to
    keep them
Moist, cool, and green; and shade the violets,
That they may bind the moss in leafy nets.
A filbert hedge with wild briar overtwined,
And clumps of woodbine taking the soft wind
Upon their summer thrones; there too should
    be
The frequent chequer of a youngling tree,
That with a score of light green brethren
    shoots
From the quaint mossiness of aged roots:
Round which is heard a spring-head of clear
    waters,
Babbling so wildly of its lovely daughters,
The spreading blue-bells: it may haply mourn
That such fair clusters should be rudely torn
From their fresh beds, and scatter'd thought-
    lessly
By infant hands, left on the path to die.

Open afresh your round of starry folds,
Ye ardent marigolds!
Dry up the moisture from your golden lids,
For great Apollo bids
That in these days your praises should be
    sung
On many harps, which he has lately strung;
And when again your dewiness he kisses,
Tell him, I have you in my world of blisses:
So haply when I rove in some far vale,
His mighty voice may come upon the gale.

Here are sweet peas, on tip-toe for a flight
With wings of gentle flush o'er delicate white,
And taper fingers catching at all things,
To bind them all about with tiny rings.

Linger awhile upon some bending planks
That lean against a streamlet's rushy banks,
And watch intently Nature's gentle doings:
They will be found softer than ring-dove's
    cooings.
How silent comes the water round that bend!
Not the minutest whisper does it send
To the o'erhanging sallows: blades of grass
Slowly across the chequer'd shadows pass.
Why, you might read two sonnets, ere they
    reach
To where the hurrying freshnesses aye preach
A natural sermon o'er their pebbly beds;
Where swarms of minnows show their little
    heads,

Staying their wavy bodies 'gainst the streams,
To taste the luxury of sunny beams
Temper'd with coolness. How they ever
wrestle
With their own sweet delight, and ever nestle
Their silver bellies on the pebbly sand!
If you but scantily hold out the hand,
That very instant not one will remain;
But turn your eye, and they are there again.
The ripples seem right glad to reach those
cresses,
And cool themselves among the em'rald
tresses;
The while they cool themselves, they fresh-
ness give,
And moisture, that the bowery green may
live:
So keeping up an interchange of favours,
Like good men in the truth of their behav-
iours.
Sometimes goldfinches one by one will drop
From low-hung branches: little space they
stop.
But sip, and twitter, and their feathers sleek;
Then off at once, as in a wanton freak:
Or perhaps, to show their black and golden
wings,
Pausing upon their yellow flutterings.
Were I in such a place, I sure should pray
That nought less sweet might call my
thoughts away,
Than the soft rustle of a maiden's gown

Fanning away the dandelion's down;
Than the light music of her nimble toes
Patting against the sorrel as she goes.
How she would start, and blush, thus to be
    caught
Playing in all her innocence of thought!
O let me lead her gently o'er the brook,
Watch her half-smiling lips and downward
    look;
O let me for one moment touch her wrist;
Let me one moment to her breathing list;
And as she leaves me, may she often turn
Her fair eyes looking through her locks au-
    burne.
What next? A tuft of evening primroses,
O'er which the mind may hover till it dozes;
O'er which it well might take a pleasant sleep,
But that 'tis ever startled by the leap
Of buds into ripe flowers; or by the flitting
Of divers moths, that aye their rest are quit-
    ting;
Or by the moon lifting her silver rim
Above a cloud, and with a gradual swim
Coming into the blue with all her light.
O Maker of sweet poets! dear delight
Of this fair world and all its gentle livers;
Spangler of clouds, halo of crystal rivers,
Mingler with leaves, and dew and tumbling
    streams,
Closer of lovely eyes to lovely dreams,
Lover of loneliness, and wandering,
Of upcast eye, and tender pondering!

Thee must I praise above all other glories
That smile us on to tell delightful stories.
For what has made the sage or poet write
But the fair paradise of Nature's light?
In the calm grandeur of a sober line,
We see the waving of the mountain pine;
And when a tale is beautifully staid,
We feel the safety of a hawthorn glade:
When it is moving on luxurious wings,
The soul is lost in pleasant smotherings:
Fair dewy roses brush against our faces,
And flowering laurels spring from diamond
　　vases;
O'erhead we see the jasmine and sweet briar,
And bloomy grapes laughing from green at-
　　tire,
While at our feet, the voice of crystal bubbles
Charms　us　at　once　away　from　all　our
　　troubles:
So that we feel uplifted from the world,
Walking upon the white clouds wreath'd and
　　curl'd.
So felt he, who first told how Psyche went
On the smooth wind to realms of wonder-
　　ment;
What Psyche felt, and Love, when their full
　　lips
First touch'd; what amorous and fondling
　　nips
They gave each other's cheeks; with all their
　　sighs,

And how they kist each other's tremulous
    eyes:
The silver lamp, — the ravishment — the
    wonder —
The darkness — loneliness — the fearful
    thunder;
Their woes gone by, and both to heaven up-
    flown,
To bow for gratitude before Jove's throne.
So did he feel, who pull'd the boughs aside,
That we might look into a forest wide,
To catch a glimpse of Fauns, and Dryades
Coming with softest rustle through the trees;
And garlands woven of flowers wild, and
    sweet,
Upheld on ivory wrists, or sporting feet:
Telling us how fair, trembling Syrinx fled
Arcadian Pan, with such a fearful dread.
Poor nymph, — poor Pan, — how he did
    weep to find
Nought but a lovely sighing of the wind
Along the reedy stream; a half-heard strain,
Full of sweet desolation — balmy pain.

What first inspir'd a bard of old to sing
Narcissus pining o'er the untainted spring
In some delicious ramble, he had found
A little space, with boughs all woven round;
And in the midst of all, a clearer pool
Than e'er reflected in its pleasant cool
The blue sky, here and there serenely peep-
    ing,

Through tendril wreaths fantastically creep-
　　ing.
And on the bank a lonely flower he spied,
A meek and forlorn flower, with nought of
　　pride,
Drooping its beauty o'er the watery clear-
　　ness,
To woo its own sad image into nearness:
Deaf to light Zephyrus, it would not move;
But still would seem to droop, to pine, to
　　love.
So while the Poet stood in this sweet spot,
Some fainter gleamings o'er his fancy shot;
Nor was it long ere he had told the tale
Of young Narcissus, and sad Echo's bale.

Where had he been, from whose warm head
　　outflew
That sweetest of all songs, that ever new,
That aye refreshing, pure deliciousness,
Coming ever to bless
The wanderer by moonlight? to him bringing
Shapes from the invisible world, unearthly
　　singing
From out the middle air, from flowery nests,
And from the pillowy silkiness that rests
Full in the speculation of the stars.
Ah! surely he had burst our mortal bars:
Into some wond'rous region he had gone,
To search for thee, divine Endymion!

He was a Poet, sure a lover too,

Who stood on Latmus' top, what time there
  blew
Soft breezes from the myrtle vale below:
And brought, in faintness solemn, sweet and
  slow,
A hymn from Dian's temple; while upswell-
  ing,
The incense went to her own starry dwelling.
But though her face was clear as infant's eyes,
Though she stood smiling o'er the sacrifice,
The Poet wept at her so piteous fate,
Wept that such beauty should be desolate:
So in fine wrath some golden sounds he won,
And gave meek Cynthia her Endymion.

Queen of the wide air; thou most lovely
  queen
Of all the brightness that mine eyes have
  seen!
As thou exceedest all things in thy shine,
So every tale does this sweet tale of thine.
O for three words of honey, that I might
Tell but one wonder of thy bridal night!

Where distant ships do seem to show their
  keels,
Phœbus awhile delay'd his mighty wheels,
And turn'd to smile upon thy bashful eyes,
Ere he his unseen pomp would solemnise.
The evening weather was so bright, and clear,
That men of health were of unusual cheer;
Stepping like Homer at the trumpet's call,

Or young Apollo on the pedestal:
And lovely women were as fair and warm
As Venus looking sideways in alarm.
The breezes were ethereal, and pure,
And crept through half-closed lattices to cure
The languid sick; it cool'd their fever'd sleep,
And soothed them into slumbers full and
  deep.
Soon they awoke clear eyed: nor burnt with
  thirsting,
Nor with hot fingers, nor with temples burst-
  ing:
And springing up, they met the wond'ring
  sight
Of their dear friends, nigh foolish with de-
  light;
Who feel their arms, and breasts, and kiss,
  and stare,
And on their placid foreheads part the hair.
Young men and maidens at each other gazed,
With hands held back, and motionless,
  amazed
To see the brightness in each other's eyes;
And so they stood, fill'd with a sweet surprise,
Until their tongues were loosed in poesy.
Therefore no lover did of anguish die:
But the soft numbers, in that moment spo-
  ken,
Made silken ties, that never may be broken.
Cynthia! I cannot tell the greater blisses
That follow'd thine, and thy dear shepherd's
  kisses:

Was there a Poet born? — but now no
  more —
My wand'ring spirit must no farther soar.

Specimen of an Induction to a Poem

Lo! I must tell a tale of chivalry;
For large white plumes are dancing in mine
  eye.
Not like the formal crest of latter days,
But bending in a thousand graceful ways;
So graceful, that it seems no mortal hand,
Or e'en the touch of Archimago's wand,
Could charm them into such an attitude.
We must think rather, that in playful mood
Some mountain breeze had turn'd its chief
  delight
To show this wonder of its gentle might.
Lo! I must tell a tell of chivalry;
For while I muse, the lance points slantingly
Athwart the morning air: some lady sweet,
Who cannot feel for cold her tender feet,
From the worn top of some old battlement
Hails it with tears, her stout defender sent;
And from her own pure self no joy dis-
  sembling,
Wraps round her ample robe with happy
  trembling.
Sometimes, when the good knight his rest
  would take,
It is reflected, clearly, in a lake,

With the young ashen boughs, 'gainst which
    it rests,
And th' half-seen mossiness of linnets' nests.
Ah! shall I ever tell its cruelty,
When the fire flashes from a warrior's eye,
And his tremendous hand is grasping it,
And his dark brow for very wrath is knit?
Or when his spirit, with more calm intent,
Leaps to the honours of a tournament,
And makes the gazers round about the ring
Stare at the grandeur of the balancing!
No, no! this is far off: — then how shall I
Revive the dying tones of minstrelsy,
Which linger yet about lone gothic arches,
In dark green ivy, and among wild larches?
How sing the splendour of the revelries,
When butts of wine are drunk off to the lees?
And that bright lance, against the fretted wall,
Beneath the shade of stately banneral,
Is slung with shining cuirass, sword, and
    shield?
Where ye may see a spur in bloody field.
Light-footed damsels move with gentle paces
Round the wide hall, and show their happy
    faces;
Or stand in courtly talk by fives and sevens:
Like those fair stars that twinkle in the heav-
    ens.
Yet must I tell a tale of chivalry:
Or wherefore comes that steed so proudly
    by?

Wherefore more proudly does the gentle
  knight
Rein in the swelling of his ample might?

Spenser! thy brows are archèd, open, kind,
And come like a clear sunrise to my mind;
And always does my heart with pleasure
  dance,
When I think on thy noble countenance:
Where never yet was aught more earthly seen
Than the pure freshness of thy laurels green.
Therefore, great bard, I not so fearfully
Call on thy gentle spirit to hover nigh
My daring steps: or if thy tender care,
Thus startled unaware,
Be jealous that the foot of other wight
Should madly follow that bright path of light
Traced by thy lov'd Libertas; he will speak,
And tell thee that my prayer is very meek;
That I will follow with due reverence,
And start with awe at mine own strange
  pretence.
Him thou wilt hear; so I will rest in hope
To see wide plains, fair trees, and lawny slope;
The morn, the eve, the light, the shade, the
  flowers;
Clear streams, smooth lakes, and overlooking
  towers.

Calidore

A Fragment

Young Calidore is paddling o'er the lake;
His healthful spirit eager and awake
To feel the beauty of a silent eve,
Which seem'd full loth this happy world to
    leave,
The light dwelt o'er the scene so lingeringly.
He bares his forehead to the cool blue sky,
And smiles at the far clearness all around,
Until his heart is well-nigh overwound,
And turns for calmness to the pleasant green
Of easy slopes, and shadowy trees that lean
So elegantly o'er the waters' brim
And show their blossoms trim.
Scarce can his clear and nimble eyesight fol-
    low
The freaks and dartings of the black-wing'd
    swallow,
Delighting much to see it, half at rest,
Dip so refreshingly its wings and breast
'Gainst the smooth surface, and to mark
    anon
The widening circles into nothing gone.

And now the sharp keel of his little boat
Comes up with ripple, and with easy float,
And glides into a bed of water-lilies:
Broad-leaved are they, and their white cano-
    pies

Are upward turn'd to catch the heavens' dew
Near to a little island's point they grew;
Whence Calidore might have the goodliest
view
Of this sweet spot of earth. The bowery shore
Went off in gentle windings to the hoar
And light blue mountains: but no breathing
man,
With a warm heart, and eye prepared to scan
Nature's clear beauty, could pass lightly by
Objects that look'd out so invitingly
On either side. These gentle Calidore
Greeted, as he had known them long before.

The sidelong view of swelling leafiness,
Which the glad setting sun in gold doth dress,
Whence, ever and anon, the jay outsprings,
And scales upon the beauty of its wings.
The lonely turret, shatter'd and outworn,
Stands venerably proud; too proud to mourn
Its long-lost grandeur: fir-trees grow around,
Aye dropping their hard fruit upon the
ground.

The little chapel, with the cross above,
Upholding wreaths of ivy; the white dove,
That on the windows spreads his feathers
light,
And seems from purple clouds to wing its
flight.
Green tufted islands casting their soft shades
Across the lake; sequester'd leafy glades,

That through the dimness of their twilight
    show
Large dock-leaves, spiral foxgloves, or the
    glow
Of the wild cat's eyes, or the silvery stems
Of delicate birch-trees, or long grass which
    hems
A little brook. The youth had long been view-
    ing
These pleasant things, and heaven was be-
    dewing
The mountain flowers, when his glad senses
    caught
A trumpet's silver voice. Ah! it was fraught
With many joys for him: the warder's ken
Had found white coursers prancing in the
    glen:
Friends very dear to him he soon will see;
So pushes off his boat most eagerly.
And soon upon the lake he skims along,
Deaf to the nightingale's first under-song;
Nor minds he the white swans that dream so
    sweetly,
His spirit flies before him so completely.

And now he turns a jutting point of land,
Whence may be seen the castle gloomy and
    grand:
Nor will a bee buzz round two swelling
    peaches,
Before the point of his light shallop reaches

Those marble steps that through the water
  dip:
Now over them he goes with hasty trip,
And scarcely stays to ope the folding doors;
Anon he leaps along the oaken floors
Of halls and corridors.
Delicious sounds! those little bright-eyed
  things
That float about the air on azure wings,
Had been less heartfelt by him than the clang
Of clattering hoofs: into the court he sprang,
Just as two noble steeds, and palfreys twain,
Were slanting out their necks with loosen'd
  rein;
While from beneath the threat'ning portcul-
  lis
They brought their happy burthens. What a
  kiss,
What gentle squeeze he gave each lady's
  hand!
How tremblingly their delicate ankles
  spann'd!
Into how sweet a trance his soul was gone,
While whisperings of affection
Made him delay to let their tender feet
Come to the earth; with an incline so sweet
From their low palfreys o'er his neck they
  bent:
And whether there were tears of languish-
  ment,
Or that the evening dew had pearl'd their
  tresses,

He feels a moisture on his cheek, and blesses,
With lips that tremble, and with glistening
    eye,
All the soft luxury
That nestled in his arms. A dimpled hand,
Fair as some wonder out of fairyland,
Hung from his shoulder like the drooping
    flowers
Of whitest cassia, fresh from summer show-
    ers:
And this he fondled with his happy cheek,
As if for joy he would no further seek:
When the kind voice of good Sir Clerimond
Came to his ear, like something from beyond
His present being: so he gently drew
His warm arms, thrilling now with pulses
    new,
From their sweet thrall, and forward gently
    bending,
Thank'd heaven that his joy was never-
    ending;
While 'gainst his forehead he devoutly press'd
A hand heaven made to succour the
    distress'd;
A hand that from the world's bleak promon-
    tory
Had lifted Calidore for deeds of glory.

Amid the pages, and the torches' glare,
There stood a knight, patting the flowing hair
Of his proud horse's mane: he was withal
A man of elegance, and stature tall:

So that the waving of his plumes would be
High as the berries of a wild ash tree,
Or as the wingèd cap of Mercury.
His armour was so dexterously wrought
In shape, that sure no living man had thought
It hard, and heavy steel: but that indeed
It was some glorious form, some splendid
    weed,
In which a spirit new come from the skies
Might live, and show itself to human eyes.
'Tis the far-famed, the brave Sir Gondibert,
Said the good man to Calidore alert;
While the young warrior with a step of grace
Came up, — a courtly smile upon his face,
And mailèd hand held out, ready to greet
The large-eyed wonder and ambitious heat
Of the aspiring boy; who as he led
Those smiling ladies, often turn'd his head
To admire the visor arch'd so gracefully
Over a knightly brow; while they went by,
The lamps that from the high roof'd hall
    were pendent,
And gave the steel a shining quite transcen-
    dent.

Soon in a pleasant chamber they are seated;
The sweet-lipp'd ladies have already greeted
All the green leaves that round the window
    clamber,
To show their purple stars, and bells of am-
    ber.
Sir Gondibert has doff'd his shining steel,

Gladdening in the free and airy feel
Of a light mantle; and while Clerimond
Is looking round about him with a fond
And placid eye, young Calidore is burning
To hear of knightly deeds, and gallant spurn-
    ing
Of all unworthiness; and how the strong of
    arm
Kept off dismay, and terror, and alarm
From lovely woman: while brimful of this,
He gave each damsel's hand so warm a kiss,
And had such manly ardour in his eye,
That each at other look'd half-staringly:
And then their features started into smiles,
Sweet as blue heavens o'er enchanted isles.

Softly the breezes from the forest came,
Softly they blew aside the taper's flame;
Clear was the song from Philomel's far
    bower;
Grateful the incense from the lime-tree
    flower;
Mysterious, wild, the far-heard trumpet's
    tone;
Lovely the moon in ether, all alone:
Sweet too, the converse of these happy mor-
    tals,
As that of busy spirits when the portals
Are closing in the west; or that soft humming
We hear around when Hesperus is coming.
Sweet be their sleep. * * * *

To Some Ladies

What though, while the wonders of nature
   exploring,
  I cannot your light, mazy footsteps attend;
Nor listen to accents, that almost adoring,
   Bless Cynthia's face, the enthusiast's
   friend?

Yet over the steep, whence the mountain
   stream rushes,
  With you, kindest friends, in idea I muse;
Mark the clear tumbling crystal, its passionate gushes,
  Its spray, that the wild flower kindly be-
   dews.

Why linger ye so, the wild labyrinth strolling?
  Why breathless, unable your bliss to declare?
Ah! you list to the nightingale's tender con-
  doling,
  Responsive to sylphs, in the moonbeamy
  air.

'Tis morn, and the flowers with dew are yet
   drooping,
  I see you are treading the verge of the sea:
And now! ah, I see it — you just now are
   stooping
  To pick up the keepsake intended for me.

If a cherub, on pinions of silver descending,
   Had brought me a gem from the fretwork
     of heaven;
And, smiles with his star-cheering voice
   sweetly blending,
   The blessings of Tighe had melodiously
     given;

It had not created a warmer emotion
   Than the present, fair nymphs, I was blest
     with from you;
Than the shell, from the bright golden sands
   of the ocean,
   Which the emerald waves at your feet
     gladly threw.

For, indeed, 'tis a sweet and peculiar pleasure
   (And blissful is he who such happiness
     finds),
To possess but a span of the hour of leisure
   In elegant, pure, and aerial minds.

On receiving a Curious Shell and a Copy of Verses from the Same Ladies

Hast thou from the caves of Golconda, a gem
   Pure as the ice-drop that froze on the
     mountain?
Bright as the humming-bird's green diadem,
   When it flutters in sunbeams that shine
     through a fountain?

Hast thou a goblet for dark sparkling wine;

That goblet right heavy, and massy, and
  gold?
And splendidly marked with the story divine
  Of Armida the fair, and Rinaldo the bold?

Hast thou a steed with a mane richly flow-
  ing?
  Hast thou a sword that thine enemy's smart
  is?
Hast thou a trumpet rich melodies blowing?
  And wear'st thou the shield of the famed
  Britomartis?

What is it that hangs from thy shoulder so
  brave,
  Embroider'd with many a spring-peering
  flower?
Is it a scarf that thy fair lady gave?
  And hastest thou now to that fair lady's
  bower?

Ah! courteous Sir Knight, with large joy thou
  art crown'd;
  Full many the glories that brighten thy
  youth!
I will tell thee my blisses, which richly
  abound
  In magical powers to bless and to soothe.

On this scroll thou seest written in characters
  fair
  A sunbeamy tale of a wreath, and a chain:

And, warrior, it nurtures the property rare
  Of charming my mind from the trammels
  of pain.

This canopy mark: 'tis the work of a fay;
  Beneath its rich shade did King Oberon
  languish,
When lovely Titania was far, far away,
  And cruelly left him to sorrow and anguish.

There, oft would he bring from his soft-
  sighing lute
  Wild strains to which, spell-bound, the
  nightingales listen'd!
The wondering spirits of heaven were mute,
  And tears 'mong the dewdrops of morning
  oft glisten'd.

In this little dome, all those melodies strange,
  Soft, plaintive, and melting, for ever will
  sigh;
Nor e'er will the notes from their tenderness
  change,
  Nor e'er will the music of Oberon die.

So when I am in a voluptuous vein,
  I pillow my head on the sweets of the rose,
And list to the tale of the wreath, and the
  chain,
  Till its echoes depart; then I sink to repose.

Adieu! valiant Eric! with joy thou art
39

crown'd,
  Full many the glories that brighten thy
    youth,
I too have my blisses, which richly abound
  In magical powers to bless and to soothe.

To * * * *

Hadst thou lived in days of old,
O what wonders had been told
Of thy lively countenance,
And thy humid eyes, that dance
In the midst of their own brightness,
In the very fane of lightness;
Over which thine eyebrows, leaning,
Picture out each lovely meaning:
In a dainty bend they lie,
Like the streaks across the sky,
Or the feathers from a crow
Fallen on a bed of snow:
Of thy dark hair, that extends
Into many graceful bends;
As the leaves of hellebore
Turn to whence they sprung before;
And behind each ample curl
Peeps the richness of a pearl.
Downward too flows many a tress
With a glossy waviness,
Full, and round like globes that rise
From the censer to the skies
Through sunny air. Add too the sweetness
Of thy honey'd voice; the neatness
Of thine ankle lightly turn'd:

With those beauties, scarce discern'd,
Kept with such sweet privacy,
That they seldom meet the eye
Of the little loves that fly
Round about with eager pry.
Saving when, with freshening lave,
Thou dipp'st them in the taintless wave;
Like twin water-lilies, born
In the coolness of the morn.
O, if thou hadst breathèd then,
Now the Muses had been ten.
Couldst thou wish for lineage higher
Than twin-sister of Thalia?
At least for ever, evermore,
Will I call the Graces four.

Hadst thou lived when chivalry
Lifted up her lance on high,
Tell me what thou wouldst have been?
Ah! I see the silver sheen
Of thy broider'd floating vest
Cov'ring half thine ivory breast:
Which, O heavens! I should see,
But that cruel destiny
Has placed a golden cuirass there,
Keeping secret what is fair.
Like sunbeams in a cloudlet nested,
Thy locks in knightly casque are rested;
O'er which bend four milky plumes
Like the gentle lily's blooms
Springing from a costly vase.
See with what a stately pace

Comes thine alabaster steed;
Servant of heroic deed!
O'er his loins, his trappings glow
Like the northern lights on snow.
Mount his back! thy sword unsheath!
Sign of the enchanter's death;
Bane of every wicked spell;
Silencer of dragon's yell.
Alas! thou this wilt never do,
Thou art an enchantress too,
And wilt never surely spill
Blood of those whose eyes can kill.

To Hope

When by my solitary hearth I sit,
  And hateful thoughts enwrap my soul in
    gloom;
When no fair dreams before my 'mind's eye'
  flit,
  And the bare heath of life presents no
    bloom;
Sweet Hope! ethereal balm upon me shed,
And wave thy silver pinions o'er my head.

Whene'er I wander, at the fall of night,
  Where woven boughs shut out the moon's
    bright ray,
Should sad Despondency my musings fright,
  And frown, to drive fair Cheerfulness away,
Peep with the moonbeams through the leafy
  roof,
And keep that fiend Despondence far aloof.

Should Disappointment, parent of Despair,
  Strive for her son to seize my careless heart
When, like a cloud, he sits upon the air,
  Preparing on his spell-bound prey to dart:
Chase him away, sweet Hope, with visage
  bright,
And fright him, as the morning frightens
  night.

Whene'er the fate of those I hold most dear
  Tells to my fearful breast a tale of sorrow,
O bright-eyed Hope, my morbid fancy cheer;
  Let me awhile thy sweetest comforts bor-
  row:
Thy heaven-born radiance around me shed,
And wave thy silver pinions o'er my head!

Should e'er unhappy love my bosom pain,
  From cruel parents, or relentless fair,
O let me think it is not quite in vain
  To sigh out sonnets to the midnight air!
Sweet Hope! ethereal balm upon me shed,
And wave thy silver pinions o'er my head.

In the long vista of the years to roll,
  Let me not see our country's honour fade,
O let me see our land retain her soul,
  Her pride, her freedom; and not freedom's
  shade.
From thy bright eyes unusual brightness
  shed —
Beneath thy pinions canopy my head!

43

Let me not see the patriot's high bequest,
  Great liberty! how great in plain attire!
With the base purple of a court oppress'd,
  Bowing her head, and ready to expire:
But let me see thee stoop from heaven on
    wings
That fill the skies with silver glitterings!

And as, in sparkling majesty, a star
  Gilds the bright summit of some gloomy
    cloud:
Brightening the half-veil'd face of heaven
    afar:
  So, when dark thoughts my boding spirit
    shroud,
Sweet Hope! celestial influence round me
    shed,
Waving thy silver pinions o'er my head.

Imitation of Spenser

. . .

Now Morning from her orient chamber
    came,
And her first footsteps touch'd a verdant
    hill:
Crowning its lawny crest with amber
    flame,
Silv'ring the untainted gushes of its rill;
Which, pure from mossy beds, did down
    distil,
And after parting beds of simple flow-
    ers,

44

By many streams a little lake did fill,
Which round its marge reflected woven
  bowers,
And, in its middle space, a sky that never
 lowers.

  There the kingfisher saw his plumage
   bright,
  Vying with fish of brilliant dye below;
  Whose silken fins, and golden scales'
   light
  Cast upward, through the waves, a ruby
   glow:
  There saw the swan his neck of archèd
   snow,
  And oar'd himself along with majesty:
  Sparkled his jetty eyes; his feet did show
  Beneath the waves like Afric's ebony,
And on his back a fay reclined volup-
 tuously.

  Ah! could I tell the wonders of an isle
  That in that fairest lake had placèd been,
  I could e'en Dido of her grief beguile;
  Or rob from aged Lear his bitter teen:
  For sure so fair a place was never seen
  Of all that ever charm'd romantic eye:
  It seem'd an emerald in the silver sheen
  Of the bright waters; or as when on high,
Through clouds of fleecy white, laughs the
 cærulean sky.

And all around it dipp'd luxuriously
Slopings of verdure through the glossy
    tide,
Which, as it were in gentle amity,
Rippled delighted up the flowery side;
As if to glean the ruddy tears it tried,
Which fell profusely from the rose-tree
    stem!
Haply it was the workings of its pride,
In strife to throw upon the shore a gem
Outvying all the buds in Flora's diadem.

'Woman! when I behold thee flippant, vain'

Woman! when I behold thee flippant, vain,
    Inconstant, childish, proud, and full of fan-
    cies;
    Without that modest softening that en-
    hances
The downcast eye, repentant of the pain
That its mild light creates to heal again;
    E'en then, elate, my spirit leaps and
    prances,
    E'en then my soul with exultation dances,
For that to love, so long, I've dormant lain:
But when I see thee meek, and kind, and
    tender,
    Heavens! how desperately do I adore
Thy winning graces; — to be thy defender
    I hotly burn — to be a Calidore —
A very Red Cross Knight — a stout

46

Leander —
   Might I be loved by thee like these of yore.

Light feet, dark violet eyes, and parted hair;
  Soft dimpled hands, white neck and creamy
    breast;
  Are things on which the dazzled senses rest
Till the fond, fixed eyes forget they stare.
From such fine pictures, heavens! I cannot
    dare
  To turn my admiration, though unpossess'd
  They be of what is worthy, — though not
    drest
In lovely modesty, and virtues rare.
Yet these I leave as thoughtless as a lark:
  These lures I straight forget, — e'en ere I
    dine,
Or thrice my palate moisten: but when I mark
  Such charms with mild intelligences shine,
My ear is open like a greedy shark,
  To catch the tunings of a voice divine.
Ah! who can e'er forget so fair a being?
  Who can forget her half-retiring sweets?
  God! she is like a milk-white lamb that
    bleats
For man's protection. Surely the All-seeing,
Who joys to see us with his gifts agreeing,
  Will never give him pinions, who entreats
  Such innocence to ruin, — who vilely
    cheats
A dove-like bosom. In truth there is no free-
  ing

One's thoughts from such a beauty; when I
  hear
  A lay that once I saw her hand awake,
Her form seems floating palpable, and near:
  Had I e'er seen her from an arbour take
A dewy flower, oft would that hand appear,
  And o'er my eyes the trembling moisture
  shake.

EPISTLES

'Among the rest a shepheard (though but
  young
  Yet hartned to his pipe) with all the skill
His few yeeres could, began to fill his quill.'
          — BROWNE, *Britannia's Pastorals*

To George Felton Mathew

Sweet are the pleasures that to verse belong,
And doubly sweet a brotherhood in song;
Nor can remembrance, Mathew! bring to
  view
A fate more pleasing, a delight more true
Than that in which the brother Poets joy'd,
Who, with combinèd powers, their wit
  employ'd
To raise a trophy to the drama's muses.
The thought of this great partnership dif-
  fuses
Over the genius-loving heart, a feeling
Of all that's high, and great, and good, and
  healing.

Too partial friend! fain would I follow thee

Past each horizon of fine poesy;
Fain would I echo back each pleasant note,
As o'er Sicilian seas clear anthems float
'Mong the light skimming gondolas far
     parted,
Just when the sun his farewell beam has
     darted:
But 'tis impossible; far different cares
Beckon me sternly from soft 'Lydian airs,'
And hold my faculties so long in thrall,
That I am oft in doubt whether at all
I shall again see Phœbus in the morning:
Or flush'd Aurora in the roseate dawning!
Or a white Naiad in a rippling stream;
Or a rapt seraph in a moonlight beam;
Or again witness what with thee I've seen,
The dew by fairy feet swept from the green,
After a night of some quaint jubilee
Which every elf and fay had come to see:
When bright processions took their airy
     march
Beneath the curvèd moon's triumphal arch.

But might I now each passing moment give
To the coy muse, with me she would not live
In this dark city, nor would condescend
'Mid contradictions her delights to lend.
Should e'er the fine-eyed maid to me be kind,
Ah! surely it must be whene'er I find
Some flowery spot, sequester'd, wild, roman-
     tic,
That often must have seen a poet frantic;

Where oaks, that erst the Druid knew, are
    growing,
And flowers, the glory of one day, are blow-
    ing;
Where the dark-leaved laburnum's drooping
    clusters
Reflect athwart the stream their yellow lus-
    tres,
And intertwined the cassia's arms unite,
With its own drooping buds, but very white.
Where on one side are covert branches hung,
'Mong which the nightingales have always
    sung
In leafy quiet; where to pry, aloof
Atween the pillars of the sylvan roof,
Would be to find where violet beds were
    nestling,
And where the bee with cowslip bells was
    wrestling.
There must be too a ruin dark and gloomy,
To say, 'Joy not too much in all that's
    bloomy.'

Yet that is vain — O Mathew! lend thy aid
To find a place where I may greet the
    maid —
Where we may soft humanity put on,
And sit, and rhyme, and think on Chatter-
    ton;
And that warm-hearted Shakespeare sent to
    meet him

Four laurell'd spirits, heavenward to entreat
    him.
With reverence would we speak of all the
    sages
Who have left streaks of light athwart their
    ages:
And thou shouldst moralize on Milton's
    blindness,
And mourn the fearful dearth of human kind-
    ness
To those who strove with the bright golden
    wing
Of genius, to flap away each sting
Thrown by the pitiless world. We next could
    tell
Of those who in the cause of freedom fell;
Of our own Alfred, of Helvetian Tell;
Of him whose name to ev'ry heart's a solace,
High-minded and unbending William Wal-
    lace.
While to the rugged north our musing turns,
We well might drop a tear for him and Burns.

Felton! without incitements such as these,
How vain for me the niggard Muse to tease!
For thee, she will thy every dwelling grace,
And make 'a sunshine in a shady place':
For thou wast once a flow'ret blooming wild,
Close to the source, bright, pure, and unde-
    filed,
Whence gush the streams of song: in happy
    hour

Came chaste Diana from her shady bower,
Just as the sun was from the east uprising;
And, as for him some gift she was devising,
Beheld thee, pluck'd thee, cast thee in the
    stream
To meet her glorious brother's greeting
    beam.
I marvel much that thou hast never told
How, from a flower, into a fish of gold
Apollo changed thee: how thou next didst
    seem
A black-eyed swan upon the widening
    stream;
And when thou first didst in that mirror trace
The placid features of a human face;
That thou hast never told thy travels strange,
And all the wonders of the mazy range
O'er pebbly crystal, and o'er golden sands;
Kissing thy daily food from Naiads' pearly
    hands.

To my Brother George

Full many a dreary hour have I past,
My brain bewilder'd, and my mind o'ercast
With heaviness; in seasons when I've thought
No sphery strains by me could e'er be caught
From the blue dome, though I to dimness
    gaze
On the far depth where sheeted lightning
    plays;
Or, on the wavy grass outstretch'd supinely,

Pry 'mong the stars, to strive to think di-
    vinely:
That I should never hear Apollo's song,
Though feathery clouds were floating all
    along
The purple west, and, two bright streaks
    between,
The golden lyre itself were dimly seen:
That the still murmur of the honey-bee
Would never teach a rural song to me:
That the bright glance from beauty's eyelids
    slanting
Would never make a lay of mine enchanting,
Or warm my breast with ardour to unfold
Some tale of love and arms in time of old.

But there are times, when those that love the
    bay,
Fly from all sorrowing far, far away;
A sudden glow comes on them, nought they
    see
In water, earth, or air, but poesy.
It has been said, dear George, and true I hold
    it,
(For knightly Spenser to Libertas told it)
That when a Poet is in such a trance,
In air he sees white coursers paw and prance,
Bestridden of gay knights, in gay apparel,
Who at each other tilt in playful quarrel;
And what we, ignorantly, sheet-lightning call,
Is the swift opening of their wide portal,

When the bright warder blows his trumpet
    clear,
Whose tones reach nought on earth but
    Poet's ear,
When these enchanted portals open wide,
And through the light the horsemen swiftly
    glide,
The Poet's eye can reach those golden halls,
And view the glory of their festivals:
Their ladies fair, that in the distance seem
Fit for the silvering of a seraph's dream;
Their rich brimmed goblets, that incessant
    run,
Like the bright spots that move about the
    sun;
And when upheld, the wine from each bright
    jar
Pours with the lustre of a falling star.
Yet further off are dimly seen their bowers,
Of which no mortal eye can reach the flow-
    ers;
And 'tis right just, for well Apollo knows
'Twould make the Poet quarrel with the rose.
All that's reveal'd from that far seat of
    blisses,
Is, the clear fountains' interchanging kisses,
As gracefully descending, light and thin,
Like silver streaks across a dolphin's fin,
When he upswimmeth from the coral caves,
And sports with half his tail above the waves.

These wonders strange he sees, and many
    more,
Whose head is pregnant with poetic lore:
Should he upon an evening ramble fare
With forehead to the soothing breezes bare,
Would he nought see but the dark, silent
    blue,
With all its diamonds trembling through and
    through?
Or the coy moon, when in the waviness
Of whitest clouds she does her beauty dress,
And staidly paces higher up, and higher,
Like a sweet nun in holiday attire?
Ah, yes! much more would start into his
    sight —
The revelries and mysteries of night:
And should I ever see them, I will tell you
Such tales as needs must with amazement
    spell you.

These are the living pleasures of the bard:
But richer far posterity's award.
What does he murmur with his latest breath,
While his proud eye looks through the film
    of death?
'What though I leave this dull and earthly
    mould,
Yet shall my spirit lofty converse hold
With after times. — The patriot shall feel
My stern alarum, and unsheath his steel;
Or in the senate thunder out my numbers,
To startle princes from their easy slumbers.

The sage will mingle with each moral theme
My happy thoughts sententious: he will teem
With lofty periods when my verses fire him,
And then I'll stoop from heaven to inspire
    him.
Lays have I left of such a dear delight
That maids will sing them on their bridal
    night;
Gay villagers, upon a morn of May,
When they have tired their gentle limbs with
    play
And form'd a snowy circle on the grass,
And placed in midst of all that lovely lass
Who chosen is their queen, — with her fine
    head
Crowned with flowers purple, white, and red:
For there the lily and the musk-rose sighing,
Are emblems true of hapless lovers dying:
Between her breasts, that never yet felt
    trouble,
A bunch of violets full blown, and double,
Serenely sleep: — she from a casket takes
A little book, — and then a joy awakes
About each youthful heart, — with stifled
    cries,
And rubbing of white hands, and sparkling
    eyes:
For she's to read a tale of hopes and fears:
One that I foster'd in my youthful years:
The pearls, that on each glistening circlet
    sleep,
Gush ever and anon with silent creep,

Lured by the innocent dimples. To sweet rest
Shall the dear babe, upon its mother's breast,
Be lull'd with songs of mine. Fair world,
    adieu!
Thy dales and hills are fading from my view:
Swiftly I mount, upon wide-spreading pin-
    ions,
Far from the narrow bounds of thy domin-
    ions.
Full joy I feel, while thus I cleave the air,
That my soft verse will charm thy daughters
    fair,
And warm thy sons!' Ah, my dear friend and
    brother,
Could I, at once, my mad ambition smother,
For tasting joys like these, sure I should be
Happier, and dearer to society.
At times, 'tis true, I've felt relief from pain
When some bright thought has darted
    through my brain:
Through all that day I've felt a greater plea-
    sure
Than if I'd brought to light a hidden treasure.
As to my sonnets, though none else should
    heed them,
I feel delighted, still, that you should read
    them.
Of late, too, I have had much calm enjoy-
    ment,
Stretch'd on the grass at my best-loved em-
    ployment

Of scribbling lines for you. These things I
    thought
While, in my face, the freshest breeze I
    caught.
E'en now I'm pillow'd on a bed of flowers
That crowns a lofty clift, which proudly tow-
    ers
Above the ocean waves. The stalks and blades
Chequer my tablet with their quivering
    shades.
On one side is a field of drooping oats,
Through which the poppies show their
    scarlet coats;
So pert and useless, that they bring to mind
The scarlet coats that pester humankind.
And on the other side, outspread, is seen
Ocean's blue mantle, streak'd with purple
    and green!
Now, 'tis I see a canvas'd ship, and now
Mark the bright silver curling round her
    prow;
I see the lark down-dropping to his nest,
And the broad-wing'd sea-gull never at rest;
For when no more he spreads his feathers
    free,
His breast is dancing on the restless sea.
Now I direct my eyes into the west,
Which at this moment is in sunbeams drest:
Why westward turn? 'Twas but to say adieu!
'Twas but to kiss my hand, dear George, to
    you!

To Charles Cowden Clarke

Oft have you seen a swan superbly frowning,
And with proud breast his own white shadow
   crowning;
He slants his neck beneath the waters bright
So silently, it seems a beam of light
Come from the galaxy: anon he sports, —
With outspread wings the Naiad Zephyr
   courts,
Or ruffles all the surface of the lake
In striving from its crystal face to take
Some diamond water-drops, and them to
   treasure
In milky nest, and sip them off at leisure.
But not a moment can he there insure them,
Nor to such downy rest can he allure them;
For down they rush as though they would be
   free,
And drop like hours into eternity.
Just like that bird am I in loss of time,
Whene'er I venture on the stream of rhyme;
With shatter'd boat, oar snapt, and canvas
   rent,
I slowly sail, scarce knowing my intent;
Still scooping up the water with my fingers,
In which a trembling diamond never lingers.

By this, friend Charles, you may full plainly
   see
Why I have never penn'd a line to thee:

Because my thoughts were never free and
    clear,
And little fit to please a classic ear;
Because my wine was of too poor a savour
For one whose palate gladdens in the flavour
Of sparkling Helicon: — small good it were
To take him to a desert rude and bare,
Who had on Baiæ's shore reclined at ease,
While Tasso's page was floating in a breeze
That gave soft music from Armida's bowers,
Mingled with fragrance from her rarest flow-
    ers:
Small good to one who had by Mulla's
    stream
Fondled the maidens with the breasts of
    cream;
Who had beheld Belphœbe in a brook,
And lovely Una in a leafy nook,
And Archimago leaning o'er his book:
Who had of all that's sweet tasted, and seen,
From silvery ripple, up to beauty's queen;
From the sequester'd haunts of gay Titania,
To the blue dwelling of divine Urania:
One who of late had ta'en sweet forest walks
With him who elegantly chats and talks —
The wrong'd Libertas — who has told you
    stories
Of laurel chaplets, and Apollo's glories;
Of troops chivalrous prancing through a city,
And tearful ladies, made for love and pity:
With many else which I have never known.

Thus have I thought; and days on days have
  flown
Slowly, or rapidly — unwilling still
For you to try my dull, unlearned quill.
Nor should I now, but that I've known you
  long;
That you first taught me all the sweets of
  song:
The grand, the sweet, the terse, the free, the
  fine:
What swell'd with pathos, and what right di-
  vine:
Spenserian vowels that elope with ease,
And float along like birds o'er summer seas:
Miltonian storms, and more, Miltonian ten-
  derness,
Michael in arms, and more, meek Eve's fair
  slenderness.
Who read for me the sonnet swelling loudly
Up to its climax, and then dying proudly?
Who found for me the grandeur of the ode,
Growing, like Atlas, stronger from its load?
Who let me taste that more than cordial
  dram,
The sharp, the rapier-pointed epigram?
Show'd me that epic was of all the king,
Round, vast, and spanning all, like Saturn's
  ring?
You too upheld the veil from Clio's beauty,
And pointed out the patriot's stern duty;
The might of Alfred, and the shaft of Tell;
The hand of Brutus, that so grandly fell

Upon a tyrant's head. Ah! had I never seen
Or known your kindness, what might I have
   been?
What my enjoyments in my youthful years,
Bereft of all that now my life endears?
And can I e'er these benefits forget?
And can I e'er repay the friendly debt?
No, doubly no; — yet should these rhymings
   please,
I shall roll on the grass with twofold ease;
For I have long time been my fancy feeding
With hopes that you would one day think the
   reading
Of my rough verses not an hour misspent;
Should it e'er be so, what a rich content!
Some weeks have pass'd since last I saw the
   spires
In lucent Thames reflected: — warm desires
To see the sun o'erpeep the eastern dimness.
And morning shadows streaking into slim-
   ness
Across the lawny fields, and pebbly water;
To mark the time as they grow broad, and
   shorter;
To feel the air that plays about the hills,
And sips its freshness from the little rills;
To see high, golden corn wave in the light
When Cynthia smiles upon a summer's night,
And peers among the cloudlets, jet and white,
As though she were reclining in a bed
Of bean-blossoms, in heaven freshly shed.
No sooner had I stepp'd into these pleasures,

Than I began to think of rhymes and mea-
sures:
The air that floated by me seem'd to say,
'Write! thou wilt never have a better day.'
And so I did. When many lines I'd written,
Though with their grace I was not oversmit-
ten,
Yet, as my hand was warm, I thought I'd bet-
ter
Trust to my feelings, and write you a letter.
Such an attempt required an inspiration
Of a peculiar sort, — a consummation; —
Which, had I felt, these scribblings might
have been
Verses from which the soul would never
wean;
But many days have passed since last my
heart
Was warm'd luxuriously by divine Mozart;
By Arne delighted, or by Handel madden'd;
Or by the song of Erin pierced and sadden'd:
What time you were before the music sitting,
And the rich notes to each sensation fitting.
Since I have walk'd with you through shady
lanes
That freshly terminate in open plains,
And revell'd in a chat that ceased not,
When, at night-fall, among your books we
got:
No, nor when supper came, nor after that, —
Nor when reluctantly I took my hat;
No, nor till cordially you shook my hand

Mid-way between our homes: — your ac-
cents bland
Still sounded in my ears, when I no more
Could hear your footsteps touch the gravelly
floor.
Sometimes I lost them, and then found again;
You changed the footpath for the grassy
plain.
In those still moments I have wish'd you joys
That well you know to honour: — 'Life's very
toys,
With him,' said I, 'will take a pleasant charm;
It cannot be that aught will work him harm.'
These thoughts now come o'er me with all
their might: —
Again I shake your hand, — friend Charles,
good-night.

SONNETS

1
To my Brother George

Many the wonders I this day have seen:
  The sun, when first he kist away the tears
  That fill'd the eyes of morn; — the laurell'd
    peers
Who from the feathery gold of evening
    lean; —
The ocean with its vastness, its blue green,
  Its ships, its rocks, its caves, its hopes, its
    fears,
  Its voice mysterious, which whoso hears
Must think on what will be, and what has
    been.
E'en now, dear George, while this for you I
    write,
  Cynthia is from her silken curtains peeping
So scantly, that it seems her bridal night,
  And she her half-discover'd revels keeping.
But what, without the social thought of thee,
Would be the wonders of the sky and sea?

2
*To * * * * **

Had I a man's fair form, then might my sighs
  Be echoed swiftly through that ivory shell,
  Thine ear, and find thy gentle heart; so well
Would passion arm me for the enterprise:
But ah! I am no knight whose foeman dies;
  No cuirass glistens on my bosom's swell;
  I am no happy shepherd of the dell
Whose lips have trembled with a maiden's
      eyes.
Yet must I dote upon thee, — call thee sweet,
  Sweeter by far than Hybla's honey'd roses
  When steep'd in dew rich to intoxication.
Ah! I will taste that dew, for me 'tis meet,
  And when the moon her pallid face dis-
      closes,
I'll gather some by spells, and incantation.

3
Written on the Day that Mr. Leigh Hunt left Prison

What though, for showing truth to flatter'd
      state,
  Kind Hunt was shut in prison, yet has he,
  In his immortal spirit, been as free
As the sky-searching lark, and as elate.
Minion of grandeur! think you he did wait?
  Think you he nought but prison walls did
      see,
  Till, so unwilling, thou unturn'dst the key?
Ah, no! far happier, nobler was his fate!

In Spenser's halls he stray'd, and bowers fair,
  Culling enchanted flowers; and he flew
With daring Milton through the fields of air:
  To regions of his own his genius true
Took happy flights. Who shall his fame impair
  When thou art dead, and all thy wretched
    crew?

4

'How many bards gild the lapses of time!'

How many bards gild the lapses of time!
  A few of them have ever been the food
  Of my delighted fancy, — I could brood
Over their beauties, earthly, or sublime:
And often, when I sit me down to rhyme,
  These will in throngs before my mind in-
    trude:
  But no confusion, no disturbance rude
Do they occasion; 'tis a pleasing chime.
So the unnumber'd sounds that evening
    store;
  The songs of birds — the whispering of the
    leaves —
  The voice of waters — the great bell that
    heaves
With solemn sound, — and thousand others
    more,
  That distance of recognizance bereaves,
Make pleasing music, and not wild uproar.

5

To a Friend who sent me some Roses

As late I rambled in the happy fields,
  What time the skylark shakes the tremulous
  dew
  From his lush clover covert; — when anew
Adventurous knights take up their dinted
  shields;
I saw the sweet flower wild nature yields,
  A fresh-blown musk-rose: 'twas the first
  that threw
  Its sweets upon the summer: graceful it
  grew
As is the wand that queen Titania wields.
And, as I feasted on its fragrancy,
  I thought the garden-rose it far excell'd;
But when, O Wells! thy roses came to me,
  My sense with their deliciousness was
  spell'd:
Soft voices had they, that with tender plea
  Whisper'd of peace, and truth, and friendli-
  ness unquell'd.

6

To G. A. W.

Nymph of the downward smile and sidelong
  glance,
  In what diviner moments of the day
  Art thou most lovely? when gone far astray
Into the labyrinths of sweet utterance?
Or when serenely wandering in a trance

Of sober thought? Or when starting away,
    With careless robe to meet the morning ray,
Thou spar'st the flowers in thy mazy dance?
Haply 'tis when thy ruby lips part sweetly,
    And so remain, because thou listenest:
But thou to please were nurtured so com-
        pletely
    That I can never tell what mood is best,
I shall as soon pronounce which Grace more
        neatly
    Trips it before Apollo than the rest.

7
'O solitude! if I must with thee dwell'

O solitude! if I must with thee dwell,
    Let it not be among the jumbled heap
    Of murky buildings: climb with me the
        steep, —
Nature's observatory — whence the dell,
Its flowery slopes, its river's crystal swell,
    May seem a span; let me thy vigils keep
    'Mongst boughs pavilion'd, where the
        deer's swift leap
Startles the wild bee from the foxglove bell.
But though I'll gladly trace these scenes with
        thee,
    Yet the sweet converse of an innocent mind,
    Whose words are images of thoughts re-
        fined,
Is my soul's pleasure; and it sure must be
    Almost the highest bliss of human-kind,
When to thy haunts two kindred spirits flee.

8
To my Brothers

Small, busy flames play through the fresh-
    laid coals,
    And their faint cracklings o'er our silence
    creep
    Like whispers of the household gods that
    keep
A gentle empire o'er fraternal souls,
And while, for rhymes, I search around the
    poles,
    Your eyes are fix'd, as in poetic sleep,
    Upon the lore so voluble and deep,
That aye at fall of night our care condoles.
This is your birth-day, Tom, and I rejoice
    That thus it passes smoothly, quietly.
Many such eves of gently whispering noise
    May we together pass, and calmly try
What are this world's true joys, — ere the
    great voice
    From its fair face shall bid our spirits fly.

9

'Keen fitful gusts are whispering here and there'

Keen fitful gusts are whispering here and
    there
    Among the bushes, half leafless and dry;
    The stars look very cold about the sky,
And I have many miles on foot to fare;
Yet feel I little of the cool bleak air,
    Or of the dead leaves rustling drearily,

Or of those silver lamps that burn on high,
Or of the distance from home's pleasant lair:
For I am brimful of the friendliness
  That in a little cottage I have found;
Of fair-haired Milton's eloquent distress,
  And all his love for gentle Lycid' drown'd,
Of lovely Laura in her light green dress,
  And faithful Petrarch gloriously crown'd.

10

'To one who has been long in city pent,'

To one who has been long in city pent,
  'Tis very sweet to look into the fair
  And open face of heaven, — to breathe a
  prayer
Full in the smile of the blue firmament.
Who is more happy, when, with heart's con-
    tent,
  Fatigued he sinks into some pleasant lair
  Of wavy grass, and reads a debonair
And gentle tale of love and languishment?
Returning home at evening, with an ear
  Catching the notes of Philomel, — an eye
Watching the sailing cloudlet's bright career,
  He mourns that day so soon has glided by,
E'en like the passage of an angel's tear
  That falls through the clear ether silently.

11

On first looking into Chapman's Homer

Much have I travell'd in the realms of gold,

And many goodly states and kingdoms
  seen;
  Round many western islands have I been
Which bards in fealty to Apollo hold.
Oft of one wide expanse had I been told,
  That deep-brow'd Homer ruled as his de-
  mesne:
  Yet did I never breathe its pure serene
Till I heard Chapman speak out loud and
  bold:
Then felt I like some watcher of the skies
  When a new planet swims into his ken;
Or like stout Cortez when with eagle eyes
  He stared at the Pacific — and all his men
Look'd at each other with a wild surmise —
  Silent, upon a peak in Darien.

12

On leaving some Friends at an Early Hour

Give me a golden pen, and let me lean
  On heap'd-up flowers, in regions clear, and
  far;
  Bring me a tablet whiter than a star,
Or hand of hymning angel, when 'tis seen
The silver strings of heavenly harp atween:
  And let there glide by many a pearly car,
  Pink robes, and wavy hair, and diamond
  jar,
And half-discover'd wings, and glances keen.
The while let music wander round my ears,
  And as it reaches each delicious ending,

Let me write down a line of glorious
    tone,
And full of many wonders of the spheres:
    For what a height my spirit is contending!
    'Tis not content so soon to be alone.

13
Addressed to Haydon

High-mindedness, a jealousy for good,
    A loving-kindness for the great man's fame,
    Dwells here and there with people of no
        name,
In noisome alley, and in pathless wood:
And where we think the truth least under-
    stood,
    Oft may be found a 'singleness of aim,'
    That ought to frighten into hooded shame
A money-mongering, pitiable brood.
How glorious this affection for the cause
    Of stedfast genius, toiling gallantly!
What when a stout unbending champion
    awes
    Envy and Malice to their native sty!
Unnumber'd souls breathe out a still ap-
    plause,
    Proud to behold him in his country's eye.

14
Addressed to the Same

Great spirits now on earth are sojourning:
    He of the cloud, the cataract, the lake,
    Who on Helvellyn's summit, wide awake,

Catches his freshness from Archangel's wing:
He of the rose, the violet, the spring,
   The social smile, the chain for Freedom's
      sake:
   And lo! whose stedfastness would never
      take
A meaner sound than Raphael's whispering.
And other spirits there are standing apart
   Upon the forehead of the age to come;
These, these will give the world another
      heart,
   And other pulses. Hear ye not the hum
Of mighty workings? —
   Listen awhile, ye nations, and be dumb.

15

On the Grasshopper and Cricket

The poetry of earth is never dead:
   When all the birds are faint with the hot
      sun,
   And hide in cooling trees, a voice will run
From hedge to hedge about the new-mown
      mead.
That is the Grasshopper's — he takes the
      lead
   In summer luxury, — he has never done
   With his delights; for when tired out with
      fun,
He rests at ease beneath some pleasant weed.
The poetry of earth is ceasing never:
   On a lone winter evening, when the frost
      Has wrought a silence, from the stove

there shrills
The Cricket's song, in warmth increasing
  ever,
  And seems to one in drowsiness half lost,
    The Grasshopper's among some grassy
    hills.

16

To Kosciusko

Good Kosciusko! thy great name alone
  Is a full harvest whence to reap high feel-
    ing;
  It comes upon us like the glorious pealing
Of the wide spheres — an everlasting tone.
And now it tells me, that in worlds unknown,
  The names of heroes burst from clouds
    concealing,
  And change to harmonies, for ever stealing
Through cloudless blue, and round each
  silver throne.
It tells me too, that on a happy day,
  When some good spirit walks upon the
    earth,
Thy name with Alfred's, and the great of
  yore,
  Gently commingling, gives tremendous
  birth
To a loud hymn, that sounds far, far away
To where the great God lives for evermore.

17
Happy is England

Happy is England! I could be content
  To see no other verdure than its own;
  To feel no other breezes than are blown
Through its tall woods with high romances
    blent;
Yet do I sometimes feel a languishment
  For skies Italian, and an inward groan
  To sit upon an Alp as on a throne,
And half forget what world or worldling
    meant.
Happy is England, sweet her artless daugh-
    ters:
  Enough their simple loveliness for me,
    Enough their whitest arms in silence
    clinging:
  Yet do I often warmly burn to see
    Beauties of deeper glance, and hear their
    singing,
And float with them about the summer wa-
    ters.

'As I lay in my bed slepe full unmete
Was unto me, but why that I ne might
Rest I ne wist, for there n'as erthly wight
(As I suppose) had more of hertis ese
Than I, for I n'ad sicknesse nor disese.'

— CHAUCER

What is more gentle than a wind in summer?
What is more soothing than the pretty hum-
    mer
That stays one moment in an open flower,
And buzzes cheerily from bower to bower?
What is more tranquil than a musk-rose
    blowing
In a green island, far from all men's know-
    ing?
More healthful than the leafiness of dales?
More secret than a nest of nightingales?
More serene than Cordelia's countenance?
More full of visions than a high romance?
What, but thee, Sleep? Soft closer of our eyes!
Low murmurer of tender lullabies!
Light hoverer around our happy pillows!
Wreather of poppy buds, and weeping wil-
    lows!
Silent entangler of a beauty's tresses!
Most happy listener! when the morning
    blesses
Thee for enlivening all the cheerful eyes

That glance so brightly at the new sun-rise.

But what is higher beyond thought than thee?
Fresher than berries of a mountain tree?
More strange, more beautiful, more smooth,
    more regal,
Than wings of swans, than doves, than dim-
    seen eagle?
What is it? And to what shall I compare it?
It has a glory, and nought else can share it:
The thought thereof is awful, sweet, and holy,
Chasing away all worldliness and folly:
Coming sometimes like fearful claps of thun-
    der;
Or the low rumblings earth's regions under;
And sometimes like a gentle whispering
Of all the secrets of some wondrous thing
That breathes about us in the vacant air;
So that we look around with prying stare,
Perhaps to see shapes of light, aerial limning;
And catch soft floatings from a faint-heard
    hymning;
To see the laurel wreath, on high suspended,
That is to crown our name when life is ended.
Sometimes it gives a glory to the voice,
And from the heart up-springs, rejoice! re-
    joice!
Sounds which will reach the Framer of all
    things,
And die away in ardent mutterings.

No one who once the glorious sun has seen,

And all the clouds, and felt his bosom clean
For his great Maker's presence, but must
   know
What 'tis I mean, and feel his being glow:
Therefore no insult will I give his spirit,
By telling what he sees from native merit.

O Poesy! for thee I hold my pen,
That am not yet a glorious denizen
Of thy wide heaven — Should I rather kneel
Upon some mountain-top until I feel
A glowing splendour round about me hung,
And echo back the voice of thine own
   tongue?
O Poesy! for thee I grasp my pen,
That am not yet a glorious denizen
Of thy wide heaven; yet, to my ardent prayer,
Yield from thy sanctuary some clear air,
Smoothed for intoxication by the breath
Of flowering bays, that I may die a death
Of luxury, and my young spirit follow
The morning sunbeams to the great Apollo,
Like a fresh sacrifice; or, if I can bear
The o'erwhelming sweets, 'twill bring me to
   the fair
Visions of all places: a bowery nook
Will be elysium — an eternal book
Whence I may copy many a lovely saying
About the leaves, and flowers — about the
   playing
Of nymphs in woods and fountains; and the
   shade

Keeping a silence round a sleeping maid;
And many a verse from so strange influence
That we must ever wonder how, and whence
It came. Also imaginings will hover
Round my fire-side, and haply there discover
Vistas of solemn beauty, where I'd wander
In happy silence, like the clear Meander
Through its lone vales; and where I found a
    spot
Of awfuller shade, or an enchanted grot,
Or a green hill o'erspread with chequer'd
    dress
Of flowers, and fearful from its loveliness,
Write on my tablets all that was permitted,
All that was for our human senses fitted.
Then the events of this wide world I'd seize
Like a strong giant, and my spirit tease,
Till at its shoulders it should proudly see
Wings to find out an immortality.

Stop and consider! life is but a day;
A fragile dewdrop on its perilous way
From a tree's summit; a poor Indian's sleep
While his boat hastens to the monstrous steep
Of Montmorenci. Why so sad a moan?
Life is the rose's hope while yet unblown;
The reading of an ever-changing tale;
The light uplifting of a maiden's veil;
A pigeon tumbling in clear summer air;
A laughing schoolboy, without grief or care,
Riding the springy branches of an elm.
O for ten years, that I may overwhelm

Myself in poesy! so I may do the deed
That my own soul has to itself decreed.
Then I will pass the countries that I see
In long perspective, and continually
Taste their pure fountains. First the realm
    I'll pass
Of Flora, and old Pan: sleep in the grass,
Feed upon apples red, and strawberries,
And choose each pleasure that my fancy sees;
Catch the white-handed nymphs in shady
    places,
To woo sweet kisses from averted faces, —
Play with their fingers, touch their shoulders
    white
Into a pretty shrinking with a bite
As hard as lips can make it: till agreed,
A lovely tale of human life we'll read.
And one will teach a tame dove how it best
May fan the cool air gently o'er my rest;
Another, bending o'er her nimble tread,
Will set a green robe floating round her head,
And still will dance with ever varied ease,
Smiling upon the flowers and the trees;
Another will entice me on, and on,
Through almond blossoms and rich cinna-
    mon;
Till in the bosom of a leafy world
We rest in silence, like two gems upcurl'd
In the recesses of a pearly shell.
And can I ever bid these joys farewell?
Yes, I must pass them for a nobler life,
Where I may find the agonies, the strife

Of human hearts: for lo! I see afar,
O'er-sailing the blue cragginess, a car
And steeds with streamy manes — the chari-
    oteer
Looks out upon the winds with glorious fear;
And now the numerous tramplings quiver
    lightly
Along a huge cloud's ridge; and now with
    sprightly
Wheel downward come they into fresher
    skies,
Tipt round with silver from the sun's bright
    eyes.
Still downward with capacious whirl they
    glide;
And now I see them on a green hill's side
In breezy rest among the nodding stalks.
The charioteer with wondrous gesture talks
To the trees and mountains; and there soon
    appear
Shapes of delight, of mystery, and fear,
Passing along before a dusky space
Made by some mighty oaks: as they would
    chase
Some ever-fleeting music, on they sweep.
Lo! how they murmur, laugh, and smile, and
    weep:
Some with upholden hand and mouth severe;
Some with their faces muffled to the ear
Between their arms; some, clear in youthful
    bloom,
Go glad and smilingly athwart the gloom;

Some looking back, and some with upward
    gaze;
Yes, thousands in a thousand different ways
Flit onward — now a lovely wreath of girls
Dancing their sleek hair into tangled curls;
And now broad wings. Most awfully intent
The driver of those steeds is forward bent,
And seems to listen: O that I might know
All that he writes with such a hurrying glow!

The visions all are fled — the car is fled
Into the light of heaven, and in their stead
A sense of real things comes doubly strong,
And, like a muddy stream, would bear along
My soul to nothingness: but I will strive
Against all doubtings, and will keep alive
The thought of that same chariot, and the
    strange
Journey it went.
                  Is there so small a range
In the present strength of manhood, that the
    high
Imagination cannot freely fly
As she was wont of old? prepare her steeds,
Paw up against the light, and do strange
    deeds
Upon the clouds? Has she not shown us all?
From the clear space of ether, to the small
Breath of new buds unfolding? From the
    meaning
Of Jove's large eyebrow, to the tender green-
    ing

Of April meadows? Here her altar shone,
E'en in this isle; and who could paragon
The fervid choir that lifted up a noise
Of harmony, to where it aye will poise
Its mighty self of convoluting sound,
Huge as a planet, and like that roll round,
Eternally around a dizzy void?
Ay, in those days the Muses were nigh cloy'd
With honours: nor had any other care
Than to sing out and soothe their wavy hair.

Could all this be forgotten? Yes, a schism
Nurtured by foppery and barbarism
Made great Apollo blush for this his land.
Men were thought wise who could not under-
    stand
His glories; with a puling infant's force
They sway'd about upon a rocking-horse,
And thought it Pegasus. Ah, dismal-soul'd!
The winds of heaven blew, the ocean roll'd
Its gathering waves — ye felt it not. The blue
Bared its eternal bosom, and the dew
Of summer nights collected still to make
The morning precious: beauty was awake!
Why were ye not awake? But ye were dead
To things ye knew not of; — were closely wed
To musty laws lined out with wretched rule
And compass vile; so that ye taught a school
Of dolts to smooth, inlay, and clip, and fit,
Till, like the certain wands of Jacob's wit,
Their verses tallied. Easy was the task:
A thousand handicraftsmen wore the mask

Of Poesy. Ill-fated, impious race!
That blasphemed the bright Lyrist to his
    face,
And did not know it, — no, they went about,
Holding a poor, decrepit standard out,
Mark'd with most flimsy mottoes, and in
    large
The name of one Boileau!
                          O ye whose charger
It is to hover round our pleasant hills!
Whose congregated majesty so fills
My boundly reverence, that I cannot trace
Your hallow'd names, in this unholy place,
So near those common folk; did not their
    shames
Affright you? Did our old lamenting Thames
Delight you? Did ye never cluster round
Delicious Avon, with a mournful sound,
And weep? Or did ye wholly bid adieu
To regions where no more the laurel grew?
Or did ye stay to give a welcoming
To some lone spirits who could proudly sing
Their youth away, and die? 'Twas even so.
But let me think away those times of woe:
Now 'tis a fairer season; ye have breathed
Rich benedictions o'er us; ye have wreathed
Fresh garlands: for sweet music has been
    heard
In many places; some has been upstirr'd
From out its crystal dwelling in a lake,
By a swan's ebon bill; from a thick brake,
Nested and quiet in a valley mild,

Bubbles a pipe; fine sounds are floating wild
About the earth: happy are ye and glad.

These things are doubtless; yet in truth we've
   had
Strange thunders from the potency of song;
Mingled indeed with what is sweet and
   strong,
From majesty: but in clear truth the themes
Are ugly clubs, the poets Polyphemes
Disturbing the grand sea. A drainless shower
Of light is poesy; 'tis the supreme of power;
'Tis might half slumb'ring on its own right
   arm:
The very archings of her eyelids charm
A thousand willing agents to obey,
And still she governs with the mildest sway:
But strength alone, though of the Muses
   born,
Is like a fallen angel: trees uptorn,
Darkness, and worms, and shrouds, and sep-
   ulchres
Delight it; for it feeds upon the burrs
And thorns of life; forgetting the great end
Of poesy, that it should be a friend
To soothe the cares, and lift the thoughts of
   man.

Yet I rejoice: a myrtle fairer than
E'er grew in Paphos, from the bitter weeds
Lifts its sweet head into the air, and feeds
A silent space with ever-sprouting green.

All tenderest birds there find a pleasant
  screen,
Creep through the shade with jaunty flutter-
  ing,
Nibble the little cuppèd flowers and sing.
Then let us clear away the choking thorns
From round its gentle stem; let the young
  fawns,
Yeanèd in after-times, when we are flown,
Find a fresh sward beneath it, overgrown
With simple flowers: let there nothing be
More boisterous than a lover's bended knee;
Nought more ungentle than the placid look
Of one who leans upon a closed book;
Nought more untranquil than the grassy
  slopes
Between two hills. All hail, delightful hopes!
As she was wont, th' imagination
Into most lovely labyrinths will be gone,
And they shall be accounted poet kings
Who simply tell the most heart-easing things.
Oh may these joys be ripe before I die!
Will not some say that I presumptuously
Have spoken? that from hastening disgrace
'Twere better far to hide my foolish face?
That whining boyhood should with rever-
  ence bow
Ere the dread thunderbolt could reach me?
  How!
If I do hide myself, it sure shall be
In the very fane, the light of Poesy:
If I do fall, at least I will be laid

Beneath the silence of a poplar shade;
And over me the grass shall be smooth
    shaven;
And there shall be a kind memorial graven.
But off, Despondence! miserable bane!
They should not know thee, who athirst to
    gain
A noble end, are thirsty every hour.
What though I am not wealthy in the dower
Of spanning wisdom; though I do not know
The shiftings of the mighty winds that blow
Hither and thither all the changing thoughts
Of man: though no great minist'ring reason
    sorts
Out the dark mysteries of human souls
To clear conceiving: yet there ever rolls
A vast idea before me, and I glean
Therefrom my liberty; thence too I've seen
The end and aim of Poesy. 'Tis clear
As anything most true; as that the year
Is made of the four seasons — manifest
As a large cross, some old cathedral's crest,
Lifted to the white clouds. Therefore
    should I
Be but the essence of deformity,
A coward, did my very eyelids wink
At speaking out what I have dared to think.
Ah! rather let me like a madman run
Over some precipice; let the hot sun
Melt my Dedalian wings, and drive me down
Convulsed and headlong! Stay! an inward
    frown

Of conscience bids me be more calm awhile.
An ocean dim, sprinkled with many an isle,
Spreads awfully before me. How much toil!
How many days! what desperate turmoil!
Ere I can have explored its widenesses.
Ah, what a task! upon my bended knees,
I could unsay those — no, impossible!
Impossible!
         For sweet relief I'll dwell
On humbler thoughts, and let this strange
    assay
Begun in gentleness die so away.
E'en now all tumult from my bosom fades:
I turn full-hearted to the friendly aids
That smooth the path of honour; brother-
    hood,
And friendliness, the nurse of mutual good.
The hearty grasp that sends a pleasant son-
    net
Into the brain ere one can think upon it;
The silence when some rhymes are coming
    out;
And when they're come, the very pleasant
    rout:
The message certain to be done to-morrow.
'Tis perhaps as well that it should be to bor-
    row
Some precious book from out its snug retreat,
To cluster round it when we next shall meet.
Scarce can I scribble on: for lovely airs
Are fluttering round the room like doves in
    pairs;

Many delights of that glad day recalling,
When first my senses caught their tender fall-
ing.
And with these airs come forms of elegance
Stooping their shoulders o'er a horse's
prance,
Careless, and grand — fingers soft and round
Parting luxuriant curls; and the swift bound
Of Bacchus from his chariot, when his eye
Made Ariadne's cheek look blushingly.
Thus I remember all the pleasant flow
Of words at opening a portfolio.
Things such as these are ever harbingers
To trains of peaceful images: the stirs
Of a swan's neck unseen among the rushes;
A linnet starting all about the bushes:
A butterfly, with golden wings broad parted,
Nestling a rose, convulsed as though it
smarted
With over-pleasure — many, many more,
Might I indulge at large in all my store
Of luxuries: yet I must not forget
Sleep, quiet with his poppy coronet:
For what there may be worthy in these
rhymes
I partly owe to him: and thus, the chimes
Of friendly voices had just given place
To as sweet a silence, when I 'gan retrace
The pleasant day, upon a couch at ease.
It was a poet's house who keeps the keys
Of pleasure's temple. Round about were
hung

The glorious features of the bards who sung
In other ages — cold and sacred busts
Smiled at each other. Happy he who trusts
To clear Futurity his darling fame!
Then there were fauns and satyrs taking aim
At swelling apples with a frisky leap
And reaching fingers, 'mid a luscious heap
Of vine-leaves. Then there rose to view a fane
Of liny marble, and thereto a train
Of nymphs approaching fairly o'er the sward:
One, loveliest, holding her white hand toward
The dazzling sun-rise; two sisters sweet
Bending their graceful figures till they meet
Over the trippings of a little child:
And some are hearing, eagerly, the wild
Thrilling liquidity of dewy piping.
See, in another picture, nymphs are wiping
Cherishingly Diana's timorous limbs;
A fold of lawny mantle dabbling swims
At the bath's edge, and keeps a gentle mo-
    tion
With the subsiding crystal: as when ocean
Heaves calmly its broad swelling smoothness
    o'er
Its rocky marge, and balances once more
The patient weeds, that now unshent by foam
Feel all about their undulating home.
Sappho's meek head was there half smiling
    down
At nothing; just as though the earnest frown
Of over-thinking had that moment gone
From off her brow, and left her all alone.

Great Alfred's too, with anxious, pitying eyes,
As if he always listen'd to the sighs
Of the goaded world; and Kosciusko's, worn
By horrid suffrance — mightily forlorn.

Petrarch, outstepping from the shady green,
Starts at the sight of Laura; nor can wean
His eyes from her sweet face. Most happy
   they!
For over them was seen a free display
Of outspread wings, and from between them
   shone
The face of Poesy: from off her throne
She overlook'd things that I scarce could tell.
The very sense of where I was might well
Keep Sleep aloof: but more than that there
   came
Thought after thought to nourish up the
   flame
Within my breast; so that the morning light
Surprised me even from a sleepless night;
And up I rose refresh'd, and glad, and gay,
Resolving to begin that very day
These lines; and howsoever they be done,
I leave them as a father does his son.

■ ■ ■ ■

ENDYMION
A POETIC ROMANCE

■ ■ ■ ■

'The stretchèd metre of an antique song.'

INSCRIBED
TO THE MEMORY
OF
THOMAS CHATTERTON
1818

PREFACE

Knowing within myself the manner in which this Poem has been produced, it is not without a feeling of regret that I make it public.

What manner I mean, will be quite clear to the reader, who must soon perceive great inexperience, immaturity, and every error denoting a feverish attempt, rather than a deed accomplished. The two first books, and indeed the two last, I feel sensible are not of such completion as to warrant their passing the press; nor should they if I thought a year's castigation would do them any good; — it will not: the foundations are too sandy. It is just that this youngster should die away: a sad thought for me, if I had not some hope that while it is dwindling I may be plotting, and fitting myself for verses fit to live.

This may be speaking too presumptuously, and may deserve a punishment: but no feeling man will be forward to inflict it: he will leave me alone, with the conviction that there is not a fiercer hell than the failure in a great object. This is not written with the least atom of purpose to forestall criticisms of course, but from the desire I have to conciliate men who are competent to look, and who do look with a zealous eye, to the honour of English literature.

The imagination of a boy is healthy, and the mature imagination of a man is healthy; but there is a space of life between, in which the soul is in a ferment, the character undecided, the way of life uncertain, the ambition thick-sighted: thence proceeds mawkishness, and all the thousand bitters which those men I speak of must necessarily taste in going over the following pages.

I hope I have not in too late a day touched the beautiful mythology of Greece, and dulled its brightness: for I wish to try once more, before I bid it farewell.

TEIGNMOUTH, 10 APRIL 1818

BOOK I

A thing of beauty is a joy for ever:
Its loveliness increases; it will never
Pass into nothingness; but still will keep
A bower quiet for us, and a sleep
Full of sweet dreams, and health, and quiet
  breathing.
Therefore, on every morrow, are we wreath-
  ing
A flowery band to bind us to the earth,
Spite of despondence, of the inhuman dearth
Of noble natures, of the gloomy days,
Of all the unhealthy and o'er-darken'd ways
Made for our searching: yes, in spite of all,
Some shape of beauty moves away the pall
From our dark spirits. Such the sun, the
  moon,
Trees old and young, sprouting a shady boon
For simple sheep; and such are daffodils
With the green world they live in; and clear
  rills
That for themselves a cooling covert make
'Gainst the hot season; the mid-forest brake,

Rich with a sprinkling of fair musk-rose
   blooms:
And such too is the grandeur of the dooms
We have imagined for the mighty dead;
All lovely tales that we have heard or read:
An endless fountain of immortal drink,
Pouring unto us from the heaven's brink.

  Nor do we merely feel these essences
For one short hour; no, even as the trees
That whisper round a temple become soon
Dear as the temple's self, so does the moon,
The passion poesy, glories infinite,
Haunt us till they become a cheering light
Unto our souls, and bound to us so fast,
That, whether there be shine, or gloom
   o'ercast,
They always must be with us, or we die.
  Therefore, 'tis with full happiness that I
Will trace the story of Endymion.
The very music of the name has gone
Into my being, and each pleasant scene
Is growing fresh before me as the green
Of our own valleys: so I will begin
Now while I cannot hear the city's din;
Now while the early budders are just new
And run in mazes of the youngest hue
About old forests; while the willow trails
Its delicate amber; and the dairy pails
Bring home increase of milk. And, as the year
Grows lush in juicy stalks, I'll smoothly steer
My little boat, for many quiet hours,

With streams that deepen freshly into bow-
    ers.
Many and many a verse I hope to write,
Before the daisies, vermeil rimm'd and white,
Hide in deep herbage; and ere yet the bees
Hum about globes of clover and sweet peas,
I must be near the middle of my story.
O may no wintry season, bare and hoary,
See it half-finish'd: but let Autumn bold,
With universal tinge of sober gold,
Be all about me when I make an end.
And now at once, adventuresome, I send
My herald thought into a wilderness:
There let its trumpet blow, and quickly dress
My uncertain path with green, that I may
    speed
Easily onward, thorough flowers and weed.

   Upon the sides of Latmos was outspread
A mighty forest; for the moist earth fed
So plenteously all weed-hidden roots
Into o'erhanging boughs, and precious fruits.
And it had gloomy shades, sequester'd deep,
Where no man went; and if from shepherd's
    keep
A lamb stray'd far a-down those inmost
    glens,
Never again saw he the happy pens
Whither his brethren, bleating with content,
Over the hills at every nightfall went.
Among the shepherds 'twas believèd ever,

101

That not one fleecy lamb which thus did
    sever
From the white flock, but pass'd unworried
By any wolf, or pard with prying head,
Until it came to some unfooted plains
Where fed the herds of Pan: aye, great his
    gains
Who thus one lamb did lose. Paths there
    were many,
Winding through palmy fern, and rushes
    fenny,
And ivy banks; all leading pleasantly
To a wide lawn, whence one could only see
Stems thronging all around between the swell
Of turf and slanting branches; who could tell
The freshness of the space of heaven above,
Edged round with dark tree-tops? through
    which a dove
Would often beat its wings, and often too
A little cloud would move across the blue.

   Full in the middle of this pleasantness
There stood a marble altar, with a tress
Of flowers budded newly; and the dew
Had taken fairy phantasies to strew
Daisies upon the sacred sward last eve,
And so the dawnèd light in pomp receive.
For 'twas the morn: Apollo's upward fire
Made every eastern cloud a silvery pyre
Of brightness so unsullied, that therein
A melancholy spirit well might win
Oblivion, and melt out his essence fine

Into the winds: rain-scented eglantine
Gave temperate sweets to that well-wooing
    sun:
The lark was lost in him; cold springs had
    run
To warm their chilliest bubbles in the grass;
Man's voice was on the mountains; and the
    mass
Of nature's lives and wonders pulsed tenfold,
To feel this sun-rise and its glories old.

  Now while the silent workings of the dawn
Were busiest, into that self-same lawn
All suddenly, with joyful cries, there sped
A troop of little children garlanded;
Who gathering round the altar, seem'd to
    pry
Earnestly round as wishing to espy
Some folk of holiday; nor had they waited
For many moments, ere their ears were sated
With a faint breath of music, which even then
Fill'd out its voice, and died away again.
Within a little space again it gave
Its airy swellings, with a gentle wave,
To light-hung leaves, in smoothest echoes
    breaking
Through copse-clad valleys, — ere their
    death, o'ertaking
The surgy murmurs of the lonely sea.

  And now, as deep into the wood as we

Might mark a lynx's eye, there glimmer'd
  light
Fair faces and a rush of garments white,
Plainer and plainer showing, till at last
Into the widest alley they all past,
Making directly for the woodland altar.
O kindly muse! let not my weak tongue falter
In telling of this goodly company,
Of their old piety, and of their glee:
But let a portion of ethereal dew
Fall on my head, and presently unmew
My soul; that I may dare, in wayfaring,
To stammer where old Chaucer used to sing.

   Leading the way, young damsels danced
  along,
Bearing the burden of a shepherd song;
Each having a white wicker, overbrimm'd
With April's tender younglings: next, well
  trimm'd,
A crowd of shepherds with as sunburnt looks
As may be read of in Arcadian books;
Such as sat listening round Apollo's pipe,
When the great deity, for earth too ripe,
Let his divinity o'erflowing die
In music, through the vales of Thessaly:
Some idly trail'd their sheep-hooks on the
  ground,
And some kept up a shrilly mellow sound
With ebon-tippèd flutes: close after these,
Now coming from beneath the forest trees,
A venerable priest full soberly

Begirt, with minist'ring looks: always his eye
Stedfast upon the matted turf he kept,
And after him his sacred vestments swept.
From his right hand there swung a vase,
    milk-white,
Of mingled wine, out-sparkling generous
    light;
And in his left he held a basket full
Of all sweet herbs that searching eye could
    cull:
Wild thyme, and valley-lilies whiter still
Than Leda's love, and cresses from the rill.
His aged head, crownèd with beechen
    wreath,
Seem'd like a poll of ivy in the teeth
Of winter hoar. Then came another crowd
Of shepherds, lifting in due time aloud
Their share of the ditty. After them appear'd,
Up-follow'd by a multitude that rear'd
Their voices to the clouds, a fair-wrought
    car,
Easily rolling, so as scarce to mar
The freedom of three steeds of dapple brown:
Who stood therein did seem of great renown
Among the throng. His youth was fully
    blown,
Showing like Ganymede to manhood grown;
And, for those simple times, his garments
    were
A chieftain king's: beneath his breast, half
    bare,
Was hung a silver bugle, and between
105

His nervy knees there lay a boar-spear keen.
A smile was on his countenance; he seem'd
To common lookers-on, like one who
    dream'd
Of idleness in groves Elysian:
But there were some who feelingly could scan
A lurking trouble in his nether lip,
And see that oftentimes the reins would slip
Through his forgotten hands: then would
    they sigh
And think of yellow leaves, of owlets' cry,
Of logs piled solemnly. — Ah, well-a-day,
Why should our young Endymion pine away?

   Soon the assembly, in a circle ranged,
Stood silent round the shrine: each look was
    changed
To sudden veneration: women meek
Beckon'd their sons to silence; while each
    cheek
Of virgin bloom paled gently for slight fear.
Endymion too, without a forest peer,
Stood, wan, and pale, and with an awèd face,
Among his brothers of the mountain chase.
In midst of all, the venerable priest
Eyed them with joy from greatest to the least,
And, after lifting up his aged hands,
Thus spake he: 'Men of Latmos! shepherd
    bands!
Whose care it is to guard a thousand flocks:
Whether descended from beneath the rocks
That overtop your mountains; whether come

From valleys where the pipe is never dumb;
Or from your swelling downs, where sweet
   air stirs
Blue hare-bells lightly, and where prickly
   furze
Buds lavish gold; or ye, whose precious
   charge
Nibble their fill at ocean's very marge,
Whose mellow reeds are touch'd with sounds
   forlorn
By the dim echoes of old Triton's horn:
Mothers and wives! who day by day prepare
The scrip, with needments, for the mountain
   air;
And all ye gentle girls who foster up
Udderless lambs, and in a little cup
Will put choice honey for a favour'd youth:
Yea, every one attend! for in good truth
Our vows are wanting to our great god Pan.
Are not our lowing heifers sleeker than
Night-swollen mushrooms? Are not our wide
   plains
Speckled with countless fleeces? Have not
   rains
Green'd over April's lap? No howling sad
Sickens our fearful ewes; and we have had
Great bounty from Endymion our lord.
The earth is glad: the merry lark has pour'd
His early song against yon breezy sky,
That spreads so clear o'er our solemnity.'

Thus ending, on the shrine he heap'd a
    spire
Of teeming sweets, enkindling sacred fire;
Anon he stain'd the thick and spongy sod
With wine, in honour of the shepherd-god.
Now while the earth was drinking it, and
    while
Bay leaves were crackling in the fragrant pile,
And gummy frankincense was sparkling
    bright
'Neath smothering parsley, and a hazy light
Spread greyly eastward, thus a chorus sang:

  'O thou, whose mighty palace roof doth
    hang
From jagged trunks, and overshadoweth
Eternal whispers, glooms, the birth, life,
    death
Of unseen flowers in heavy peacefulness;
Who lov'st to see the hamadryads dress
Their ruffled locks where meeting hazels
    darken;
And through whole solemn hours dost sit,
    and hearken
The dreary melody of bedded reeds —
In desolate places, where dank moisture
    breeds
The pipy hemlock to strange overgrowth,
Bethinking thee, how melancholy loth
Thou wast to lose fair Syrinx — do thou now,
By thy love's milky brow!

By all the trembling mazes that she ran,
Hear us, great Pan!

  'O thou, for whose soul-soothing quiet,
    turtles
Passion their voices cooingly 'mong myrtles,
What time thou wanderest at eventide
Through sunny meadows, that outskirt the
    side
Of thine enmossèd realms: O thou, to whom
Broad-leavèd fig-trees even now foredoom
Their ripen'd fruitage; yellow-girted bees
Their golden honeycombs; our village leas
Their fairest-blossom'd beans and poppied
    corn;
The chuckling linnet its five young unborn,
To sing for thee; low-creeping strawberries
Their summer coolness; pent-up butterflies
Their freckled wings; yea, the fresh-budding
    year
All its completions — be quickly near,
By every wind that nods the mountain pine,
O forester divine!

  'Thou, to whom every faun and satyr flies
For willing service; whether to surprise
The squatted hare while in half-sleeping fit;
Or upward ragged precipices flit
To save poor lambkins from the eagle's maw;
Or by mysterious enticement draw
Bewilder'd shepherds to their path again;
Or to tread breathless round the frothy main,

109

And gather up all fancifullest shells
For thee to tumble into Naiads' cells,
And, being hidden, laugh at their out-
    peeping;
Or to delight thee with fantastic leaping,
The while they pelt each other on the crown
With silvery oak-apples, and fir-cones
    brown —
By all the echoes that about thee ring,
Hear us, O satyr king!

  'O Hearkener to the loud-clapping shears,
While ever and anon to his shorn peers
A ram goes bleating: Winder of the horn,
When snouted wild-boars routing tender
    corn
Anger our huntsman: Breather round our
    farms,
To keep off mildews, and all weather harms:
Strange ministrant of undescribèd sounds,
That come a-swooning over hollow grounds,
And wither drearily on barren moors:
Dread opener of the mysterious doors
Leading to universal knowledge — see,
Great son of Dryope,
The many that are come to pay their vows
With leaves about their brows!

  'Be still the unimaginable lodge
For solitary thinkings; such as dodge
Conception to the very bourne of heaven,
Then leave the naked brain: be still the leaven

That spreading in this dull and clodded
    earth,
Gives it a touch ethereal — a new birth:
Be still a symbol of immensity;
A firmament reflected in a sea;
An element filling the space between;
An unknown — but no more: we humbly
    screen
With uplift hands our foreheads, lowly bend-
    ing,
And giving out a shout most heaven-rending,
Conjure thee to receive our humble Pæan,
Upon thy Mount Lycean!'

   Even while they brought the burden to a
    close
A shout from the whole multitude arose,
That linger'd in the air like dying rolls
Of abrupt thunder, when Ionian shoals
Of dolphins bob their noses through the
    brine.
Meantime, on shady levels, mossy fine,
Young companies nimbly began dancing
To the swift treble pipe, and humming string.
Ay, those fair living forms swam heavenly
To tunes forgotten — out of memory:
Fair creatures! whose young children's chil-
    dren bred
Thermopylæ its heroes — not yet dead,
But in old marbles ever beautiful.
High genitors, unconscious did they cull
Time's sweet firstfruits — they danced to

weariness,
And then in quiet circles did they press
The hillock turf, and caught the latter end
Of some strange history, potent to send
A young mind from its bodily tenement.
Or they might watch the quoit-pitchers, in-
    tent
On either side; pitying the sad death
Of Hyacinthus, when the cruel breath
Of Zephyr slew him, — Zephyr penitent,
Who now, ere Phœbus mounts the firma-
    ment,
Fondles the flower amid the sobbing rain.
The archers too, upon a wider plain,
Beside the feathery whizzing of the shaft,
And the dull twanging bowstring, and the
    raft
Branch down sweeping from a tall ash top,
Call'd up a thousand thoughts to envelope
Those who would watch. Perhaps, the trem-
    bling knee
And frantic gape of lonely Niobe,
Poor, lonely Niobe! when her lovely young
Were dead and gone, and her caressing
    tongue
Lay a lost thing upon her paly lip,
And very, very deadliness did nip
Her motherly cheeks. Aroused from this sad
    mood
By one, who at a distance loud halloo'd,
Uplifting his strong bow into the air,
Many might after brighter visions stare:

After the Argonauts, in blind amaze
Tossing about on Neptune's restless ways,
Until, from the horizon's vaulted side,
There shot a golden splendour far and wide,
Spangling those million poutings of the brine
With quivering ore: 'twas even an awful shine
From the exaltation of Apollo's bow;
A heavenly beacon in their dreary woe.
Who thus were ripe for high contemplating,
Might turn their steps towards the sober ring
Where sat Endymion and the aged priest
'Mong shepherds gone in eld, whose looks
    increased
The silvery setting of their mortal star.
There they discoursed upon the fragile bar
That keeps us from our homes ethereal;
And what our duties there: to nightly call
Vesper, the beauty-crest of summer weather;
To summon all the downiest clouds together
For the sun's purple couch; to emulate
In minist'ring the potent rule of fate
With speed of fire-tail'd exhalations;
To tint her pallid cheek with bloom, who cons
Sweet poesy by moonlight: besides these,
A world of other unguess'd offices.
Anon they wander'd, by divine converse,
Into Elysium; vying to rehearse
Each one his own anticipated bliss.
One felt heart-certain that he could not miss
His quick-gone love, among fair blossom'd
    boughs,
Where every zephyr-sigh pouts, and endows

Her lips with music for the welcoming.
Another wish'd, 'mid that eternal spring,
To meet his rosy child, with feathery sails,
Sweeping, eye-earnestly, through almond
  vales:
Who, suddenly, should stoop through the
  smooth wind
And with the balmiest leaves his temples
  bind;
And, ever after, through those regions be
His messenger, his little Mercury.
Some were athirst in soul to see again
Their fellow huntsmen o'er the wide cham-
  paign
In times long past; to sit with them, and talk
Of all the chances in their earthly walk;
Comparing, joyfully, their plenteous stores
Of happiness, to when upon the moors,
Benighted, close they huddled from the cold,
And shared their famish'd scrips. Thus all
  out-told
Their fond imaginations, — saving him
Whose eyelids curtain'd up their jewels dim,
Endymion: yet hourly had he striven
To hide the cankering venom, that had riven
His fainting recollections. Now indeed
His senses had swoon'd off: he did not heed
The sudden silence, or the whispers low,
Or the old eyes dissolving at his woe,
Or anxious calls, or close of trembling palms,
Or maiden's sigh, that grief itself embalms;
But in the self-same fixèd trance he kept,

Like one who on the earth had never stept,
Ay, even as dead-still as a marble man,
Frozen in that old tale Arabian.

  Who whispers him so pantingly and close?
Peona, his sweet sister: of all those,
His friends, the dearest. Hushing signs she
    made,
And breathed a sister's sorrow to persuade
A yielding up, a cradling on her care.
Her eloquence did breathe away the curse:
She led him, like some midnight spirit nurse
Of happy changes in emphatic dreams,
Along a path between two little streams, —
Guarding his forehead, with her round elbow,
From low-grown branches, and his footsteps
    slow
From stumbling over stumps and hillocks
    small;
Until they came to where these streamlets
    fall,
With mingled bubblings and a gentle rush,
Into a river, clear, brimful, and flush
With crystal mocking of the trees and sky.
A little shallop, floating there hard by,
Pointed its beak over the fringèd bank;
And soon it lightly dipt, and rose, and sank,
And dipt again, with the young couple's
    weight, —
Peona guiding, through the water straight,
Towards a bowery island opposite;
Which gaining presently, she steerèd light

Into a shady, fresh, and ripply cove,
Where nested was an arbour, overwove
By many a summer's silent fingering;
To whose cool bosom she was used to bring
Her playmates, with their needle broidery,
And minstrel memories of times gone by.

So she was gently glad to see him laid
Under her favourite bower's quiet shade,
On her own couch, new made of flower
    leaves,
Dried carefully on the cooler side of sheaves
When last the sun his autumn tresses shook,
And the tann'd harvesters rich armfuls took.
Soon was he quieted to slumbrous rest:
But, ere it crept upon him, he had prest
Peona's busy hand against his lips,
And still, a-sleeping, held her finger-tips
In tender pressure. And as a willow keeps
A patient watch over the stream that creeps
Windingly by it, so the quiet maid
Held her in peace: so that a whispering blade
Of grass, a wailful gnat, a bee bustling
Down in the blue-bells, or a wren light rus-
    tling
Among sere leaves and twigs, might all be
    heard.

O magic sleep! O comfortable bird,
That broodest o'er the troubled sea of the
    mind
Till it is hush'd and smooth! O unconfined

Restraint! imprison'd liberty! great key
To golden palaces, strange minstrelsy,
Fountains grotesque, new trees, bespangled
    caves,
Echoing grottoes, full of tumbling waves
And moonlight; ay, to all the mazy world
Of silvery enchantment! — who, upfurl'd
Beneath thy drowsy wing a triple hour,
But renovates and lives? — Thus, in the
    bower,
Endymion was calm'd to life again.
Opening his eyelids with a healthier brain,
He said: 'I feel this thine endearing love
All through my bosom: thou art as a dove
Trembling its closèd eyes and sleekèd wings
About me; and the pearliest dew not brings
Such morning incense from the fields of May,
As do those brighter drops that twinkling
    stray
From those kind eyes, — the very home and
    haunt
Of sisterly affection. Can I want
Aught else, aught nearer heaven, than such
    tears?
Yet dry them up, in bidding hence all fears
That, any longer, I will pass my days
Alone and sad. No, I will once more raise
My voice upon the mountain-heights; once
    more
Make my horn parley from their foreheads
    hoar;

Again my trooping hounds their tongues shall
    loll
Around the breathèd boar: again I'll poll
The fair-grown yew-tree, for a chosen bow:
And, when the pleasant sun is getting low,
Again I'll linger in a sloping mead
To hear the speckled thrushes, and see feed
Our idle sheep. So be thou cheerèd, sweet!
And, if thy lute is here, softly entreat
My soul to keep in its resolvèd course.'

    Hereat Peona, in their silver source,
Shut her pure sorrow-drops with glad ex-
    claim,
And took a lute, from which there pulsing
    came
A lively prelude, fashioning the way
In which her voice should wander. 'Twas a
    lay
More subtle-cadencèd, more forest wild
Than Dryope's lone lulling of her child;
And nothing since has floated in the air
So mournful strange. Surely some influence
    rare
Went, spiritual, through the damsel's hand;
For still, with Delphic emphasis, she spann'd
The quick invisible strings, even though she
    saw
Endymion's spirit melt away and thaw
Before the deep intoxication.
But soon she came, with sudden burst, upon
Her self-possession — swung the lute aside,

And earnestly said: 'Brother, 'tis vain to hide
That thou dost know of things mysterious,
Immortal, starry; such alone could thus
Weigh down thy nature. Hast thou sinn'd in
    aught
Offensive to the heavenly powers? Caught
A Paphian dove upon a message sent?
Thy deathful bow against some deer-herd
    bent,
Sacred to Dian? Haply, thou hast seen
Her naked limbs among the alders green;
And that, alas! is death. No, I can trace
Something more high perplexing in thy face!'

  Endymion look'd at her, and press'd her
    hand,
And said, 'Art thou so pale, who was so bland
And merry in our meadows? How is this?
Tell me thine ailment: tell me all amiss!
Ah! thou hast been unhappy at the change
Wrought suddenly in me. What indeed more
    strange?
Or more complete to overwhelm surmise?
Ambition is no sluggard: 'tis no prize,
That toiling years would put within my grasp,
That I have sigh'd for: with so deadly gasp
No man e'er panted for a mortal love.
So all have set my heavier grief above
These things which happen. Rightly have
    they done:
I, who still saw the horizontal sun
Heave his broad shoulder o'er the edge of

the world,
Out-facing Lucifer, and then had hurl'd
My spear aloft, as signal for the chase —
I, who, for very sport of heart, would race
With my own steed from Araby; pluck down
A vulture from his towery perching; frown
A lion into growling, loth retire —
To lose, at once, all my toil-breeding fire,
And sink thus low! but I will ease my breast
Of secret grief, here in this bowery nest.

    'This river does not see the naked sky,
Till it begins to progress silverly
Around the western border of the wood,
Whence, from a certain spot, its winding
    flood
Seems at the distance like a crescent moon:
And in that nook, the very pride of June,
Had I been used to pass my weary eves;
The rather for the sun unwilling leaves
So dear a picture of his sovereign power,
And I could witness his most kingly hour,
When he doth tighten up the golden reins,
And paces leisurely down amber plains
His snorting four. Now when his chariot last
Its beams against the zodiac-lion cast,
There blossom'd suddenly a magic bed
Of sacred ditamy, and poppies red:
At which I wonder'd greatly, knowing well
That but one night had wrought this flowery
    spell;
And, sitting down close by, began to muse

What it might mean. Perhaps, thought I, Morpheus,
In passing here, his owlet pinions shook;
Or, it may be, ere matron Night uptook
Her ebon urn, young Mercury, by stealth,
Had dipt his rod in it: such garland wealth
Came not by common growth. Thus on I thought,
Until my head was dizzy and distraught.
Moreover, through the dancing poppies stole
A breeze, most softly lulling to my soul;
And shaping visions all about my sight
Of colours, wings, and bursts of spangly light:
The which became more strange, and strange, and dim,
And then were gulph'd in a tumultuous swim:
And then I fell asleep. Ah, can I tell
The enchantment that afterwards befell?
Yet it was but a dream: yet such a dream
That never tongue, although it overteem
With mellow utterance, like a cavern spring,
Could figure out and to conception bring
All I beheld and felt. Methought I lay
Watching the zenith, where the milky way
Among the stars in virgin splendour pours;
And travelling my eye, until the doors
Of heaven appeared to open for my flight,
I became loth and fearful to alight
From such high soaring by a downward glance;
So kept me stedfast in that airy trance,

Spreading imaginary pinions wide.
When, presently, the stars began to glide,
And faint away, before my eager view:
At which I sigh'd that I could not pursue,
And dropt my vision to the horizon's verge;
And lo! from opening clouds, I saw emerge
The loveliest moon, that ever silver'd o'er
A shell for Neptune's goblet; she did soar
So passionately bright, my dazzled soul
Commingling with her argent spheres did
    roll
Through clear and cloudy, even when she
    went
At last into a dark and vapoury tent —
Whereat, methought, the lidless-eyèd train
Of planets all were in the blue again.
To commune with those orbs, once more I
    raised
My sight right upward: but it was quite dazed
By a bright something, sailing down apace,
Making me quickly veil my eyes and face:
Again I look'd, and, O ye deities,
Who from Olympus watch our destinies!
Whence that completed form of all complete-
    ness?
Whence came that high perfection of all
    sweetness?
Speak, stubborn earth, and tell me where, O
    where
Hast thou a symbol of her golden hair?
Not oat-sheaves drooping in the western sun;
Not — thy soft hand, fair sister! let me shun

Such follying before thee — yet she had,
Indeed, locks bright enough to make me
  mad;
And they were simply gordian'd up and
  braided,
Leaving, in naked comeliness, unshaded,
Her pearl round ears, white neck, and orbèd
  brow;
The which were blended in, I know not how,
With such a paradise of lips and eyes,
Blush-tinted cheeks, half smiles, and faintest
  sighs,
That, when I think thereon, my spirit clings
And plays about its fancy, till the stings
Of human neighbourhood envenom all.
Unto what awful power shall I call?
To what high fane? — Ah! see her hovering
  feet,
More bluely vein'd, more soft, more whitely
  sweet
Than those of sea-born Venus, when she rose
From out her cradle shell. The wind out-
  blows
Her scarf into a fluttering pavilion;
'Tis blue, and over-spangled with a million
Of little eyes, as though thou wert to shed,
Over the darkest, lushest blue-bell bed,
Handfuls of daisies.' — 'Endymion, how
  strange!
Dream within dream!' — 'She took an airy
  range,
And then, towards me, like a very maid,

123

Came blushing, waning, willing, and afraid,
And press'd me by the hand: Ah! 'twas too
　　much;
Methought I fainted at the charmèd touch,
Yet held my recollection, even as one
Who dives three fathoms where the waters
　　run
Gurgling in beds of coral: for anon,
I felt upmounted in that region
Where falling stars dart their artillery forth,
And eagles struggle with the buffeting north
That balances the heavy meteor-stone; —
Felt too, I was not fearful, nor alone,
But lapp'd and lull'd along the dangerous
　　sky.
Soon, as it seem'd, we left our journeying
　　high,
And straightway into frightful eddies
　　swoop'd;
Such as aye muster where grey time has
　　scoop'd
Huge dens and caverns in a mountain's side:
There hollow sounds aroused me, and I
　　sigh'd
To faint once more by looking on my bliss —
I was distracted; madly did I kiss
The wooing arms which held me, and did
　　give
My eyes at once to death: but 'twas to live,
To take in draughts of life from the gold fount
Of kind and passionate looks; to count, and
　　count

The moments, by some greedy help that
    seem'd
A second self, that each might be redeem'd
And plunder'd of its load of blessedness.
Ah, desperate mortal! I even dared to press
Her very cheek against my crownèd lip,
And, at that moment, felt my body dip
Into a warmer air: a moment more,
Our feet were soft in flowers. There was store
Of newest joys upon that alp. Sometimes
A scent of violets, and blossoming limes,
Loiter'd around us; then of honey cells,
Made delicate from all white-flower bells, —
And once, above the edges of our nest,
An arch face peep'd, — an Oread as I
    guess'd.

  'Why did I dream that sleep o'erpower'd
    me
In midst of all this heaven? Why not see,
Far off, the shadows of his pinions dark,
And stare them from me? But no, like a spark
That needs must die, although its little beam
Reflects upon a diamond, my sweet dream
Fell into nothing — into stupid sleep.
And so it was, until a gentle creep,
A careful moving caught my waking ears,
And up I started: Ah! my sighs, my tears,
My clenchèd hands; — for lo! the poppies
    hung
Dew-dabbled on their stalks, the ouzel sung
A heavy ditty, and the sullen day

125

Had chidden herald Hesperus away,
With leaden looks: the solitary breeze
Bluster'd, and slept, and its wild self did tease
With wayward melancholy; and I thought,
Mark me, Peona! that sometimes it brought
Faint fare-thee-wells, and sigh-shrilled
    adieus! —
Away I wander'd — all the pleasant hues
Of heaven and earth had faded: deepest
    shades
Were deepest dungeons; heaths and sunny
    glades
Were full of pestilent light; our taintless rills
Seem'd sooty, and o'erspread with upturn'd
    gills
Of dying fish; the vermeil rose had blown
In frightful scarlet, and its thorns outgrown
Like spikèd aloe. If an innocent bird
Before my heedless footsteps stirr'd, and
    stirr'd
In little journeys, I beheld in it
A disguised demon, missionèd to knit
My soul with under darkness; to entice
My stumblings down some monstrous preci-
    pice:
Therefore I eager follow'd, and did curse
The disappointment. Time, that aged nurse,
Rock'd me to patience. Now, thank gentle
    heaven,
These things, with all their comfortings, are
    given
To my down-sunken hours, and with thee,

Sweet sister, help to stem the ebbing sea
Of weary life.'

            Thus ended he, and both
Sat silent: for the maid was very loth
To answer; feeling well that breathèd words
Would all be lost, unheard, and vain as
    swords
Against the enchased crocodile, or leaps
Of grasshoppers against the sun. She weeps,
And wonders; struggles to devise some blame
To put on such a look as would say, *Shame
On this poor weakness!* but, for all her strife,
She could as soon have crush'd away the life
From a sick dove. At length, to break the
    pause,
She said with trembling chance: 'Is this the
    cause?
This all? Yet it is strange, and sad, alas!
That one who through this middle earth
    should pass
Most like a sojourning demi-god, and leave
His name upon the harp-string, should
    achieve
No higher bard than simple maidenhood,
Singing alone, and fearfully, — how the blood
Left his young cheek; and how he used to
    stray
He knew not where: and how he would say,
    nay,
If any said 'twas love: and yet 'twas love;
What could it be but love? How a ring-dove

Let fall a sprig of yew-tree in his path
And how he died: and then, that love doth
    scathe
The gentle heart, as northern blasts do roses;
And then the ballad of his sad life closes
With sighs, and an alas! — Endymion!
Be rather in the trumpet's mouth, — anon
Among the winds at large — that all may
    hearken!
Although, before the crystal heavens darken,
I watch and dote upon the silver lakes
Pictured in western cloudiness, that takes
The semblance of gold rocks and bright gold
    sands,
Islands, and creeks, and amber-fretted
    strands
With horses prancing o'er them, palaces
And towers of amethyst, — would I so tease
My pleasant days, because I could not mount
Into those regions? The Morphean fount
Of that fine element that visions, dreams,
And fitful whims of sleep are made of,
    streams
Into its airy channels with so subtle,
So thin a breathing, not the spider's shuttle,
Circled a million times within the space
Of a swallow's nest-door, could delay a trace,
A tinting of its quality: how light
Must dreams themselves be; seeing they're
    more slight
Than the mere nothing that engenders them!
Then wherefore sully the entrusted gem

Of high and noble life with thoughts so sick?
Why pierce high-fronted honour to the quick
For nothing but a dream?' Hereat the youth
Look'd up: a conflicting of shame and ruth
Was in his plaited brow: yet his eyelids
Widen'd a little, as when Zephyr bids
A little breeze to creep between the fans
Of careless butterflies; amid his pains
He seem'd to taste a drop of manna-dew,
Full palatable; and a colour grew
Upon his cheek, while thus he lifeful spake.

'Peona! ever have I long'd to slake
My thirst for the world's praises: nothing
    base,
No merely slumberous phantasm, could un-
    lace
The stubborn canvas for my voyage
    prepared —
Though now 'tis tatter'd; leaving my bark
    bared
And sullenly drifting: yet my higher hope
Is of too wide, too rainbow-large a scope,
To fret at myriads of earthly wrecks.
Wherein lies happiness? In that which becks
Our ready minds to fellowship divine,
A fellowship with essence; till we shine,
Full alchemized, and free of space. Behold
The clear religion of heaven! Fold
A rose-leaf round thy finger's taperness,
And soothe thy lips: hist! when the airy stress
Of music's kiss impregnates the free winds,

And with a sympathetic touch unbinds
Æolian magic from their lucid wombs:
Then old songs waken from enclouded
    tombs;
Old ditties sigh above their father's grave;
Ghosts of melodious prophesyings rave
Round every spot where trod Apollo's foot;
Bronze clarions awake, and faintly bruit,
Where long ago a giant battle was;
And, from the turf, a lullaby doth pass
In every place where infant Orpheus slept.
Feel we these things? — that moment have
    we stept
Into a sort of oneness, and our state
Is like a floating spirit's. But there are
Richer entanglements, enthralments far
More self-destroying, leading, by degrees,
To the chief intensity: the crown of these
Is made of love and friendship, and sits high
Upon the forehead of humanity.
All its more ponderous and bulky worth
Is friendship, whence there ever issues forth
A steady splendour; but at the tip-top,
There hangs by unseen film, an orbèd drop
Of light, and that is love: its influence,
Thrown in our eyes, genders a novel sense,
At which we start and fret; till in the end,
Melting into its radiance, we blend,
Mingle, and so become a part of it, —
Nor with aught else can our souls interknit
So wingedly: when we combine therewith,
Life's self is nourish'd by its proper pith,

And we are nurtured like a pelican brood.
Ay, so delicious is the unsating food,
That men, who might have tower'd in the
    van
Of all the congregated world, to fan
And winnow from the coming step of time
All chaff of custom, wipe away all slime
Left by men-slugs and human serpentry,
Have been content to let occasion die,
Whilst they did sleep in love's Elysium.
And, truly, I would rather be struck dumb
Than speak against this ardent listlessness:
For I have ever thought that it might bless
The world with benefits unknowingly;
As does the nightingale, up-perchèd high,
And cloister'd among cool and bunchèd
    leaves —
She sings but to her love, nor e'er conceives
How tiptoe Night holds back her dark-grey
    hood.
Just so may love, although 'tis understood
The mere commingling of passionate breath,
Produce more than our searching witnesseth:
What I know not: but who, of men, can tell
That flowers would bloom, or that green fruit
    would swell
To melting pulp, that fish would have bright
    mail,
The earth its dower of river, wood, and vale,
The meadows runnels, runnels pebble-
    stones,
The seed its harvest, or the lute its tones,

Tones ravishment, or ravishment its sweet,
If human souls did never kiss and greet?

'Now, if this earthly love has power to make
Men's being mortal, immortal; to shake
Ambition from their memories, and brim
Their measure of content; what merest whim,
Seems all this poor endeavour after fame,
To one, who keeps within his stedfast aim
A love immortal, an immortal too.
Look not so wilder'd; for these things are
     true,
And never can be born of atomies
That buzz about our slumbers, like brain-
     flies,
Leaving us fancy-sick. No, no, I'm sure,
My restless spirit never could endure
To brood so long upon one luxury,
Unless it did, though fearfully, espy
A hope beyond the shadow of a dream.
My sayings will the less obscurèd seem
When I have told thee how my waking sight
Has made me scruple whether that same
     night
Was pass'd in dreaming. Hearken, sweet
     Peona!
Beyond the matron-temple of Latona,
Which we should see but for these darkening
     boughs,
Lies a deep hollow, from whose ragged brows
Bushes and trees do lean all round athwart,

And meet so nearly, that with wings out-
  raught,
And spreaded tail, a vulture could not glide
Past them, but he must brush on every side.
Some moulder'd steps lead into this cool cell,
Far as the slabbèd margin of a well,
Whose patient level peeps its crystal eye
Right upward, through the bushes, to the sky.
Oft have I brought thee flowers, on their
  stalks set
Like vestal primroses, but dark velvet
Edges them round, and they have golden pits:
'Twas there I got them, from the gaps and
  slits
In a mossy stone, that sometimes was my
  seat,
When all above was faint with mid-day heat.
And there in strife no burning thoughts to
  heed,
I'd bubble up the water through a reed;
So reaching back to boyhood: make me ships
Of moulted feathers, touchwood, alder chips,
With leaves stuck in them; and the Neptune
  be
Of their petty ocean. Oftener, heavily,
When lovelorn hours had left me less a child,
I sat contemplating the figures wild
Of o'erhead clouds melting the mirror
  through,
Upon a day, while thus I watch'd, by flew
A cloudy Cupid, with his bow and quiver;

So plainly character'd, no breeze would
  shiver
The happy chance: so happy, I was fain
To follow it upon the open plain,
And, therefore, was just going; when, behold!
A wonder, fair as any I have told —
The same bright face I tasted in my sleep,
Smiling in the clear well. My heart did leap
Through the cool depth. — It moved as if to
  flee —
I started up, when lo! refreshfully,
There came upon my face, in plenteous
  showers,
Dew-drops, and dewy buds, and leaves, and
  flowers,
Wrapping all objects from my smother'd
  sight,
Bathing my spirit in a new delight.
Ay, such a breathless honey-feel of bliss
Alone preserved me from the drear abyss
Of death, for the fair form had gone again.
Pleasure is oft a visitant; but pain
Clings cruelly to us, like the gnawing sloth
On the deer's tender haunches: late, and loth,
'Tis scared away by slow-returning pleasure.
How sickening, how dark the dreadful leisure
Of weary days, made deeper exquisite,
By a foreknowledge of unslumbrous night!
Like sorrow came upon me, heavier still,
Than when I wander'd from the poppy hill:
And a whole age of lingering moments crept
Sluggishly by, ere more contentment swept

Away at once the deadly yellow spleen.
Yes, thrice have I this fair enchantment seen;
Once more been tortured with renewèd life.
When last the wintry gusts gave over strife
With the conquering sun of spring, and left
    the skies
Warm and serene, but yet with moisten'd
    eyes
In pity of the shatter'd infant buds, —
That time thou didst adorn, with amber
    studs,
My hunting-cap, because I laugh'd and
    smiled,
Chatted with thee, and many days exiled
All torment from my breast; — 'twas even
    then,
Straying about, yet, coop'd up in the den
Of helpless discontent, — hurling my lance
From place to place, and following at chance,
At last, by hap, through some young trees it
    struck,
And, plashing among bedded pebbles, stuck
In the middle of a brook, — whose silver
    ramble
Down twenty little falls, through reeds and
    bramble,
Tracing along, it brought me to a cave,
Whence it ran brightly forth, and white did
    lave
The nether sides of mossy stones and
    rock, —

'Mong which it gurgled blithe adieus, to
   mock
Its own sweet grief at parting. Overhead
Hung a lush screen of drooping weeds, and
   spread
Thick, as to curtain up some wood-nymph's
   home.
"Ah! impious mortal, whither do I roam?"
Said I, low-voiced: "Ah, whither! 'Tis the grot
Of Proserpine, when Hell, obscure and hot,
Doth her resign: and where her tender hands
She dabbles, on the cool and sluicy sands;
Or 'tis the cell of Echo, where she sits,
And babbles thorough silence, till her wits
Are gone in tender madness, and anon,
Faints into sleep, with many a dying tone
Of sadness. O that she would take my vows,
And breathe them sighingly among the
   boughs,
To sue her gentle ears for whose fair head,
Daily, I pluck sweet flowerets from their bed,
And weave them dyingly — send honey-
   whispers
Round every leaf, that all those gentle lispers
May sigh my love unto her pitying!
O charitable Echo! hear, and sing
This ditty to her! — tell her" — So I stay'd
My foolish tongue, and listening, half afraid,
Stood stupefied with my own empty folly,
And blushing for the freaks of melancholy.
Salt tears were coming, when I heard my
   name

Most fondly lipp'd, and then these accents
    came:
"Endymion! the cave is secreter
Than the isle of Delos. Echo hence shall stir
No sighs but sigh-warm kisses, or light noise
Of thy combing hand, the while it travelling
    cloys
And trembles through my labyrinthine hair."
At that oppress'd, I hurried in. — Ah! where
Are those swift moments? Whither are they
    fled?
I'll smile no more, Peona; nor will wed
Sorrow, the way to death; but patiently
Bear up against it: so farewell, sad sigh;
And come instead demurest meditation,
To occupy me wholly, and to fashion
My pilgrimage for the world's dusky brink.
No more will I count over, link by link,
My chain of grief: no longer strive to find
A half-forgetfulness in mountain wind
Blustering about my ears: ay, thou shalt see,
Dearest of sisters, what my life shall be;
What a calm round of hours shall make my
    days.
There is a paly flame of hope that plays
Where'er I look: but yet, I'll say 'tis
    nought —
And here I bid it die. Have not I caught,
Already, a more healthy countenance?
By this the sun is setting; we may chance
Meet some of our near-dwellers with my car.'

137

This said, he rose, faint-smiling like a star
Through autumn mists, and took Peona's
    hand:
They stept into the boat, and launch'd from
    land.

Book II

O sovereign power of love! O grief! O balm!
All records, saving thine, come cool, and
    calm,
And shadowy, through the mist of passèd
    years:
For others, good or bad, hatred and tears
Have become indolent; but touching thine,
One sigh doth echo, one poor sob doth pine,
One kiss brings honey-dew from buried days.
The woes of Troy, towers smothering o'er
    their blaze,
Stiff-holden shields, far-piercing spears, keen
    blades,
Struggling, and blood, and shrieks — all
    dimly fades
Into some backward corner of the brain;
Yet, in our very souls, we feel amain
The close of Troilus and Cressid sweet.
Hence, pageant history! hence, gilded cheat!
Swart planet in the universe of deeds!
Wide sea, that one continuous murmur
    breeds
Along the pebbled shore of memory!

Many old rotten-timber'd boats there be
Upon thy vaporous bosom, magnified
To goodly vessels; many a sail of pride,
And golden-keel'd, is left unlaunch'd and
    dry.
But wherefore this? What care, though owl
    did fly
About the great Athenian admiral's mast?
What care, though striding Alexander past
The Indus with his Macedonian numbers?
Though old Ulysses tortured from his slum-
    bers
The glutted Cyclops, what care? — Juliet
    leaning
Amid her window-flowers, — sighing, —
    weaning
Tenderly her fancy from its maiden snow,
Doth more avail than these: the silver flow
Of Hero's tears, the swoon of Imogen,
Fair Pastorella in the bandit's den,
Are things to brood on with more ardency
Than the death-day of empires. Fearfully
Must such conviction come upon his head,
Who, thus far, discontent, has dared to tread,
Without one muse's smile, or kind behest,
The path of love and poesy. But rest,
In chafing restlessness, is yet more drear
Than to be crush'd, in striving to uprear
Love's standard on the battlements of song.
So once more days and nights aid me along,
Like legion'd soldiers.

　　　　　Brain-sick shepherd prince,
What promise hast thou faithful guarded
　　since
The day of sacrifice? Or, have new sorrows
Come with the constant dawn upon thy mor-
　　rows?
Alas! 'tis his old grief. For many days,
Has he been wandering in uncertain ways:
Through wilderness, and woods of mossèd
　　oaks;
Counting his woe-worn minutes, by the
　　strokes
Of the lone wood-cutter; and listening still,
Hour after hour, to each lush-leav'd rill.
Now he is sitting by a shady spring,
And elbow-deep with feverous fingering
Stems the upbursting cold: a wild rose-tree
Pavilions him in bloom, and he doth see
A bud which snares his fancy: lo! but now
He plucks it, dips its stalk in the water: how!
It swells, it buds, it flowers beneath his sight;
And, in the middle, there is softly pight
A golden butterfly; upon whose wings
There must be surely character'd strange
　　things,
For with wide eye he wonders, and smiles
　　oft.

　　Lightly this little herald flew aloft,
Follow'd by glad Endymion's claspèd hands:
Onward it flies. From languor's sullen bands
His limbs are loosed, and eager, on he hies

Dazzled to trace it in the sunny skies.
It seem'd he flew, the way so easy was;
And like a new-born spirit did he pass
Through the green evening quiet in the sun,
O'er many a heath, through many a wood-
   land dun,
Through buried paths, where sleepy twilight
   dreams
The summer time away. One track unseams
A wooded cleft, and, far away, the blue
Of ocean fades upon him; then, anew,
He sinks adown a solitary glen,
Where there was never sound of mortal men,
Saving, perhaps, some snow-light cadences
Melting to silence, when upon the breeze
Some holy bark let forth an anthem sweet,
To cheer itself to Delphi. Still his feet
Went swift beneath the merry-wingèd guide,
Until it reach'd a splashing fountain's side
That, near a cavern's mouth, for ever pour'd
Unto the temperate air; then high it soar'd,
And, downward, suddenly began to dip,
As if, athirst with so much toil, 'twould sip
The crystal spout-head; so it did, with touch
Most delicate, as though afraid to smutch
Even with mealy gold the waters clear.
But, at that very touch, to disappear
So fairy-quick, was strange! Bewilderèd,
Endymion sought around, and shook each
   bed
Of covert flowers in vain; and then he flung
Himself along the grass. What gentle tongue,

What whisperer disturb'd his gloomy rest?
It was a nymph uprisen to the breast
In the fountain's pebbly margin, and she
    stood
'Mong lilies, like the youngest of the brood.
To him her dripping hand she softly kist,
And anxiously began to plait and twist
Her ringlets round her fingers, saying: 'Youth!
Too long, alas, hast thou starved on the ruth,
The bitterness of love: too long indeed,
Seeing thou art so gentle. Could I weed
Thy soul of care, by heavens, I would offer
All the bright riches of my crystal coffer
To Amphitrite; all my clear-eyed fish,
Golden, or rainbow-sided, or purplish,
Vermilion-tail'd, or finn'd with silvery gauze;
Yea, or my veinèd pebble-floor, that draws
A virgin light to the deep; my grotto-sands,
Tawny and gold, oozed slowly from far lands
By my diligent springs: my level lilies, shells,
My charming-rod, my potent river spells;
Yes, everything, even to the pearly cup
Meander gave me, — for I bubbled up
To fainting creatures in a desert wild.
But woe is me, I am but as a child
To gladden thee; and all I dare to say,
Is, that I pity thee; that on this day
I've been thy guide; that thou must wander
    far
In other regions, past the scanty bar
To mortal steps, before thou canst be ta'en
From every wasting sigh, from every pain,

Into the gentle bosom of thy love.
Why it is thus, one knows in heaven above:
But, a poor Naiad, I guess not. Farewell!
I have a ditty for my hollow cell.'

Hereat she vanish'd from Endymion's gaze,
Who brooded o'er the water in amaze:
The dashing fount pour'd on, and where its
    pool
Lay, half asleep, in grass and rushes cool,
Quick waterflies and gnats were sporting still,
And fish were dimpling, as if good nor ill
Had fallen out that hour. The wanderer,
Holding his forehead, to keep off the burr
Of smothering fancies, patiently sat down;
And, while beneath the evening's sleepy
    frown
Glow-worms began to trim their starry
    lamps,
Thus breathed he to himself: 'Whoso en-
    camps
To take a fancied city of delight,
O what a wretch is he! and when 'tis his,
After long toil and travelling, to miss
The kernel of his hopes, how more than vile!
Yet, for him there's refreshment even in toil;
Another city doth he set about,
Free from the smallest pebble-bead of doubt
That he will seize on trickling honey-combs:
Alas! he finds them dry; and then he foams,
And onward to another city speeds.
But this is human life: the war, the deeds,

The disappointment, the anxiety,
Imagination's struggles, far and nigh,
All human; bearing in themselves this good,
That they are still the air, the subtle food,
To make us feel existence, and to show
How quiet death is. Where soil is men grow,
Whether to weeds or flowers; but for me,
There is no depth to strike in: I can see
Nought earthly worth my compassing; so
  stand
Upon a misty, jutting head of land —
Alone? No, no; and by the Orphean lute,
When mad Eurydice is listening to 't,
I'd rather stand upon this misty peak,
With not a thing to sigh for, or to seek,
But the soft shadow of my thrice-seen love,
Than be — I care not what. O meekest dove
Of heaven! O Cynthia, ten-times bright and
  fair!
From thy blue throne, now filling all the air,
Glance but one little beam of temper'd light
Into my bosom, that the dreadful might
And tyranny of love be somewhat scared!
Yet do not so, sweet queen; one torment
  spared
Would give a pang to jealous misery,
Worse than the torment's self: but rather tie
Large wings upon my shoulders, and point
  out
My love's far dwelling. Though the playful
  rout
Of Cupids shun thee, too divine art thou,

Too keen in beauty, for thy silver prow
Not to have dipp'd in love's most gentle
  stream.
O be propitious, nor severely deem
My madness impious; for, by all the stars
That tend thy bidding, I do think the bars
That kept my spirit in are burst — that I
Am sailing with thee through the dizzy sky!
How beautiful thou art! The world how deep!
How tremulous-dazzlingly the wheels sweep
Around their axle! Then these gleaming reins,
How lithe! When this thy chariot attains
Its airy goal, haply some bower veils
Those twilight eyes? Those eyes! — my spirit
  fails;
Dear goddess, help! or the wide-gaping air
Will gulph me — help!' — At this, with
  madden'd stare,
And lifted hands, and trembling lips, he
  stood;
Like old Deucalion mountain'd o'er the
  flood,
Or blind Orion hungry for the morn.
And, but from the deep cavern there was
  borne
A voice, he had been froze to senseless stone;
Nor sigh of his, nor plaint, nor passion'd
  moan
Had more been heard. Thus swell'd it forth:
  'Descend,
Young mountaineer! descend where alleys
  bend

Into the sparry hollows of the world!
Oft hast thou seen bolts of the thunder hurl'd
As from thy threshold; day by day hast been
A little lower than the chilly sheen
Of icy pinnacles, and dipp'dst thine arms
Into the deadening ether that still charms
Their marble being; now, as deep profound
As those are high, descend! He ne'er is
     crown'd
With immortality, who fears to follow
Where airy voices lead: so through the hol-
     low,
The silent mysteries of earth, descend!'

   He heard but the last words, nor could
     contend
One moment in reflection: for he fled
Into the fearful deep, to hide his head
From the clear moon, the trees, and coming
     madness.

   'Twas far too strange and wonderful for
     sadness;
Sharpening, by degrees, his appetite
To dive into the deepest. Dark, nor light,
The region; nor bright, nor sombre wholly,
But mingled up; a gleaming melancholy;
A dusky empire and its diadems;
One faint eternal eventide of gems.
Ay, millions sparkled on a vein of gold,
Along whose track the prince quick footsteps
     told,

147

With all its lines abrupt and angular:
Out-shooting sometimes, like a meteor-star,
Through a vast antre; then the metal woof,
Like Vulcan's rainbow, with some monstrous
    roof
Curves hugely: now, far in the deep abyss,
It seems an angry lightning, and doth hiss
Fancy into belief: anon it leads
Through winding passages, where sameness
    breeds
Vexing conceptions of some sudden change;
Whether to silver grots, or giant range
Of sapphire columns, or fantastic bridge
Athwart a flood of crystal. On a ridge
Now fareth he, that o'er the vast beneath
Towers like an ocean-cliff, and whence he
    seeth
A hundred waterfalls, whose voices come
But as the murmuring surge. Chilly and
    numb
His bosom grew, when first he, far away,
Descried an orbèd diamond, set to fray
Old Darkness from his throne: 'twas like the
    sun
Uprisen o'er chaos: and with such a stun
Came the amazement, that, absorb'd in it,
He saw not fiercer wonders — past the wit
Of any spirit to tell, but one of those
Who, when this planet's sphering time doth
    close,
Will be its high remembrancers: who they?
The mighty ones who have made eternal day

For Greece and England. While astonishment
With deep-drawn sighs was quieting, he went
Into a marble gallery, passing through
A mimic temple, so complete and true
In sacred custom, that he well-nigh fear'd
To search it inwards; whence far off appear'd,
Through a long pillar'd vista, a fair shrine,
And, just beyond, on light tiptoe divine,
A quiver'd Dian. Stepping awfully,
The youth approach'd; oft turning his veil'd
    eye
Down sidelong aisles, and into niches old:
And, when more near against the marble cold
He had touch'd his forehead, he began to
    thread
All courts and passages, where silence dead,
Roused by his whispering footsteps,
    murmur'd faint:
And long he traversed to and fro, to acquaint
Himself with every mystery, and awe;
Till, weary, he sat down before the maw
Of a wide outlet, fathomless and dim,
To wild uncertainty and shadows grim.
There, when new wonders ceased to float
    before,
And thoughts of self came on, how crude
    and sore
The journey homeward to habitual self!
A mad-pursuing of the fog-born elf,
Whose flitting lantern, through rude nettle-
    brier,
Cheats us into a swamp, into a fire,

Into the bosom of a hated thing.

What misery most drowningly doth sing
In lone Endymion's ear, now he has raught
The goal of consciousness? Ah, 'tis the
   thought,
The deadly feel of solitude: for lo!
He cannot see the heavens, nor the flow
Of rivers, nor hill-flowers running wild
In pink and purple chequer, nor, up-piled,
The cloudy rack slow journeying in the west,
Like herded elephants; nor felt, nor prest
Cool grass, nor tasted the fresh slumberous
   air;
But far from such companionship to wear
An unknown time, surcharged with grief,
   away,
Was now his lot. And must he patient stay,
Tracing fantastic figures with his spear?
'No!' exclaimed he, 'why should I tarry here?'
No! loudly echoed times innumerable.
At which he straightway started, and 'gan tell
His paces back into the temple's chief;
Warming and glowing strong in the belief
Of help from Dian: so that when again
He caught her airy form, thus did he plain,
Moving more near the while: 'O Haunter
   chaste
Of river sides, and woods, and heathy waste,
Where with thy silver bow and arrows keen
Art thou now forested? O woodland Queen,

What smoothest air thy smoother forehead
    woos?
Where dost thou listen to the wide halloos
Of thy disparted nymphs? Through what dark
    tree
Glimmers thy crescent? Wheresoe'er it be,
'Tis in the breath of heaven: thou dost taste
Freedom as none can taste it, nor dost waste
Thy loveliness in dismal elements;
But, finding in our green earth sweet con-
    tents,
There livest blissfully. Ah, if to thee
It feels Elysian, how rich to me,
An exiled mortal, sounds its pleasant name!
Within my breast there lives a choking
    flame —
O let me cool 't the zephyr-boughs among!
A homeward fever parches up my tongue —
O let me slake it at the running springs!
Upon my ear a noisy nothing rings —
O let me once more hear the linnet's note!
Before mine eyes thick films and shadows
    float —
O let me 'noint them with the heaven's light:
Dost thou now lave thy feet and ankles white?
O think how sweet to me the freshening
    sluice!
Dost thou now please thy thirst with berry-
    juice?
O think how this dry palate would rejoice!
If in soft slumber thou dost hear my voice,
O think how I should love a bed of

flowers! —
Young goddess! let me see my native bowers!
Deliver me from this rapacious deep!'

Thus ending loudly, as he would o'erleap
His destiny, alert he stood: but when
Obstinate silence came heavily again,
Feeling about for its old couch of space
And airy cradle, lowly bow'd his face,
Desponding, o'er the marble floor's cold
     thrill.
But 'twas not long; for, sweeter than the rill
To its old channel, or a swollen tide
To margin sallows, were the leaves he spied,
And flowers, and wreaths, and ready myrtle
     crowns
Up heaping through the slab: refreshment
     drowns
Itself, and strives its own delights to hide —
Nor in one spot alone; the floral pride
In a long whispering birth enchanted grew
Before his footsteps; as when heaved anew
Old ocean rolls a lengthen'd wave to the
     shore,
Down whose green back the short-lived
     foam, all hoar,
Bursts gradual, with a wayward indolence.

Increasing still in heart, and pleasant sense,
Upon his fairy journey on he hastes;
So anxious for the end, he scarcely wastes

One moment with his hand among the
   sweets:
Onward he goes — he stops — his bosom
   beats
As plainly in his ear, as the faint charm
Of which the throbs were born. This still
   alarm,
This sleepy music, forced him walk tiptoe;
For it came more softly than the east could
   blow
Arion's magic to the Atlantic isles;
Or than the west, made jealous by the smiles
Of throned Apollo, could breathe back the
   lyre
To seas Ionian and Tyrian.

   O did he ever live, that lonely man,
Who loved — and music slew not? 'Tis the
   pest
Of love, that fairest joys give most unrest;
That things of delicate and tenderest worth
Are swallow'd all, and make a searèd dearth,
By one consuming flame: it doth immerse
And suffocate true blessings in a curse.
Half-happy, by comparison of bliss,
Is miserable. 'Twas even so with this
Dew-dropping melody, in the Carian's ear;
First heaven, then hell, and then forgotten
   clear,
Vanish'd in elemental passion.

   And down some swart abysm he had gone,

Had not a heavenly guide benignant led
To where thick myrtle branches, 'gainst his
    head
Brushing, awaken'd: then the sounds again
Went noiseless as a passing noontide rain
Over a bower, where little space he stood;
For as the sunset peeps into a wood,
So saw he panting light, and towards it went
Through winding alleys; and lo, wonder-
    ment!
Upon soft verdure saw, one here, one there,
Cupids a-slumbering on their pinions fair.

  After a thousand mazes overgone,
At last, with sudden step, he came upon
A chamber, myrtle-wall'd, embower'd high,
Full of light, incense, tender minstrelsy,
And more of beautiful and strange beside:
For on a silken couch of rosy pride,
In midst of all, there lay a sleeping youth
Of fondest beauty; fonder, in fair sooth,
Than sighs could fathom, or contentment
    reach:
And coverlids gold-tinted like the peach,
Or ripe October's faded marigolds,
Fell sleek about him in a thousand folds —
Not hiding up an Apollonian curve
Of neck and shoulder, nor the tenting swerve
Of knee from knee, nor ankles pointing light;
But rather, giving them to the fill'd sight
Officiously. Sideway his face reposed
On one white arm, and tenderly unclosed,

By tenderest pressure, a faint damask mouth
To slumbery pout: just as the morning south
Disparts a dew-lipp'd rose. Above his head,
Four lily stalks did their white honours wed
To make a coronal; and round him grew
All tendrils green, of every bloom and hue,
Together intertwined and trammell'd fresh:
The vine of glossy sprout; the ivy mesh,
Shading its Ethiop berries; and woodbine,
Of velvet leaves and bugle-blooms divine;
Convolvulus in streakèd vases flush;
The creeper, mellowing for an autumn blush;
And virgin's bower, trailing airily;
With others of the sisterhood. Hard by,
Stood serene Cupids watching silently.
One, kneeling to a lyre, touch'd the strings,
Muffling to death the pathos with his wings;
And, ever and anon, uprose to look
At the youth's slumber; while another took
A willow bough, distilling odorous dew,
And shook it on his hair; another flew
In through the woven roof, and fluttering-
    wise
Rain'd violets upon his sleeping eyes.

   At these enchantments, and yet many more,
The breathless Latmian wonder'd o'er and
    o'er;
Until, impatient in embarrassment,
He forthright pass'd, and lightly treading
    went

To that same feather'd lyrist, who straight-
    way,
Smiling, thus whisper'd: 'Though from up-
    per day
Thou art a wanderer, and thy presence here
Might seem unholy, be of happy cheer!
For 'tis the nicest touch of human honour,
When some ethereal and high-favouring do-
    nor
Presents immortal bowers to mortal sense;
As now 'tis done to thee, Endymion. Hence
Was I in no wise startled. So recline
Upon these living flowers. Here is wine,
Alive with sparkles — never, I aver,
Since Ariadne was a vintager,
So cool a purple: taste these juicy pears,
Sent me by sad Vertumnus, when his fears
Were high about Pomona; here is cream,
Deepening to richness from a snowy gleam;
Sweeter than that nurse Amalthea skimm'd
For the boy Jupiter: and here, undimm'd
By any touch, a bunch of blooming plums
Ready to melt between an infant's gums:
And here is manna pick'd from Syrian trees,
In starlight, by the three Hesperides.
Feast on, and meanwhile I will let thee know
Of all these things around us.' He did so,
Still brooding o'er the cadence of his lyre;
And thus: 'I need not any hearing tire
By telling how the sea-born goddess pined
For a mortal youth, and how she strove to
    bind

Him all in all unto her doting self.
Who would not be so prison'd? but, fond elf
He was content to let her amorous plea
Faint through his careless arms; content to
    see
An unseized heaven dying at his feet;
Content, O fool! to make a cold retreat,
When on the pleasant grass such love, love-
    lorn,
Lay sorrowing; when every tear was born
Of diverse passion; when her lips and eyes
Were closed in sullen moisture, and quick
    sighs
Came vex'd and pettish through her nostrils
    small.
Hush! no exclaim — yet, justly might'st thou
    call
Curses upon his head. — I was half glad,
But my poor mistress went distract and mad,
When the boar tusk'd him: so away she flew
To Jove's high throne, and by her plainings
    drew
Immortal tear-drops down the Thunderer's
    beard;
Whereon, it was decreed he should be rear'd
Each summer-time to life. Lo! this is he,
That same Adonis, safe in the privacy
Of this still region all his winter-sleep.
Ay, sleep; for when our love-sick queen did
    weep
Over his wanèd corse, the tremulous shower

Heal'd up the wound, and, with a balmy
    power,
Medicined death to a lengthen'd drowsiness:
The which she fills with visions, and doth
    dress
In all this quiet luxury; and hath set
Us young immortals, without any let,
To watch his slumber through. 'Tis well-nigh
    pass'd,
Even to a moment's filling up, and fast
She scuds with summer breezes, to pant
    through
The first long kiss, warm firstling, to renew
Embower'd sports in Cytherea's isle.
Look, how those wingèd listeners all this
    while
Stand anxious: see! behold!' — This clamant
    word
Broke through the careful silence; for they
    heard
A rustling noise of leaves, and out there
    flutter'd
Pigeons and doves: Adonis something
    mutter'd,
The while one hand, that erst upon his thigh
Lay dormant, moved convulsed and gradu-
    ally
Up to his forehead. Then there was a hum
Of sudden voices, echoing, 'Come! come!
Arise! awake! Clear summer has forth walk'd
Unto the clover-sward, and she has talk'd
Full soothingly to every nested finch:

Rise, Cupids! or we'll give the blue-bell pinch
To your dimpled arms. Once more sweet life
    begin!'
At this, from every side they hurried in,
Rubbing their sleepy eyes with lazy wrists,
And doubling overhead their little fists
In backward yawns. But all were soon alive:
For as delicious wine doth, sparkling, dive
In nectar'd clouds and curls through water
    fair,
So from the arbour roof down swell'd an air
Odorous and enlivening; making all
To laugh, and play, and sing, and loudly call
For their sweet queen: when lo! the wreathèd
    green
Disparted, and far upward could be seen
Blue heaven, and a silver car, air-borne,
Whose silent wheels, fresh wet from clouds
    of morn,
Spun off a drizzling dew, — which falling
    chill
On soft Adonis' shoulders, made him still
Nestle and turn uneasily about.
Soon were the white doves plain, with necks
    stretched out,
And silken traces lighten'd in descent;
And soon, returning from love's banishment,
Queen Venus leaning downward open-arm'd:
Her shadow fell upon his breast, and charm'd
A tumult to his heart, and a new life
Into his eyes. Ah, miserable strife,
But for her comforting! unhappy sight,

But meeting her blue orbs! Who, who can write
Of these first minutes? The unchariest muse
To embracements warm as theirs makes coy
    excuse.

   O it has ruffled every spirit there,
Saving Love's self, who stands superb to
    share
The general gladness: awfully he stands;
A sovereign quell is in his waving hands;
No sight can bear the lightning of his bow;
His quiver is mysterious, none can know
What themselves think of it; from forth his
    eyes
There darts strange light of varied hues and
    dyes:
A scowl is sometimes on his brow, but who
Look full upon it feel anon the blue
Of his fair eyes run liquid through their souls.
Endymion feels it, and no more controls
The burning prayer within him; so, bent low,
He had begun a plaining of his woe.
But Venus, bending forward, said: 'My child,
Favour this gentle youth; his days are wild
With love — he — but alas! too well I see
Thou know'st the deepness of his misery.
Ah, smile not so, my son: I tell thee true,
That when through heavy hours I used to
    rue
The endless sleep of this new-born Adon',
This stranger aye I pitied. For upon

A dreary morning once I fled away
Into the breezy clouds, to weep and pray
For this my love: for vexing Mars had teased
Me even to tears: thence, when a little eased,
Down-looking, vacant, through a hazy wood,
I saw this youth as he despairing stood:
Those same dark curls blown vagrant in the
    wind:
Those same full fringèd lids a constant blind
Over his sullen eyes: I saw him throw
Himself on wither'd leaves, even as though
Death had come sudden; for no jot he moved,
Yet mutter'd wildly. I could hear he loved
Some fair immortal, and that his embrace
Had zoned her through the night. There is
    no trace
Of this in heaven: I have mark'd each cheek,
And find it is the vainest thing to seek;
And that of all things 'tis kept secretest.
Endymion! one day thou wilt be blest:
So still obey the guiding hand that fends
Thee safely through these wonders for sweet
    ends.
'Tis a concealment needful in extreme;
And if I guess'd not so, the sunny beam
Thou shouldst mount up to with me. Now
    adieu!
Here must we leave thee.' — At these words
    up flew
The impatient doves, up rose the floating car,
Up went the hum celestial. High afar
The Latmian saw them minish into nought;

And, when all were clear vanish'd, still he
    caught
A vivid lightning from that dreadful bow.
When all was darken'd, with Ætnean throe
The earth closed — gave a solitary moan —
And left him once again in twilight lone.

He did not rave, he did not stare aghast,
For all those visions were o'ergone, and past,
And he in loneliness: he felt assured
Of happy times, when all he had endured
Would seem a feather to the mighty prize.
So, with unusual gladness, on he hies
Through caves, and palaces of mottled ore,
Gold dome, and crystal wall, and turquois
    floor,
Black polish'd porticoes of awful shade,
And, at the last, a diamond balustrade,
Leading afar past wild magnificence,
Spiral through ruggedest loop-holes, and
    thence
Stretching across a void, then guiding o'er
Enormous chasms, where, all foam and roar,
Streams subterranean tease their granite
    beds;
Then heighten'd just above the silvery heads
Of a thousand fountains, so that he could
    dash
The waters with his spear; but at the splash,
Done heedlessly, those spouting columns
    rose
Sudden a poplar's height, and 'gan to enclose

His diamond path with fretwork, streaming
    round
Alive, and dazzling cool, and with a sound,
Haply, like dolphin tumults, when sweet
    shells
Welcome the float of Thetis. Long he dwells
On this delight; for, every minute's space,
The streams with changèd magic interlace:
Sometimes like delicatest lattices,
Cover'd with crystal vines; then weeping
    trees,
Moving about as in a gentle wind,
Which, in a wink, to watery gauze refined,
Pour'd into shapes of curtain'd canopies,
Spangled, and rich with liquid broideries
Of flowers, peacocks, swans, and naiads fair.
Swifter than lightning went these wonders
    rare;
And then the water, into stubborn streams
Collecting, mimick'd the wrought oaken
    beams,
Pillars, and frieze, and high fantastic roof,
Of those dusk places in times far aloof
Cathedrals call'd. He bade a loth farewell
To these founts Protean, passing gulph, and
    dell,
And torrent, and ten thousand jutting shapes,
Half seen through deepest gloom, and griesly
    gapes,
Blackening on every side, and overhead
A vaulted dome like heaven's, far bespread

With starlight gems: ay, all so huge and
    strange,
The solitary felt a hurried change
Working within him into something
    dreary, —
Vex'd like a morning eagle, lost, and weary,
And purblind amid foggy midnight wolds,
But he revives at once: for who beholds
New sudden things, nor casts his mental
    slough?
Forth from a rugged arch, in the dusk below,
Came mother Cybele! alone — alone —
In sombre chariot; dark foldings thrown
About her majesty, and front death-pale,
With turrets crown'd. Four manèd lions hale
The sluggish wheels; solemn their toothèd
    maws,
Their surly eyes brow-hidden, heavy paws
Uplifted drowsily, and nervy tails
Cowering their tawny brushes. Silent sails
This shadowy queen athwart, and faints away
In another gloomy arch.

               Wherefore delay,
Young traveller, in such a mournful place?
Art thou wayworn, or canst not further trace
The diamond path? And does it indeed end
Abrupt in middle air? Yet earthward bend
Thy forehead, and to Jupiter cloud-borne
Call ardently! He was indeed wayworn;
Abrupt, in middle air, his way was lost;
To cloud-borne Jove he bowed, and there
    crost

Towards him a large eagle, 'twixt whose
    wings,
Without one impious word, himself he flings,
Committed to the darkness and the gloom:
Down, down, uncertain to what pleasant
    doom,
Swift as a fathoming plummet down he fell
Through unknown things; till exhaled aspho-
    del,
And rose, with spicy fannings interbreathed,
Came swelling forth where little caves were
    wreathed
So thick with leaves and mosses, that they
    seem'd
Large honeycombs of green, and freshly
    teem'd
With airs delicious. In the greenest nook
The eagle landed him, and farewell took.

    It was a jasmine bower, all bestrown
With golden moss. His every sense had grown
Ethereal for pleasure; 'bove his head
Flew a delight half graspable; his tread
Was Hesperean; to his capable ears
Silence was music from the holy spheres;
A dewy luxury was in his eyes;
The little flowers felt his pleasant sighs
And stirr'd them faintly. Verdant cave and
    cell
He wander'd through, oft wondering at such
    swell
Of sudden exaltation: but, 'Alas!'

Said he, 'will all this gush of feeling pass
Away in solitude? And must they wane,
Like melodies upon a sandy plain,
Without an echo? Then shall I be left
So sad, so melancholy, so bereft!
Yet still I feel immortal! O my love,
My breath of life, where art thou? High
    above,
Dancing before the morning gates of heaven?
Or keeping watch among those starry seven,
Old Atlas' children? Art a maid of the waters
One of shell-winding Triton's bright-hair'd
    daughters?
Or art, impossible! a nymph of Dian's,
Weaving a coronal of tender scions
For very idleness? Where'er thou art,
Methinks it now is at my will to start
Into thine arms; to scare Aurora's train,
And snatch thee from the morning; o'er the
    main
To scud like a wild bird, and take thee off
From thy sea-foamy cradle; or to doff
Thy shepherd vest, and woo thee 'mid fresh
    leaves.
No, no, too eagerly my soul deceives
Its powerless self: I know this cannot be.
O let me then by some sweet dreaming flee
To her entrancements: hither sleep awhile!
Hither, most gentle sleep! and soothing foil
For some few hours the coming solitude.'

Thus spake he, and that moment felt en-
   dued
With power to dream deliciously; so wound
Through a dim passage, searching till he
   found
The smoothest mossy bed and deepest,
   where
He threw himself, and just into the air
Stretching his indolent arms, he took, O bliss!
A naked waist: 'Fair Cupid, whence is this?'
A well-known voice sigh'd, 'Sweetest, here
   am I!'
At which soft ravishment, with doting cry
They trembled to each other. — Helicon!
O fountain'd hill! Old Homer's Helicon!
That thou wouldst spout a little streamlet
   o'er
These sorry pages; then the verse would soar
And sing above this gentle pair, like lark
Over his nested young: but all is dark
Around thine aged top, and thy clear fount
Exhales in mists to heaven. Ay, the count
Of mighty Poets is made up; the scroll
Is folded by the Muses; the bright roll
Is in Apollo's hand: our dazèd eyes
Have seen a new tinge in the western skies:
The world has done its duty. Yet, oh yet,
Although the sun of poesy is set,
These lovers did embrace, and we must weep
That there is no old power left to steep
A quill immortal in their joyous tears.
Long time in silence did their anxious fears

Question that thus it was; long time they lay
Fondling and kissing every doubt away;
Long time ere soft caressing sobs began
To mellow into words, and then there ran
Two bubbling springs of talk from their sweet
    lips.
'O known Unknown! from whom my being
    sips
Such darling essence, wherefore may I not
Be ever in these arms? in this sweet spot
Pillow my chin for ever? ever press
These toying hands and kiss their smooth
    excess?
Why not for ever and for ever feel
That breath about my eyes? Ah, thou wilt
    steal
Away from me again, indeed, indeed —
Thou wilt be gone away, and wilt not heed
My lonely madness. Speak, my kindest fair!
Is — is it to be so? No! Who will dare
To pluck thee from me? And, of thine own
    will
Full well I feel thou wouldst not leave
    me. Still
Let me entwine thee surer, surer — now
How can we part? Elysium! who art thou?
Who, that thou canst not be for ever here,
Or lift me with thee to some starry sphere?
Enchantress! tell me by this soft embrace,
By the most soft completion of thy face,
Those lips, O slippery blisses! twinkling eyes,
And by these tenderest, milky

sovereignties —
These tenderest, and by the nectar-wine,
The passion' — 'O loved Ida the divine!
Endymion! dearest! Ah, unhappy me!
His soul will 'scape us — O felicity!
How he does love me! His poor temples beat
To the very tune of love — how sweet, sweet,
    sweet!
Revive, dear youth, or I shall faint and die;
Revive, or these soft hours will hurry by
In trancèd dullness; speak, and let that spell
Affright this lethargy! I cannot quell
Its heavy pressure, and will press at least
My lips to thine, that they may richly feast
Until we taste the life of love again.
What! dost thou move? dost kiss? O bliss! O
    pain!
I love thee, youth, more than I can conceive;
And so long absence from thee doth bereave
My soul of any rest: yet must I hence:
Yet, can I not to starry eminence
Uplift thee; nor for very shame can own
Myself to thee. Ah, dearest! do not groan,
Or thou wilt force me from this secrecy,
And I must blush in heaven. O that I
Had done it already! that the dreadful smiles
At my lost brightness, my impassion'd wiles,
Had waned from Olympus' solemn height,
And from all serious Gods; that our delight
Was quite forgotten, save of us alone!
And wherefore so ashamed? 'Tis but to atone
For endless pleasure, by some coward

blushes:
Yet must I be a coward! Horror rushes
Too palpable before me — the sad look
Of Jove — Minerva's start — no bosom
    shook
With awe of purity — no Cupid pinion
In reverence vail'd — my crystalline domin-
    ion
Half lost, and all old hymns made nullity!
But what is this to love? O I could fly
With thee into the ken of heavenly powers,
So thou wouldst thus, for many sequent
    hours,
Press me so sweetly. Now I swear at once
That I am wise, that Pallas is a dunce —
Perhaps her love like mine is but
    unknown —
O I do think that I have been alone
In chastity! yes, Pallas has been sighing,
While every eve saw me my hair uptying
With fingers cool as aspen leaves. Sweet love,
I was as vague as solitary dove,
Nor knew that nests were built. Now a soft
    kiss —
Ay, by that kiss, I vow an endless bliss,
An immortality of passion's thine:
Ere long I will exalt thee to the shine
Of heaven ambrosial; and we will shade
Ourselves whole summers by a river glade;
And I will tell thee stories of the sky,
And breathe thee whispers of its minstrelsy,
My happy love will overwing all bounds!

O let me melt into thee! let the sounds
Of our close voices marry at their birth;
Let us entwine hoveringly! O dearth
Of human words! roughness of mortal
  speech!
Lispings empyrean will I sometimes teach
Thine honey'd tongue — lute-breathings
  which I gasp
To have thee understand, now while I clasp
Thee thus, and weep for fondness — I am
  pain'd,
Endymion: woe! woe! is grief contain'd
In the very deeps of pleasure, my sole
  life?' —
Hereat, with many sobs, her gentle strife
Melted into a languor. He return'd
Entrancèd vows and tears.

                    Ye who have yearn'd
With too much passion, will here stay and
  pity,
For the mere sake of truth; as 'tis a ditty
Not of these days, but long ago 'twas told
By a cavern wind unto a forest old;
And then the forest told it in a dream
To a sleeping lake, whose cool and level
  gleam
A poet caught as he was journeying
To Phœbus' shrine; and in it he did fling
His weary limbs, bathing an hour's space,
And after, straight in that inspired place
He sang the story up into the air,

Giving it universal freedom. There
Has it been ever sounding for those ears
Whose tips are glowing hot. The legend
    cheers
Yon sentinel stars; and he who listens to it
Must surely be self-doom'd or he will rue it:
For quenchless burnings come upon the
    heart,
Made fiercer by a fear lest any part
Should be engulphed in the eddying wind.
As much as here is penn'd doth always find
A resting-place, thus much comes clear and
    plain;
Anon the strange voice is upon the wane —
And 'tis but echoed from departing sound,
That the fair visitant at last unwound
Her gentle limbs, and left the youth
    asleep. —
Thus the tradition of the gusty deep.

    Now turn we to our former chroniclers. —
Endymion awoke, that grief of hers
Sweet paining on his ear: he sickly guess'd
How lone he was once more, and sadly
    press'd
His empty arms together, hung his head,
And most forlorn upon that widow'd bed
Sat silently. Love's madness he had known:
Often with more than tortured lion's groan
Moanings had burst from him; but now that
    rage
Had pass'd away: no longer did he wage

A rough-voiced war against the dooming
    stars.
No, he had felt too much for such harsh jars:
The lyre of his soul Æolian tuned
Forgot all violence, and but communed
With melancholy thought: O he had swoon'd
Drunken from pleasure's nipple! and his love
Henceforth was dove-like. — Loth was he to
    move
From the imprinted couch, and when he did,
'Twas with slow, languid paces, and face hid
In muffling hands. So temper'd, out he
    stray'd,
Half seeing visions that might have dismay'd
Alecto's serpents; ravishments more keen
Than Hermes' pipe, when anxious he did
    lean
Over eclipsing eyes: and at the last
It was a sounding grotto, vaulted, vast,
O'erstudded with a thousand, thousand
    pearls,
And crimson-mouthèd shells with stubborn
    curls
Of every shape and size, even to the bulk
In which whales harbour close, to brood and
    sulk
Against an endless storm. Moreover too,
Fish-semblances of green and azure hue,
Ready to snort their streams. In this cool
    wonder
Endymion sat down, and 'gan to ponder
On all his life: his youth, up to the day

When 'mid acclaim, and feasts, and garlands
    gay,
He stept upon his shepherd throne: the look
Of his white palace in wild forest nook,
And all the revels he had lorded there:
Each tender maiden whom he once thought
    fair,
With every friend and fellow-woodlander —
Pass'd like a dream before him. Then the spur
Of the old bards to mighty deeds: his plans
To nurse the golden age 'mong shepherd
    clans:
That wondrous night: the great Pan-festival:
His sister's sorrow; and his wanderings all,
Until into the earth's deep maw he rush'd:
Then all its buried magic, till it flush'd
High with excessive love. 'And now,' thought
    he,
'How long must I remain in jeopardy
Of blank amazements that amaze no more?
Now I have tasted her sweet soul to the core,
All other depths are shallow: essences,
Once spiritual, are like muddy lees,
Meant but to fertilize my earthly root,
And make my branches lift a golden fruit
Into the bloom of heaven: other light,
Though it be quick and sharp enough to
    blight
The Olympian eagle's vision, is dark,
Dark as the parentage of chaos. Hark!
My silent thoughts are echoing from these
    shells;

Or they are but the ghosts, the dying swells
Of noises far away? — list!' — Hereupon
He kept an anxious ear. The humming tone
Came louder, and behold, there as he lay,
On either side outgush'd, with misty spray,
A copious spring; and both together dash'd
Swift, mad, fantastic round the rocks, and
    lash'd
Among the conchs and shells of the lofty
    grot,
Leaving a trickling dew. At last they shot
Down from the ceiling's height, pouring a
    noise
As of some breathless racers whose hopes
    poise
Upon the last few steps, and with spent force
Along the ground they took a winding course.
Endymion follow'd — for it seem'd that one
Ever pursued, the other strove to shun —
Follow'd their languid mazes, till well-nigh
He had left thinking of the mystery, —
And was now rapt in tender hoverings
Over the vanish'd bliss. Ah! what is it sings
His dream away? What melodies are these?
They sound as through the whispering of
    trees,
Not native in such barren vaults. Give ear!

'O Arethusa, peerless nymph! why fear
Such tenderness as mine? Great Dian, why,
Why didst thou hear her prayer? O that I
Were rippling round her dainty fairness now,

Circling about her waist, and striving how
To entice her to a dive! then stealing in
Between her luscious lips and eyelids thin.
O that her shining hair was in the sun,
And I distilling from it thence to run
In amorous rillets down her shrinking form!
To linger on her lily shoulders, warm
Between her kissing breasts, and every charm
Touch raptured! — See how painfully I flow:
Fair maid, be pitiful to my great woe.
Stay, stay thy weary course, and let me lead,
A happy wooer, to the flowery mead
Where all that beauty snared me.' — 'Cruel
 god,
Desist! or my offended mistress' nod
Will stagnate all thy fountains: — tease me
 not
With syren words — Ah, have I really got
Such power to madden thee? And is it
 true —
Away, away, or I shall dearly rue
My very thoughts: in mercy then away,
Kindest Alpheus, for should I obey
My own dear will, 'twould be a deadly bane.
O, Oread-Queen! would that thou hadst a
 pain
Like this of mine, then would I fearless turn
And be a criminal. Alas, I burn,
I shudder — gentle river, get thee hence.
Alpheus! thou enchanter! every sense
Of mine was once made perfect in these
 woods.

Fresh breezes, bowery lawns, and innocent
  floods,
Ripe fruits, and lonely couch, contentment
  gave;
But ever since I heedlessly did lave
In thy deceitful stream, a panting glow
Grew strong within me; wherefore serve me
  so,
And call it love? Alas! 'twas cruelty.
Not once more did I close my happy eye
Amid the thrushes' song. Away! Avaunt!
O 'twas a cruel thing.' — 'Now thou dost
  taunt
So softly, Arethusa, that I think
If thou wast playing on my shady brink,
Thou wouldst bathe once again. Innocent
  maid!
Stifle thine heart no more; nor be afraid
Of angry powers: there are deities
Will shade us with their wings. Those fitful
  sighs
'Tis almost death to hear: O let me pour
A dewy balm upon them! — fear no more,
Sweet Arethusa! Dian's self must feel
Sometime these very pangs. Dear maiden,
  steal
Blushing into my soul, and let us fly
These dreary caverns for the open sky.
I will delight thee all my winding course,
From the green sea up to my hidden source
About Arcadian forests; and will show
The channels where my coolest waters flow

Through mossy rocks; where, 'mid exuber-
    ant green,
I roam in pleasant darkness, more unseen
Than Saturn in his exile; where I brim
Round flowery islands, and take thence a
    skim
Of mealy sweets, which myriads of bees
Buzz from their honey'd wings: and thou
    shouldst please
Thyself to choose the richest, where we might
Be incense-pillow'd every summer night.
Doff all sad fears, thou white deliciousness,
And let us be thus comforted; unless
Thou couldst rejoice to see my hopeless
    stream
Hurry distracted from Sol's temperate beam,
And pour to death along some hungry
    sands.' —
'What can I do, Alpheus? Dian stands
Severe before me: persecuting fate!
Unhappy Arethusa! thou wast late
A huntress free in —' At this, sudden fell
Those two sad streams adown a fearful dell.
The Latmian listen'd, but he heard no more,
Save echo, faint repeating o'er and o'er
The name of Arethusa. On the verge
Of that dark gulph he wept, and said: 'I urge
Thee, gentle Goddess of my pilgrimage,
By our eternal hopes, to soothe, to assuage,
If thou art powerful, these lovers' pains;
And make them happy in some happy plains.'

He turn'd — there was a whelming sound
   — he stept —
There was a cooler light; and so he kept
Towards it by a sandy path, and lo!
More suddenly than doth a moment go,
The visions of the earth were gone and
   fled —
He saw the giant sea above his head.

Book III

There are who lord it o'er their fellow-men
With most prevailing tinsel: who unpen
Their baaing vanities, to browse away
The comfortable green and juicy hay
From human pastures; or, O torturing fact!
Who, through an idiot blink, will see
    unpack'd
Fire-branded foxes to sear up and singe
Our gold and ripe-ear'd hopes. With not one
    tinge
Of sanctuary splendour, not a sight
Able to face an owl's, they still are dight
By the blear-eyed nations in empurpled vests,
And crowns, and turbans. With unladen
    breasts,
Save of blown self-applause, they proudly
    mount
To their spirit's perch, their being's high ac-
    count,
Their tip-top nothings, their dull skies, their
    thrones —
Amid the fierce intoxicating tones

Of trumpets, shoutings, and belabour'd
    drums,
And sudden cannon. Ah! how all this hums,
In wakeful ears, like uproar past and gone —
Like thunder-clouds that spake to Babylon,
And set those old Chaldeans to their
    tasks. —
Are then regalities all gilded masks?
No, there are thronèd seats unscalable
But by a patient wing, a constant spell,
Or by ethereal things that, unconfined,
Can make a ladder of the eternal wind,
And poise about in cloudy thunder-tents
To watch the abysm-birth of elements.
Ay, 'bove the withering of old-lipp'd Fate
A thousand Powers keep religious state,
In water, fiery realm, and airy bourne;
And, silent, as a consecrated urn,
Hold sphery sessions for a season due.
Yet few of these far majesties, ah, few!
Have bared their operations to this globe —
Few, who with gorgeous pageantry enrobe
Our piece of heaven — whose benevolence
Shakes hand with our own Ceres; every sense
Filling with spiritual sweets to plenitude,
As bees gorge full their cells. And by the feud
'Twixt Nothing and Creation, I here swear,
Eterne Apollo! that thy Sister fair
Is of all these the gentlier-mightiest.
When thy gold breath is misting in the west,
She unobservèd steals unto her throne,
And there she sits most meek and most alone;

As if she had not pomp subservient;
As if thine eye, high Poet! was not bent
Towards her with the Muses in thine heart;
As if the minist'ring stars kept not apart,
Waiting for silver-footed messages.
O Moon! the oldest shades 'mong oldest trees
Feel palpitations when thou lookest in.
O Moon! old boughs lisp forth a holier din
The while they feel thine airy fellowship.
Thou dost bless everywhere, with silver lip
Kissing dead things to life. The sleeping kine,
Couch'd in thy brightness, dream of fields
    divine:
Innumerable mountains rise, and rise,
Ambitious for the hallowing of thine eyes,
And yet thy benediction passeth not
One obscure hiding-place, one little spot
Where pleasure may be sent: the nested wren
Has thy fair face within its tranquil ken,
And from beneath a sheltering ivy leaf
Takes glimpses of thee; thou art a relief
To the poor patient oyster, where it sleeps,
Within its pearly house; — The mighty deeps,
The monstrous sea is thine — the myriad
    sea!
O Moon! far spooming Ocean bows to thee,
And Tellus feels his forehead's cumbrous
    load.

  Cynthia! where art thou now? What far
    abode
Of green or silvery bower doth enshrine

Such utmost beauty? Alas, thou dost pine
For one as sorrowful: thy cheek is pale
For one whose cheek is pale: thou dost bewail
His tears who weep for thee. Where dost thou
    sigh?
Ah! surely that light peeps from Vesper's eye,
Or, what a thing is love! 'Tis She, but lo!
How changed, how full of ache, how gone in
    woe!
She dies at the thinnest cloud; her loveliness
Is wan on Neptune's blue: yet there's a stress
Of love-spangles, just off yon cape of trees,
Dancing upon the waves, as if to please
The curly foam with amorous influence.
O, not so idle! for down-glancing thence,
She fathoms eddies, and runs wild about
O'erwhelming water-courses; scaring out
The thorny sharks from hiding-holes, and
    fright'ning
Their savage eyes with unaccustom'd light-
    ning.
Where will the splendour be content to
    reach?
O love! how potent hast thou been to teach
Strange journeyings! Wherever beauty dwells,
In gulph or aerie, mountains or deep dells,
In light, in gloom, in star or blazing sun,
Thou pointest out the way, and straight 'tis
    won.
Amid his toil thou gav'st Leander breath;
Thou leddest Orpheus through the gleams of
    death;

Thou madest Pluto bear thin element:
And now, O wingèd Chieftain! thou hast sent
A moon-beam to the deep, deep water-world,
To find Endymion.

              On gold sand impearl'd
With lily shells, and pebbles milky white,
Poor Cynthia greeted him, and soothed her
   light
Against his pallid face: he felt the charm
To breathlessness, and suddenly a warm
Of his heart's blood: 'twas very sweet; he
   stay'd
His wandering steps, and half-entrancèd laid
His head upon a tuft of straggling weeds,
To taste the gentle moon, and freshening
   beads,
Lash'd from the crystal roof by fishes' tails.
And so he kept, until the rosy veils
Mantling the east, by Aurora's peering hand
Were lifted from the water's breast, and
   fann'd
Into sweet air; and sober'd morning came
Meekly through billows: — when like taper-
   flame
Left sudden by a dallying breath of air,
He rose in silence, and once more 'gan fare
Along his fated way.

              Far had he roam'd,
With nothing save the hollow vast, that
   foam'd

Above, around, and at his feet; save things
More dead than Morpheus' imaginings:
Old rusted anchors, helmets, breastplates
    large
Of gone sea-warriors; brazen beaks and targe;
Rudders that for a hundred years had lost
The sway of human hand; gold vase emboss'd
With long-forgotten story, and wherein
No reveller had ever dipp'd a chin
But those of Saturn's vintage; mouldering
    scrolls,
Writ in the tongue of heaven, by those souls
Who first were on the earth; and sculptures
    rude
In ponderous stone, developing the mood
Of ancient Nox; — then skeletons of man,
Of beast, behemoth, and leviathan,
And elephant, and eagle, and huge jaw
Of nameless monster. A cold leaden awe
These secrets struck into him; and unless
Dian had chased away that heaviness,
He might have died: but now, with cheerèd
    feel,
He onward kept; wooing these thoughts to
    steal
About the labyrinth in his soul of love.

  'What is there in thee, Moon! that thou
    shouldst move
My heart so potently? When yet a child
I oft have dried my tears when thou hast
    smiled.

185

Thou seem'dst my sister: hand in hand we
    went
From eve to morn across the firmament.
No apples would I gather from the tree,
Till thou hadst cool'd their cheeks deli-
    ciously:
No tumbling water ever spake romance,
But when my eyes with thine thereon could
    dance:
No woods were green enough, no bower di-
    vine,
Until thou liftedst up thine eyelids fine:
In sowing-time ne'er would I dibble take,
Or drop a seed, till thou wast wide awake;
And, in the summer-tide of blossoming,
No one but thee hath heard me blithely sing
And mesh my dewy flowers all the night.
No melody was like a passing spright
If it went not to solemnize thy reign.
Yes, in my boyhood, every joy and pain
By thee were fashion'd to the self-same end;
And as I grew in years, still didst thou blend
With all my ardours: thou wast the deep
    glen —
Thou wast the mountain-top — the sage's
    pen —
The poet's harp — the voice of friends —
    the sun;
Thou wast the river — thou wast glory won;
Thou wast my clarion's blast — thou wast
    my steed —
My goblet full of wine — my topmost

deed: —
Thou wast the charm of women, lovely
    Moon!
O what a wild and harmonizèd tune
My spirit struck from all the beautiful!
On some bright essence could I lean, and
    lull
Myself to immortality: I prest
Nature's soft pillow in a wakeful rest.
But, gentle Orb! there came a nearer bliss —
My strange love came — Felicity's abyss!
She came, and thou didst fade, and fade
    away —
Yet not entirely; no, thy starry sway
Has been an under-passion to this hour.
Now I begin to feel thine orby power
Is coming fresh upon me: O be kind!
Keep back thine influence, and do not blind
My sovereign vision. — Dearest love, forgive
That I can think away from thee and live! —
Pardon me, airy planet, that I prize
One thought beyond thine argent luxuries!
How far beyond!' At this a surprised start
Frosted the springing verdure of his heart;
For as he lifted up his eyes to swear
How his own goddess was past all things fair,
He saw far in the concave green of the sea
An old man sitting calm and peacefully.
Upon a weeded rock this old man sat,
And his white hair was awful, and a mat
Of weeds were cold beneath his cold thin
    feet;

And, ample as the largest winding-sheet,
A cloak of blue wrapp'd up his aged bones,
O'erwrought with symbols by the deepest
  groans
Of ambitious magic: every ocean-form
Was woven in with black distinctness; storm,
And calm, and whispering, and hideous roar,
Quicksand, and whirlpool, and deserted
  shore,
Were emblem'd in the woof; with every shape
That skims, or dives, or sleeps, 'twixt cape
  and cape.
The gulphing whale was like a dot in the
  spell,
Yet look upon it, and 'twould size and swell
To its huge self; and the minutest fish
Would pass the very hardest gazer's wish,
And show his little eye's anatomy.
Then there was pictured the regality
Of Neptune; and the sea-nymphs round his
  state,
In beauteous vassalage, look up and wait.
Beside this old man lay a pearly wand,
And in his lap a book, the which he conn'd
So stedfastly, that the new denizen
Had time to keep him in amazèd ken,
To mark these shadowings, and stand in awe.

  The old man raised his hoary head and saw
The wilder'd stranger — seeming not to see,
His features were so lifeless. Suddenly

He woke as from a trance; his snow-white
 brows
Went arching up, and like two magic ploughs
Furrow'd deep wrinkles in his forehead large,
Which kept as fixedly as rocky marge,
Till round his wither'd lips had gone a smile.
Then up he rose, like one whose tedious toil
Had watch'd for years in forlorn hermitage,
Who had not from mid-life to utmost age
Eased in one accent his o'erburden'd soul,
Even to the trees. He rose: he grasp'd his
 stole,
With convulsed clenches waving it abroad,
And in a voice of solemn joy, that awed
Echo into oblivion, he said: —

'Thou art the man! Now shall I lay my head
In peace upon my watery pillow: now
Sleep will come smoothly to my weary brow.
O Jove! I shall be young again, be young!
O shell-borne Neptune, I am pierced and
 stung
With new-born life! What shall I do? Where
 go,
When I have cast this serpent-skin of
 - woe? —
I'll swim to the syrens, and one moment
 listen
Their melodies, and see their long hair glis-
 ten;
Anon upon that giant's arm I'll be,
That writhes about the roots of Sicily;

189

To northern seas I'll in a twinkling sail,
And mount upon the snortings of a whale
To some black cloud; thence down I'll madly
    sweep
On forked lightning to the deepest deep,
Where through some sucking pool I will be
    hurl'd
With rapture to the other side of the world!
O, I am full of gladness! Sisters three,
I bow full-hearted to your old decree!
Yes, every god be thank'd, and power benign,
For I no more shall wither, droop, and pine.
Thou art the man!' Endymion started back
Dismay'd; and like a wretch from whom the
    rack
Tortures hot breath, and speech of agony,
Mutter'd: 'What lonely death am I to die
In this cold region? Will he let me freeze,
And float my brittle limbs o'er polar seas?
Or will he touch me with his searing hand,
And leave a black memorial on the sand?
Or tear me piecemeal with a bony saw,
And keep me as a chosen food to draw
His magian fish through hated fire and flame?
O misery of hell! resistless, tame,
Am I to be burnt up? No, I will shout,
Until the gods through heaven's blue look
    out! —
O Tartarus! but some few days agone
Her soft arms were entwining me, and on
Her voice I hung like fruit among green
    leaves:

Her lips were all my own, and — ah, ripe
    sheaves
Of happiness! ye on the stubble droop,
But never may be garner'd. I must stoop
My head, and kiss death's foot. Love! love,
    farewell!
Is there no hope from thee? This horrid spell
Would melt at thy sweet breath. — By Dian's
    hind
Feeding from her white fingers, on the wind
I see thy streaming hair! and now, by Pan,
I care not for this old mysterious man!'

    He spake, and walking to that aged form,
Look'd high defiance. Lo! his heart 'gan
    warm
With pity, for the grey-hair'd creature wept.
Had he then wrong'd a heart where sorrow
    kept?
Had he, though blindly contumelious,
    brought
Rheum to kind eyes, a sting to human
    thought,
Convulsion to a mouth of many years?
He had in truth; and he was ripe for tears.
The penitent shower fell, as down he knelt
Before that care-worn sage, who trembling
    felt
About his large dark locks, and faltering
    spake:

'Arise, good youth, for sacred Phœbus'
    sake!
I know thine inmost bosom, and I feel
A very brother's yearning for thee steal
Into mine own: for why? thou openest
The prison-gates that have so long oppress'd
My weary watching. Though thou know'st it
    not,
Thou art commission'd to this fated spot
For great enfranchisement. O weep no more!
I am a friend to love, to loves of yore:
Ay, hadst thou never loved an unknown
    power,
I had been grieving at this joyous hour.
But even now, most miserable old,
I saw thee, and my blood no longer cold
Gave mighty pulses: in this tottering case
Grew a new heart, which at this moment
    plays
As dancingly as thine. Be not afraid,
For thou shalt hear this secret all display'd,
Now as we speed towards our joyous task.'

  So saying, this young soul in age's mask
Went forward with the Carian side by side:
Resuming quickly thus; while ocean's tide
Hung swollen at their backs, and jewell'd
    sands
Took silently their foot-prints.

                  'My soul stands
Now past the midway from mortality,

And so I can prepare without a sigh
To tell thee briefly all my joy and pain.
I was a fisher once, upon this main,
And my boat danced in every creek and bay;
Rough billows were my home by night and
    day, —
The sea-gulls not more constant; for I had
No housing from the storm and tempests
    mad,
But hollow rocks, — and they were palaces
Of silent happiness, of slumberous ease:
Long years of misery have told me so.
Ay, thus it was one thousand years ago.
One thousand years! — Is it then possible
To look so plainly through them? to dispel
A thousand years with backward glance sub-
    lime?
To breathe away as 'twere all scummy slime
From off a crystal pool, to see its deep,
And one's own image from the bottom peep?
Yes: now I am no longer wretched thrall,
My long captivity and moanings all
Are but a slime, a thin-pervading scum,
The which I breathe away, and thronging
    come
Like things of yesterday my youthful plea-
    sures.

   'I touch'd no lute, I sang not, trod no
    measures:
I was a lonely youth on desert shores.

My sports were lonely, 'mid continuous
    roars,
And craggy isles, and sea-mew's plaintive cry
Plaining discrepant between sea and sky.
Dolphins were still my playmates; shapes un-
    seen
Would let me feel their scales of gold and
    green
Nor be my desolation; and, full oft,
When a dread waterspout had rear'd aloft
Its hungry hugeness, seeming ready ripe
To burst with hoarsest thunderings, and wipe
My life away like a vast sponge of fate,
Some friendly monster, pitying my sad state,
Has dived to its foundations, gulph'd it down,
And left me tossing safely. But the crown
Of all my life was utmost quietude:
More did I love to lie in cavern rude,
Keeping in wait whole days for Neptune's
    voice,
And if it came at last, hark, and rejoice!
There blush'd no summer eve but I would
    steer
My skiff along green shelving coasts, to hear
The shepherd's pipe come clear from aery
    steep,
Mingled with ceaseless bleatings of his sheep:
And never was a day of summer shine,
But I beheld its birth upon the brine:
For I would watch all night to see unfold
Heaven's gates, and Æthon snort his morn-
    ing gold

Wide o'er the swelling streams: and con-
  stantly
At brim of day-tide, on some grassy lea,
My nets would be spread out, and I at rest.
The poor folk of the sea-country I blest
With daily boon of fish most delicate:
They knew not whence this bounty, and elate
Would strew sweet flowers on a sterile beach.

'Why was I not contented? Wherefore reach
At things which, but for thee, O Latmian!
Had been my dreary death! Fool! I began
To feel distemper'd longings: to desire
The utmost privilege that ocean's sire
Could grant in benediction: to be free
Of all his kingdom. Long in misery
I wasted, ere in one extremest fit
I plunged for life or death. To interknit
One's senses with so dense a breathing stuff
Might seem a work of pain; so not enough
Can I admire how crystal-smooth it felt,
And buoyant round my limbs. At first I dwelt
Whole days and days in sheer astonishment;
Forgetful utterly of self-intent;
Moving but with the mighty ebb and flow.
Then, like a new-fledged bird that first doth
  show
His spreaded feathers to the morrow chill,
I tried in fear the pinions of my will.
'Twas freedom! and at once I visited
The ceaseless wonders of this ocean-bed.
No need to tell thee of them, for I see

195

That thou hast been a witness — it must
    be —
For these I know thou canst not feel a drouth,
By the melancholy corners of that mouth.
So I will in my story straightway pass
To more immediate matter. Woe, alas!
That love should be my bane! Ah, Scylla, fair!
Why did poor Glaucus ever — ever dare
To sue thee to his heart? Kind stranger-
    youth!
I loved her to the very white of truth,
And she would not conceive it. Timid thing!
She fled me swift as sea-bird on the wing,
Round every isle, and point, and promon-
    tory,
From where large Hercules wound up his
    story
Far as Egyptian Nile. My passion grew
The more, the more I saw her dainty hue
Gleam delicately through the azure clear:
Until 'twas too fierce agony to bear;
And in that agony, across my grief
It flash'd, that Circe might find some
    relief —
Cruel enchantress! So above the water
I rear'd my head, and look'd for Phœbus'
    daughter.
Æœa's isle was wondering at the moon: —
It seem'd to whirl around me, and a swoon
Left me dead-drifting to that fatal power.

'When I awoke, 'twas in a twilight bower;

Just when the light of morn, with hum of
    bees,
Stole through its verdurous matting of fresh
    trees.
How sweet, and sweeter! for I heard a lyre,
And over it a sighing voice expire.
It ceased — I caught light footsteps; and anon
The fairest face that morn e'er looked upon
Push'd through a screen of roses. Starry Jove!
With tears, and smiles, and honey-words she
    wove
A net whose thraldom was more bliss than
    all
The range of flower'd Elysium. Thus did fall
The dew of her rich speech: "Ah! art awake?
O let me hear thee speak, for Cupid's sake!
I am so oppress'd with joy! Why, I have shed
An urn of tears, as though thou wert cold
    dead;
And now I find thee living, I will pour
From these devoted eyes their silver store,
Until exhausted of the latest drop,
So it will pleasure thee, and force thee stop
Here, that I too may live; but if beyond
Such cool and sorrowful offerings, thou art
    fond
Of soothing warmth, of dalliance supreme;
If thou art ripe to taste a long love-dream;
If smiles, if dimples, tongues for ardour mute,
Hang in thy vision like a tempting fruit,
O let me pluck it for thee!" Thus she link'd
Her charming syllables, till indistinct

Their music came to my o'er-sweeten'd soul;
And then she hover'd over me, and stole
So near, that if no nearer it had been
This furrow'd visage thou hadst never seen.

'Young man of Latmos! thus particular
Am I, that thou may'st plainly see how far
This fierce temptation went: and thou may'st
    not
Exclaim, How then? was Scylla quite forgot?

'Who could resist? Who in this universe?
She did so breathe ambrosia; so immerse
My fine existence in a golden clime.
She took me like a child of suckling time,
And cradled me in roses. Thus condemn'd,
The current of my former life was stemm'd,
And to this arbitrary queen of sense
I bow'd a trancèd vassal: nor would thence
Have moved, even though Amphion's harp
    had woo'd
Me back to Scylla o'er the billows rude.
For as Apollo each eve doth devise
A new apparelling for western skies;
So every eve, nay, every spendthrift hour
Shed balmy consciousness within that bower.
And I was free of haunts umbrageous;
Could wander in the mazy forest-house
Of squirrels, foxes shy, and antler'd deer,
And birds from coverts innermost and drear
Warbling for very joy mellifluous sorrow —
To me new-born delights!

              'Now let me borrow
For moments few, a temperament as stern
As Pluto's sceptre, that my words not burn
These uttering lips, while I in calm speech
    tell
How specious heaven was changed to real
    hell.

    'One morn she left me sleeping: half awake
I sought for her smooth arms and lips, to
    slake
My greedy thirst with nectarous camel-
    draughts;
But she was gone. Whereat the barbèd shafts
Of disappointment stuck in me so sore,
That out I ran and search'd the forest o'er.
Wandering about in pine and cedar gloom
Damp awe assail'd me, for there 'gan to
    boom
A sound of moan, an agony of sound,
Sepulchral from the distance all around.
Then came a conquering earth-thunder, and
    rumbled
That fierce complain to silence; while I
    stumbled
Down a precipitous path, as if impell'd.
I came to a dark valley. Groanings swell'd
Poisonous about my ears, and louder grew,
The nearer I approach'd a flame's gaunt blue,
That glared before me through a thorny
    brake.
This fire, like the eye of gordian snake,

Bewitch'd me towards; and I soon was near
A sight too fearful for the feel of fear:
In thicket hid I cursed the haggard scene —
The banquet of my arms, my arbour queen,
Seated upon an uptorn forest root;
And all around her shapes, wizard and brute,
Laughing, and wailing, grovelling, serpent-
    ing,
Showing tooth, tusk, and venom-bag, and
    sting.
O such deformities! Old Charon's self,
Should he give up awhile his penny pelf;
And take a dream 'mong rushes Stygian,
It could not be so phantasied. Fierce, wan,
And tyrannizing was the lady's look,
As over them a gnarlèd staff she shook.
Oft-times upon the sudden she laugh'd out,
And from a basket emptied to the rout
Clusters of grapes, the which they raven'd
    quick
And roar'd for more; with many a hungry
    lick
About their shaggy jaws. Avenging, slow,
Anon she took a branch of mistletoe,
And emptied on't a black dull-gurgling phial:
Groan'd one and all, as if some piercing trial
Was sharpening for their pitiable bones.
She lifted up the charm: appealing groans
From their poor breasts went suing to her
    ear
In vain; remorseless as an infant's bier
She whisk'd against their eyes the sooty oil,

Whereat was heard a noise of painful toil,
Increasing gradual to a tempest rage,
Shrieks, yells, and groans of torture-
    pilgrimage;
Until their grievèd bodies 'gan to bloat
And puff from the tail's end to stifled throat:
Then was appalling silence: then a sight
More wildering than all that hoarse affright;
For the whole herd, as by a whirlwind
    writhen,
Went through the dismal air like one huge
    Python
Antagonizing Boreas, — and so vanish'd.
Yet there was not a breath of wind: she
    banish'd
These phantoms with a nod. Lo! from the
    dark
Came waggish fauns, and nymphs, and satyrs
    stark,
With dancing and loud revelry, — and went
Swifter than centaurs after rapine bent. —
Sighing an elephant appear'd and bow'd
Before the fierce witch, speaking thus aloud
In human accent: "Potent goddess! chief
Of pains resistless! make my being brief,
Or let me from this heavy prison fly:
Or give me to the air, or let me die!
I sue not for my happy crown again;
I sue not for my phalanx on the plain;
I sue not for my lone, my widow'd wife;
I sue not for my ruddy drops of life,
My children fair, my lovely girls and boys!

I will forget them; I will pass these joys;
Ask nought so heavenward, so too — too
   high;
Only I pray, as fairest boon, to die,
Or be deliver'd from this cumbrous flesh,
From this gross, detestable, filthy mesh,
And merely given to the cold bleak air.
Have mercy, Goddess! Circe, feel my prayer!"

  'That curst magician's name fell icy numb
Upon my wild conjecturing: truth had come
Naked and sabre-like against my heart.
I saw a fury whetting a death-dart;
And my slain spirit, overwrought with fright,
Fainted away in that dark lair of night.
Think, my deliverer, how desolate
My waking must have been! disgust and hate
And terrors manifold divided me
A spoil amongst them. I prepared to flee
Into the dungeon core of that wild wood:
I fled three days — when lo! before me stood
Glaring the angry witch. O Dis, even now,
A clammy dew is beading on my brow,
At mere remembering her pale laugh, and
   curse.
"Ha! ha! Sir Dainty! there must be a nurse
Made of rose-leaves and thistle-down, ex-
   press,
To cradle thee, my sweet, and lull thee: yes,
I am too flinty-hard for thy nice touch:
My tenderest squeeze is but a giant's clutch.
So, fairy-thing, it shall have lullabies

Unheard of yet; and it shall still its cries
Upon some breast more lily-feminine.
Oh, no — it shall not pine, and pine, and
    pine
More than one pretty, trifling thousand years;
And then 'twere pity, but fate's gentle shears
Cut short its immortality. Sea-flirt!
Young dove of the waters! truly I'll not hurt
One hair of thine: see how I weep and sigh,
That our heart-broken parting is so nigh.
And must we part? Ah, yes, it must be so.
Yet ere thou leavest me in utter woe,
Let me sob over thee my last adieus,
And speak a blessing: Mark me! thou hast
    thews
Immortal, for thou art of heavenly race:
But such a love is mine, that here I chase
Eternally away from thee all bloom
Of youth, and destine thee towards a tomb.
Hence shalt thou quickly to the watery vast;
And there, ere many days be overpast,
Disabled age shall seize thee; and even then
Thou shalt not go the way of aged men;
But live and wither, cripple and still breathe
Ten hundred years: which gone, I then be-
    queath
Thy fragile bones to unknown burial.
Adieu, sweet love, adieu!" — As shot stars
    fall,
She fled ere I could groan for mercy. Stung
And poison'd was my spirit: despair sung
A war-song of defiance 'gainst all hell.

A hand was at my shoulder to compel
My sullen steps; another 'fore my eyes
Moved on with pointed finger. In this guise
Enforcèd, at the last by ocean's foam
I found me; by my fresh, my native home.
Its tempering coolness, to my life akin,
Came salutary as I waded in;
And, with a blind voluptuous rage, I gave
Battle to the swollen billow-ridge, and drave
Large froth before me, while there yet
    remain'd
Hale strength, nor from my bones all mar-
    row drain'd.

  'Young lover, I must weep — such hellish
    spite
With dry cheek who can tell? Why thus my
    might
Proving upon this element, dismay'd,
Upon a dead thing's face my hand I laid;
I look'd — 'twas Scylla! Cursed, cursed
    Circe!
O vulture-witch, hast never heard of mercy!
Could not thy harshest vengeance be content,
But thou must nip this tender innocent
Because I loved her? — Cold, O cold indeed
Were her fair limbs, and like a common weed
The sea-swell took her hair. Dead as she was
I clung about her waist, nor ceased to pass
Fleet as an arrow through unfathom'd brine,
Until there shone a fabric crystalline,

204

Ribb'd and inlaid with coral, pebble, and
  pearl.
Headlong I darted; at one eager swirl
Gain'd its bright portal, enter'd, and behold!
'Twas vast, and desolate, and icy-cold;
And all around — But wherefore this to thee
Who in few minutes more thyself shalt
  see? —
I left poor Scylla in a niche and fled.
My fever'd parchings up, my scathing dread
Met palsy half way: soon these limbs became
Gaunt, wither'd, sapless, feeble, cramp'd, and
  lame.

  'Now let me pass a cruel, cruel space,
Without one hope, without one faintest trace
Of mitigation, or redeeming bubble
Of colour'd phantasy; for I fear 'twould
  trouble
Thy brain to loss of reason: and next tell
How a restoring chance came down to quell
One half of the witch in me.

                              'On a day,
Sitting upon a rock above the spray,
I saw grow up from the horizon's brink
A gallant vessel: soon she seem'd to sink
Away from me again, as though her course
Had been resumed in spite of hindering
  force —
So vanish'd: and not long, before arose
Dark clouds, and muttering of winds morose.

Old Æolus would stifle his mad spleen,
But could not: therefore all the billows green
Toss'd up the silver spume against the clouds.
The tempest came: I saw that vessel's shrouds
In perilous bustle; while upon the deck
Stood trembling creatures. I beheld the
    wreck;
The final gulphing; the poor struggling souls:
I heard their cries amid loud thunder-rolls.
O they had all been saved but crazèd eld
Annull'd my vigorous cravings: and thus
    quell'd
And curb'd, think on 't, O Latmian! did I sit
Writhing with pity, and a cursing fit
Against that hell-born Circe. The crew had
    gone,
By one and one, to pale oblivion;
And I was gazing on the surges prone,
With many a scalding tear and many a groan,
When at my feet emerged an old man's hand,
Grasping this scroll, and this same slender
    wand.
I knelt with pain — reach'd out my hand —
    had grasp'd
These treasures — touch'd the knuckles —
    they unclasp'd —
I caught a finger; but the downward weight
O'erpower'd me — it sank. Then 'gan abate
The storm, and through chill aguish gloom
    outburst
The comfortable sun. I was athirst
To search the book, and in the warming air

Parted its dripping leaves with eager care.
Strange matters did it treat of, and drew on
My soul page after page, till well-nigh won
Into forgetfulness; when, stupefied,
I read these words, and read again, and tried
My eyes against the heavens, and read again.
O what a load of misery and pain
Each Atlas-line bore off! — a shine of hope
Came gold around me, cheering me to cope
Strenuous with hellish tyranny. Attend!
For thou hast brought their promise to an
    end.

  ' "In the wide sea there lives a forlorn
    wretch,
Doom'd with enfeebled carcase to outstretch
His loathed existence through ten centuries,
And then to die alone. Who can devise
A total opposition? No one. So
One million times ocean must ebb and flow,
And he oppressed. Yet he shall not die,
These things accomplish'd: — If he utterly
Scans all the depths of magic, and expounds
The meanings of all motions, shapes, and
    sounds;
If he explores all forms and substances
Straight homeward to their symbol-essences;
He shall not die. Moreover, and in chief,
He must pursue this task of joy and grief
Most piously; — all lovers tempest-tost,
And in the savage overwhelming lost,
He shall deposit side by side, until

Time's creeping shall the dreary space fulfil:
Which done, and all these labours ripened,
A youth, by heavenly power loved and led,
Shall stand before him; whom he shall direct
How to consummate all. The youth elect
Must do the thing, or both will be
    destroy'd." '

  'Then,' cried the young Endymion,
    overjoy'd,
'We are twin brothers in this destiny!
Say, I entreat thee, what achievement high
Is, in this restless world, for me reserved.
What! if from thee my wandering feet had
    swerved,
Had we both perish'd?' — 'Look!' the sage
    replied,
'Dost thou not mark a gleaming through the
    tide,
Of divers brilliances? 'tis the edifice
I told thee of, where lovely Scylla lies;
And where I have enshrinèd piously
All lovers, whom fell storms have doom'd to
    die
Throughout my bondage.' Thus discoursing,
    on
They went till unobscured the porches shone;
Which hurryingly they gain'd, and enter'd
    straight.
Sure never since king Neptune held his state
Was seen such wonder underneath the stars.
Turn to some level plain where haughty Mars

Has legion'd all his battle; and behold
How every soldier, with firm foot, doth hold
His even breast: see, many steelèd squares,
And rigid ranks of iron — whence who dares
One step? Imagine further, line by line,
These warrior thousands on the field
    supine: —
So in that crystal place, in silent rows,
Poor lovers lay at rest from joys and woes. —
The stranger from the mountains, breathless,
    traced
Such thousands of shut eyes in order placed;
Such ranges of white feet, and patient lips
All ruddy, — for here death no blossom nips.
He mark'd their brows and foreheads; saw
    their hair
Put sleekly on one side with nicest care;
And each one's gentle wrists, with reverence,
Put cross-wise to its heart.

                  'Let us commence,'
Whisper'd the guide, stuttering with joy,
    'even now.'
He spake, and, trembling like an aspen-
    bough,
Began to tear his scroll in pieces small,
Uttering the while some mumblings funeral.
He tore it into pieces small as snow
That drifts unfeather'd when bleak north-
    erns blow;
And having done it, took his dark blue cloak
And bound it round Endymion: then struck

His wand against the empty air times nine.
'What more there is to do, young man, is
    thine:
But first a little patience; first undo
This tangled thread, and wind it to a clue.
Ah, gentle! 'tis as weak as spider's skein;
And shouldst thou break it — What, is it
    done so clean?
A power overshadows thee! O, brave!
The spite of hell is tumbling to its grave.
Here is a shell; 'tis pearly blank to me,
Nor mark'd with any sign or charactery —
Canst thou read aught? O read for pity's sake!
Olympus! we are safe! Now, Carian, break
This wand against yon lyre on the pedestal.'

  'Twas done: and straight with sudden swell
    and fall
Sweet music breathed her soul away, and
    sigh'd
A lullaby to silence. — 'Youth! now strew
These mincèd leaves on me, and passing
    through
Those files of dead, scatter the same around,
And thou wilt see the issue.' — 'Mid the
    sound
Of flutes and viols, ravishing his heart,
Endymion from Glaucus stood apart,
And scatter'd in his face some fragments
    light.
How lightning-swift the change! a youthful
    wight

Smiling beneath a coral diadem,
Out-sparkling sudden like an upturn'd gem,
Appear'd, and, stepping to a beauteous corse,
Kneel'd down beside it, and with tenderest
    force
Press'd its cold hand, and wept — and Scylla
    sigh'd!
Endymion, with quick hand, the charm ap-
    plied —
The nymph arose: he left them to their joy,
And onward went upon his high employ,
Showering those powerful fragments on the
    dead,
And, as he pass'd, each lifted up his head,
As doth a flower at Apollo's touch.
Death felt it to his inwards; 'twas too much:
Death fell a-weeping in his charnel-house.
The Latmian persevered along, and thus
All were reanimated. There arose
A noise of harmony, pulses and throes
Of gladness in the air — while many, who
Had died in mutual arms devout and true,
Sprang to each other madly; and the rest
Felt a high certainty of being blest.
They gazed upon Endymion. Enchantment
Grew drunken, and would have its head and
    bent.
Delicious symphonies, like airy flowers,
Budded, and swell'd, and, full-blown, shed
    full showers
Of light, soft, unseen leaves of sounds divine.
The two deliverers tasted a pure wine

Of happiness, from fairy press oozed out.
Speechless they eyed each other, and about
The fair assembly wander'd to and fro,
Distracted with the richest overflow
Of joy that ever pour'd from heaven.

                    — 'Away!'
Shouted the new-born god; 'Follow, and pay
Our piety to Neptunus supreme!'
Then Scylla, blushing sweetly from her
   dream,
They led on first, bent to her meek surprise,
Through portal columns of a giant size
Into the vaulted, boundless emerald.
Joyous all follow'd, as the leader call'd,
Down marble steps; pouring as easily
As hour-glass sand — and fast, as you might
   see
Swallows obeying the south summer's call,
Or swans upon a gentle waterfall.

  Thus went that beautiful multitude, nor
    far,
Ere from among some rocks of glittering
    spar,
Just within ken, they saw descending thick
Another multitude. Whereat more quick
Moved either host. On a wide sand they met,
And of those numbers every eye was wet;
For each their old love found. A murmuring
    rose,
Like what was never heard in all the throes

Of wind and waters: 'tis past human wit
To tell; 'tis dizziness to think of it.

This mighty consummation made, the host
Moved on for many a league; and gain'd and
    lost
Huge sea-marks; vanward swelling in array,
And from the rear diminishing away,
Till a faint dawn surprised them. Glaucus
    cried,
'Behold! behold, the palace of his pride!
God Neptune's palaces!' With noise in-
    creased,
They shoulder'd on towards that brightening
    east,
At every onward step proud domes arose
In prospect; diamond gleams and golden
    glows
Of amber 'gainst their faces levelling.
Joyous, and many as the leaves in spring,
Still onward; still the splendour gradual
    swell'd.
Rich opal domes were seen, on high upheld
By jasper pillars, letting through their shafts
A blush of coral. Copious wonder-draughts
Each gazer drank; and deeper drank more
    near:
For what poor mortals fragment up, as mere
As marble was there lavish, to the vast
Of one fair palace, that far, far surpass'd,
Even for common bulk, those olden three,
Memphis, and Babylon, and Nineveh.

As large, as bright, as colour'd as the bow
Of Iris, when unfading it doth show
Beyond a silvery shower, was the arch
Through which this Paphian army took its
    march
Into the outer courts of Neptune's state:
Whence could be seen, direct, a golden gate,
To which the leaders sped; but not half
    raught
Ere it burst open swift as fairy thought,
And made those dazzled thousands veil their
    eyes
Like callow eagles at the first sunrise.
Soon with an eagle nativeness their gaze
Ripe from hue-golden swoons took all the
    blaze,
And then, behold! large Neptune on his
    throne
Of emerald deep: yet not exalt alone;
At his right hand stood wingèd Love, and on
His left sat smiling Beauty's paragon.

Far as the mariner on highest mast
Can see all round upon the calmèd vast,
So wide was Neptune's hall: and as the blue
Doth vault the waters, so the waters drew
Their doming curtains, high, magnificent,
Awed from the throne aloof; — and when
    storm-rent
Disclosed the thunder-gloomings in Jove's
    air;

But soothed as now, flash'd sudden every-
  where,
Noiseless, sub-marine cloudlets, glittering
Death to a human eye: for there did spring
From natural west, and east, and south, and
  north,
A light as of four sunsets, blazing forth
A gold-green zenith 'bove the Sea-God's
  head.
Of lucid depth the floor, and far outspread
As breezeless lake, on which the slim canoe
Of feather'd Indian darts about, as through
The delicatest air: air verily,
But for the portraiture of clouds and sky:
This palace floor breath-air, — but for the
  amaze
Of deep-seen wonders motionless, — and
  blaze
Of the dome pomp, reflected in extremes,
Globing a golden sphere.

                    They stood in dreams
Till Triton blew his horn. The palace rang;
The Nereids danced; the Syrens faintly sang;
And the great Sea-King bow'd his dripping
  head.
Then Love took wing, and from his pinions
  shed
On all the multitude a nectarous dew.
The ooze-born Goddess beckoned and drew
Fair Scylla and her guides to conference;
And when they reach'd the throned eminence

215

She kist the sea-nymph's cheek, who sat her
    down
A toying with the doves. Then, 'Mighty crown
And sceptre of this kingdom!' Venus said,
'Thy vows were on a time to Nais paid:
Behold!' — Two copious tear-drops instant
    fell
From the God's large eyes; he smiled delec-
    table,
And over Glaucus held his blessing hands. —
'Endymion! Ah! still wandering in the bands
Of love? Now this is cruel. Since the hour
I met thee in earth's bosom, all my power
Have I put forth to serve thee. What, not yet
Escaped from dull mortality's harsh net?
A little patience, youth! 'twill not be long,
Or I am skilless quite: an idle tongue,
A humid eye, and steps luxurious,
Where these are new and strange, are omi-
    nous.
Ay, I have seen these signs in one of heaven,
When others were all blind; and were I given
To utter secrets, haply I might say
Some pleasant words; but Love will have his
    day.
So wait awhile expectant. Pr'ythee soon,
Even in the passing of thine honey-moon,
Visit thou my Cythera: thou wilt find
Cupid well-natured, my Adonis kind;
And pray persuade with thee — Ah, I have
    done,
All blisses be upon thee, my sweet son!' —

Thus the fair Goddess: while Endymion
Knelt to receive those accents halcyon.

Meantime a glorious revelry began
Before the Water-Monarch. Nectar ran
In courteous fountains to all cups outreach'd;
And plunder'd vines, teeming exhaustless,
    pleach'd
New growth about each shell and pendent
    lyre;
The which, in disentangling for their fire,
Pull'd down fresh foliage and coverture
For dainty toy. Cupid, empire-sure,
Flutter'd and laugh'd, and oft-times through
    the throng
Made a delighted way. Then dance, and song,
And garlanding, grew wild; and pleasure
    reign'd.
In harmless tendril they each other chain'd,
And strove who should be smother'd deepest
    in
Fresh crush of leaves.

                        O 'tis a very sin
For one so weak to venture his poor verse
In such a place as this. O do not curse,
High Muses! let him hurry to the ending.

All suddenly were silent. A soft blending
Of dulcet instruments came charmingly;
And then a hymn.

     'King of the stormy sea!
Brother of Jove, and co-inheritor
Of elements! Eternally before
Thee the waves awful bow. Fast, stubborn
  rock,
At thy fear'd trident shrinking, doth unlock
Its deep foundations, hissing into foam.
All mountain-rivers, lost in the wide home
Of thy capacious bosom, ever flow.
Thou frownest, and old Æolus thy foe
Skulks to his cavern, 'mid the gruff complaint
Of all his rebel tempests. Dark clouds faint
When, from thy diadem, a silver gleam
Slants over blue dominion. Thy bright team
Gulphs in the morning light, and scuds along
To bring thee nearer to that golden song
Apollo singeth, while his chariot
Waits at the doors of heaven. Thou art not
For scenes like this: an empire stern hast
  thou;
And it hath furrow'd that large front: yet now,
As newly come of heaven, dost thou sit
To blend and interknit
Subduèd majesty with this glad time.
O shell-borne King sublime!
We lay our hearts before thee evermore —
We sing, and we adore!

 'Breathe softly, flutes,
Be tender of your strings, ye soothing lutes;
Nor be the trumpet heard! O vain, O vain!
Not flowers budding in an April rain,

Nor breath of sleeping dove, nor river's
   flow, —
No, nor the Æolian twang of Love's own bow,
Can mingle music fit for the soft ear
Of goddess Cytherea!
Yet deign, white Queen of Beauty, thy fair
   eyes
On our souls' sacrifice.

   'Bright-wingèd Child!
Who has another care when thou hast smiled?
Unfortunates on earth, we see at last
All death-shadows, and glooms that overcast
Our spirits, fann'd away by thy light pinions.
O sweetest essence! sweetest of all minions!
God of warm pulses, and dishevell'd hair,
And panting bosoms bare!
Dear unseen light in darkness! eclipser
Of light in light! delicious poisoner!
Thy venom'd goblet will we quaff until
We fill — we fill!
And by thy Mother's lips —'

              Was heard no more
For clamour, when the golden palace-door
Open'd again, and from without, in shone
A new magnificence. On oozy throne
Smooth-moving came Oceanus the old,
To take a latest glimpse at his sheep-fold,
Before he went into his quiet cave
To muse for ever — Then, a lucid wave,

Scoop'd from its trembling sisters of mid-
    sea,
Afloat, and pillowing up the majesty
Of Doris, and the Ægean seer, her spouse —
Next, on a dolphin, clad in laurel boughs,
Theban Amphion leaning on his lute:
His fingers went across it — All were mute
To gaze on Amphitrite, queen of pearls,
And Thetis pearly too. —

                        The palace whirls
Around giddy Endymion; seeing he
Was there far strayed from mortality.
He could not bear it — shut his eyes in vain;
Imagination gave a dizzier pain.
'O I shall die! sweet Venus, be my stay!
Where is my lovely mistress? Well-away!
I die — I hear her voice — I feel my wing —'
At Neptune's feet he sank. A sudden ring
Of Nereids were about him, in kind strife
To usher back his spirit into life:
But still he slept. At last they interwove
Their cradling arms, and purposed to convey
Towards a crystal bower far away.

  Lo! while slow carried through the pitying
    crowd,
To his inward senses these words spake
    aloud;
Written in star-light on the dark above:
'Dearest Endymion! my entire love!
How have I dwelt in fear of fate: 'tis done —

Immortal bliss for me too hast thou won.
Arise then! for the hen-dove shall not hatch
Her ready eggs, before I'll kissing snatch
Thee into endless heaven. Awake! awake!'

  The youth at once arose: a placid lake
Came quiet to his eyes; and forest green,
Cooler than all the wonder he had seen,
Lull'd with its simple song his fluttering
  breast.
How happy once again in grassy nest!

Book IV

Muse of my native land! loftiest Muse!
O first-born on the mountains! by the hues
Of heaven on the spiritual air begot:
Long didst thou sit alone in northern grot,
While yet our England was a wolfish den;
Before our forests heard the talk of men;
Before the first of Druids was a child; —
Long didst thou sit amid our regions wild,
Rapt in a deep prophetic solitude.
There came an eastern voice of solemn
    mood: —
Yet wast thou patient. Then sang forth the
    Nine,
Apollo's garland: — yet didst thou divine
Such home-bred glory, that they cried in
    vain,
'Come hither, Sister of the Island!' Plain
Spake fair Ausonia; and once more she spake
A higher summons: — still didst thou betake
Thee to thy native hopes. O thou hast won
A full accomplishment! The thing is done,
Which undone, these our latter days had
    risen

On barren souls. Great Muse, thou know'st what prison
Of flesh and bone, curbs, and confines, and frets
Our spirit's wings: despondency besets
Our pillows; and the fresh to-morrow morn
Seems to give forth its light in very scorn
Of our dull, uninspired, snail-paced lives.
Long have I said, how happy he who shrives
To thee! But then I thought on poets gone,
And could not pray: — nor can I now — so on
I move to the end in lowliness of heart. —

  'Ah, woe is me! that I should fondly part
From my dear native land! Ah, foolish maid!
Glad was the hour, when, with thee, myriads bade
Adieu to Ganges and their pleasant fields!
To one so friendless the clear freshet yields
A bitter coolness; the ripe grape is sour:
Yet I would have, great gods! but one short hour
Of native air — let me but die at home.'

  Endymion to heaven's airy dome
Was offering up a hecatomb of vows,
When these words reach'd him. Whereupon he bows
His head through thorny-green entanglement
Of underwood, and to the sound is bent,
Anxious as hind towards her hidden fawn.

'Is no one near to help me? No fair dawn
Of life from charitable voice? No sweet say-
    ing
To set my dull and sadden'd spirit playing?
No hand to toy with mine? No lips so sweet
That I may worship them? No eyelids meet
To twinkle on my bosom? No one dies
Before me, till from these enslaving eyes
Redemption sparkles! — I am sad and lost.'

    Thou, Carian lord, hadst better have been
        tost
Into a whirlpool. Vanish into air,
Warm mountaineer! for canst thou only bear
A woman's sigh alone and in distress?
See not her charms! Is Phœbe passionless?
Phœbe is fairer far — O gaze no more: —
Yet if thou wilt behold all beauty's store,
Behold her panting in the forest grass!
Do not those curls of glossy jet surpass
For tenderness the arms so idly lain
Amongst them? Feelest not a kindred pain,
To see such lovely eyes in swimming search
After some warm delight, that seems to perch
Dovelike in the dim cell lying beyond
Their upper lids? — Hist!

                    'O for Hermes' wand,
To touch this flower into human shape!
That woodland Hyacinthus could escape
From his green prison, and here kneeling
    down

Call me his queen, his second life's fair
   crown!
Ah me, how I could love! — My soul doth
   melt
For the unhappy youth — Love! I have felt
So faint a kindness, such a meek surrender
To what my own full thoughts had made too
   tender,
That but for tears my life had fled away! —
Ye deaf and senseless minutes of the day,
And thou, old forest, hold ye this for true,
There is no lightning, no authentic dew
But in the eye of love: there's not a sound,
Melodious howsoever, can confound
The heavens and earth in one to such a death
As doth the voice of love: there's not a breath
Will mingle kindly with the meadow air,
Till it has panted round, and stolen a share
Of passion from the heart!' —

                              Upon a bough
He leant, wretched. He surely cannot now
Thirst for another love: O impious,
That he can even dream upon it thus!
Thought he, 'Why am I not as are the dead,
Since to a woe like this I have been led
Through the dark earth, and through the
   wondrous sea?
Goddess! I love thee not the less: from thee,
By Juno's smile, I turn not — no, no, no —
While the great waters are at ebb and flow.
I have a triple soul! O fond pretence —

For both, for both my love is so immense,
I feel my heart is cut for them in twain.'

And so he groan'd, as one by beauty slain.
The lady's heart beat quick, and he could
  see
Her gentle bosom heave tumultuously.
He sprang from his green covert: there she
  lay,
Sweet as a musk-rose upon new-made hay;
With all her limbs on tremble, and her eyes
Shut softly up alive. To speak he tries:
'Fair damsel, pity me! forgive that I
Thus violate thy bower's sanctity!
O pardon me, for I am full of grief —
Grief born of thee, young angel! fairest thief!
Who stolen hast away the wings wherewith
I was to top the heavens. Dear maid, sith
Thou art my executioner, and I feel
Loving and hatred, misery and weal,
Will in a few short hours be nothing to me,
And all my story that much passion slew me;
Do smile upon the evening of my days;
And, for my tortured brain begins to craze,
Be thou my nurse; and let me understand
How dying I shall kiss that lily hand. —
Dost weep for me? Then should I be content.
Scowl on, ye fates! until the firmament
Outblackens Erebus, and the full-cavern'd
  earth
Crumbles into itself. By the cloud-girth
Of Jove, those tears have given me a thirst

To meet oblivion.' — As her heart would
    burst
The maiden sobb'd awhile, and then replied:
'Why must such desolation betide
As that thou speakest of? Are not these green
    nooks
Empty of all misfortune? Do the brooks
Utter a gorgon voice? Does yonder thrush,
Schooling its half-fledged little ones to brush
About the dewy forest, whisper tales? —
Speak not of grief, young stranger, or cold
    snails
Will slime the rose to-night. Though if thou
    wilt,
Methinks 'twould be a guilt — a very
    guilt —
Not to companion thee, and sigh away
The light — the dusk — the dark — till break
    of day!'
'Dear lady,' said Endymion, ' 'tis past:
I love thee! and my days can never last.
That I may pass in patience still speak:
Let me have music dying, and I seek
No more delight — I bid adieu to all.
Didst thou not after other climates call,
And murmur about Indian streams?' — Then
    she,
Sitting beneath the midmost forest tree,
For pity sang this roundelay —

    'O Sorrow!
Why dost borrow
227

The natural hue of health, from vermeil
   lips? —
       To give maiden blushes
       To the white rose bushes?
Or is it thy dewy hand the daisy tips?

       'O Sorrow!
   Why dost borrow
The lustrous passion from a falcon-eye? —
       To give the glow-worm light?
       Or, on a moonless night,
To tinge, on syren shores, the salt sea-spry?

       'O Sorrow!
   Why dost borrow
The mellow ditties from a mourning
   tongue? —
       To give at evening pale
       Unto the nightingale,
That thou mayst listen the cold dews among?

       'O Sorrow!
   Why dost borrow
Heart's lightness from the merriment of
   May?
       A lover would not tread
       A cowslip on the head,
Though he should dance from eve till peep
   of day —
       Nor any drooping flower
       Held sacred for thy bower,
Wherever he may sport himself and play.

'To Sorrow
          I bade good morrow,
And thought to leave her far away behind;
          But cheerly, cheerly,
          She loves me dearly;
She is so constant to me, and so kind:
          I would deceive her,
          And so leave her,
But ah! she is so constant and so kind.

'Beneath my palm-trees, by the river side,
I sat a-weeping: in the whole world wide
There was no one to ask me why I wept —
          And so I kept
Brimming the water-lily cups with tears
          Cold as my fears.

'Beneath my palm-trees, by the river side,
I sat a-weeping: what enamour'd bride,
Cheated by shadowy wooer from the clouds,
          But hides and shrouds
Beneath dark palm-trees by a river side?

'And as I sat, over the light blue hills
There came a noise of revellers: the rills
Into the wide stream came of purple hue —
          'Twas Bacchus and his crew!
The earnest trumpet spake, and silver thrills
From kissing cymbals made a merry din —
          'Twas Bacchus and his kin!
Like to a moving vintage down they came,

Crown'd with green leaves, and faces all on
    flame;
All madly dancing through the pleasant val-
    ley,
        To scare thee, Melancholy!
O then, O then, thou wast a simple name!
And I forgot thee, as the berried holly
By shepherds is forgotten, when, in June,
Tall chestnuts keep away the sun and
    moon: —
        I rush'd into the folly!

'Within his car, aloft, young Bacchus stood,
Trifling his ivy-dart, in dancing mood,
        With sidelong laughing;
And little rills of crimson wine imbrued
His plump white arms, and shoulders,
    enough white,
        For Venus' pearly bite;
And near him rode Silenus on his ass,
Pelted with flowers as he on did pass
        Tipsily quaffing.

'Whence came ye, merry Damsels! whence
    came ye,
So many, and so many, and such glee?
Why have ye left your bowers desolate,
        Your lutes, and gentler fate?
"We follow Bacchus! Bacchus on the wing,
        A-conquering!
Bacchus, young Bacchus! good or ill betide,
We dance before him thorough kingdoms

wide: —
Come hither, lady fair, and joinèd be
      To our wild minstrelsy!"

'Whence came ye, jolly Satyrs! whence came
   ye,
So many, and so many, and such glee?
Why have ye left your forest haunts, why left
      Your nuts in oak-tree cleft? —
"For wine, for wine we left our kernel tree;
For wine we left our heath, and yellow
   brooms,
      And cold mushrooms;
For wine we follow Bacchus through the
   earth;
Great god of breathless cups and chirping
   mirth!
Come hither, lady fair, and joinèd be
      To our mad minstrelsy!"

'Over wide streams and mountains great we
   went,
And, save when Bacchus kept his ivy tent,
Onward the tiger and the leopard pants,
      With Asian elephants:
Onward these myriads — with song and
   dance,
With zebras striped, and sleek Arabians'
   prance,
Web-footed alligators, crocodiles,
Bearing upon their scaly backs, in files,
Plump infant laughers mimicking the coil

231

Of seamen, and stout galley-rowers' toil:
With toying oars and silken sails they glide,
      Nor care for wind and tide.

'Mounted on panthers' furs and lions'
    manes,
From rear to van they scour about the plains;
A three days' journey in a moment done;
And always, at the rising of the sun,
About the wilds they hunt with spear and
    horn,
      On spleenful unicorn.
'I saw Osirian Egypt kneel adown
      Before the vine-wreath crown!
I saw parch'd Abyssinia rouse and sing
      To the silver cymbals' ring!
I saw the whelming vintage hotly pierce
      Old Tartary the fierce!
The kings of Ind their jewel-sceptres vail,
And from their treasures scatter pearlèd hail;
Great Brahma from his mystic heaven groans,
      And all his priesthood moans;
Before young Bacchus' eye-wink turning
    pale.
Into these regions came I, following him,
Sick-hearted, weary — so I took a whim
To stray away into these forests drear,
      Alone, without a peer:
And I have told thee all thou mayest hear.

      'Young stranger!
      I've been a ranger

In search of pleasure throughout every clime:
      Alas, 'tis not for me!
      Bewitch'd I sure must be,
To lose in grieving all my maiden prime.

      'Come then, Sorrow,
      Sweetest Sorrow!
Like an own babe I nurse thee on my breast:
      I thought to leave thee,
      And deceive thee,
But now of all the world I love thee best.

      'There is not one,
      No, no, not one
But thee to comfort a poor lonely maid;
      Thou art her mother,
      And her brother,
Her playmate, and her wooer in the shade.'

O what a sigh she gave in finishing,
And look, quite dead to every worldly thing!
Endymion could not speak, but gazed on her:
And listen'd to the wind that now did stir
About the crispèd oaks full drearily,
Yet with as sweet a softness as might be
Remember'd from its velvet summer song.
At last he said: 'Poor lady! how thus long
Have I been able to endure that voice?
Fair Melody! kind Syren! I've no choice;
I must be thy sad servant evermore:
I cannot choose but kneel here and adore.
Alas, I must not think — by Phœbe, no!

Let me not think, soft Angel! shall it be so?
Say, beautifullest, shall I never think?
O thou couldst foster me beyond the brink
Of recollection! make my watchful care
Close up its bloodshot eyes, nor see despair!
Do gently murder half my soul, and I
Shall feel the other half so utterly! —
I'm giddy at that cheek so fair and smooth;
O let it blush so ever: let it soothe
My madness; let it mantle rosy-warm
With the tinge of love, panting in safe alarm.
This cannot be thy hand, and yet it is!
And this is sure thine other softling — this
Thine own fair bosom, and I am so near!
Wilt fall asleep? O let me sip that tear!
And whisper one sweet word that I may know
This is this world — sweet dewy blossom!'
　 — *Woe!*
Woe! Woe to that Endymion! Where is he? —
Even these words went echoing dismally
Through the wide forest — a most fearful
　　tone,
Like one repenting in his latest moan;
And while it died away a shade pass'd by,
As of a thunder-cloud. When arrows fly
Through the thick branches, poor ring-doves
　　sleek forth
Their timid necks and tremble; so these both
Leant to each other trembling, and sat so
Waiting for some destruction — when lo!
Foot-feather'd Mercury appeared sublime
Beyond the tall tree tops; and in less time

Than shoots the slanted hail-storm, down he
   dropt
Towards the ground; but rested not, nor stopt
One moment from his home: only the sward
He with his wand light touch'd, and heaven-
   ward
Swifter than sight was gone — even before
The teeming earth a sudden witness bore
Of his swift magic. Diving swans appear
Above the crystal circlings white and clear;
And catch the cheated eye in wild surprise,
How they can dive in sight and unseen
   rise —
So from the turf outsprang two steeds jet-
   black,
Each with large dark blue wings upon his
   back.
The youth of Caria placed the lovely dame
On one, and felt himself in spleen to tame
The other's fierceness. Through the air they
   flew,
High as the eagles. Like two drops of dew
Exhaled to Phœbus' lips, away they are gone,
Far from the earth away — unseen, alone,
Among cool clouds and winds, but that the
   free,
The buoyant life of song can floating be
Above their heads, and follow them untired.
Muse of my native land! am I inspired?
This is the giddy air, and I must spread
Wide pinions to keep here; nor do I dread
Or height, or depth, or width, or any chance

Precipitous: I have beneath my glance
Those towering horses and their mournful
  freight.
Could I thus sail, and see, and thus await
Fearless for power of thought, without thine
  aid?
There is a sleepy dusk, an odorous shade
From some approaching wonder, and behold
Those winged steeds, with snorting nostrils
  bold
Snuff at its faint extreme, and seem to tire,
Dying to embers from their native fire!

  There curl'd a purple mist around them;
  soon,
It seem'd as when around the pale new moon
Sad Zephyr droops the clouds like weeping
  willow:
'Twas Sleep slow journeying with head on
  pillow,
For the first time, since he came nigh dead-
  born
From the old womb of night, his cave forlorn
Had he left more forlorn; for the first time,
He felt aloof the day and morning's prime —
Because into his depth Cimmerian
There came a dream, showing how a young
  man,
Ere a lean bat could plump its wintry skin,
Would at high Jove's empyreal footstool win
An immortality, and how espouse
Jove's daughter, and be reckon'd of his house.

Now was he slumbering towards heaven's
    gate,
That he might at the threshold one hour wait
To hear the marriage melodies, and then
Sink downward to his dusky cave again.
His litter of smooth semilucent mist,
Diversely tinged with rose and amethyst,
Puzzled those eyes that for the centre sought;
And scarcely for one moment could be
    caught
His sluggish form reposing motionless.
Those two on wingèd steeds, with all the
    stress
Of vision search'd for him, as one would look
Athwart the sallows of a river nook
To catch a glance at silver-throated eels, —
Or from old Skiddaw's top, when fog con-
    ceals
His rugged forehead in a mantle pale,
With an eye-guess towards some pleasant
    vale,
Descry a favourite hamlet faint and far.

  These raven horses, though they foster'd
    are
Of earth's splenetic fire, dully drop
Their full-vein'd ears, nostrils blood wide,
    and stop;
Upon the spiritless mist have they outspread
Their ample feathers, are in slumber
    dead, —
And on those pinions, level in mid-air

Endymion sleepeth and the lady fair.
Slowly they sail, slowly as icy isle
Upon a calm sea drifting; and meanwhile
The mournful wanderer dreams. Behold! he
   walks
On heaven's pavement, brotherly he talks
To divine powers; from his hand full fain
Juno's proud birds are pecking pearly grain:
He tries the nerve of Phœbus' golden bow,
And asketh where the golden apples grow:
Upon his arm he braces Pallas' shield,
And strives in vain to unsettle and wield
A Jovian thunderbolt: arch Hebe brings
A full-brimm'd goblet, dances lightly, sings
And tantalizes long; at last he drinks,
And lost in pleasure, at her feet he sinks,
Touching with dazzled lips her star-light
   hand;
He blows a bugle, — an ethereal band
Are visible above: the Seasons four, —
Green-kirtled Spring, flush Summer, golden
   store
In Autumn's sickle, Winter frosty hoar,
Join dance with shadowy Hours; while still
   the blast,
In swells unmitigated, still doth last
To sway their floating morris. 'Whose is this?
Whose bugle?' he inquires: they smile — 'O
   Dis!
Why is this mortal here? Dost thou not know
Its mistress' lips? Not thou? — 'Tis Dian's:
   lo!

She rises crescented!' He looks, 'tis she,
His very goddess: good-bye earth, and sea,
And air, and pains, and care, and suffering;
Good-bye to all but love! Then doth he spring
Towards her, and awakes — and, strange,
   o'erhead,
Of those same fragrant exhalations bred,
Beheld awake his very dream: the gods
Stood smiling; merry Hebe laughs and nods;
And Phœbe bends towards him crescented.
O state perplexing! On the pinion bed,
Too well awake, he feels the panting side
Of his delicious lady. He who died
For soaring too audacious in the sun,
Where that same treacherous wax began to
   run,
Felt not more tongue-tied than Endymion.
His heart leapt up as to its rightful throne,
To that fair-shadow'd passion pulsed its
   way —
Ah, what perplexity! Ah, well-a-day!
So fond, so beauteous was his bed-fellow,
He could not help but kiss her: then he grew
Awhile forgetful of all beauty save
Young Phœbe's, golden-hair'd; and so 'gan
   crave
Forgiveness: yet he turn'd once more to look
At the sweet sleeper, — all his soul was
   shook, —
She press'd his hand in slumber; so once
   more
He could not help but kiss her and adore.

At this the shadow wept, melting away.
The Latmian started up: 'Bright goddess,
    stay!
Search my most hidden breast! By truth's
    own tongue,
I have no dædale heart; why is it wrung
To desperation? Is there nought for me
Upon the bourne of bliss, but misery?'

These words awoke the stranger of dark
    tresses:
Her dawning love-look rapt Endymion
    blesses
With 'haviour soft. Sleep yawn'd from under-
    neath.
'Thou swan of Ganges, let us no more
    breathe
This murky phantasm! thou contented
    seem'st,
Pillow'd in lovely idleness, nor dream'st
What horrors may discomfort thee and me.
Ah, shouldst thou die from my heart-
    treachery! —
Yet did she merely weep — her gentle soul
Hath no revenge in it; as it is whole
In tenderness, would I were whole in love!
Can I prize thee, fair maid, all price above,
Even when I feel as true as innocence!
I do, I do. — What is this soul then? Whence
Came it? It does not seem my own, and I
Have no self-passion or identity.

Some fearful end must be; where, where is
    it?
By Nemesis! I see my spirit flit
Alone about the dark — Forgive me, sweet!
Shall we away?' He roused the steeds; they
    beat
Their wings chivalrous into the clear air,
Leaving old Sleep within his vapoury lair.

  The good-night blush of eve was waning
    slow,
And Vesper, risen star, began to throe
In the dusk heavens silverly, when they
Thus sprang direct towards the Galaxy.
Nor did speed hinder converse soft and
    strange —
Eternal oaths and vows they interchange,
In such wise, in such temper, so aloof
Up in the winds, beneath a starry roof,
So witless of their doom, that verily
'Tis well nigh past man's search their hearts
    to see;
Whether they wept, or laugh'd or grieved, or
    toy'd —
Most like with joy gone mad, with sorrow
    cloy'd.

  Full facing their swift flight, from ebon
    streak,
The moon put forth a little diamond peak,
No bigger than an unobserved star,
Or tiny point of fairy scymitar;

Bright signal that she only stoop'd to tie
Her silver sandals, ere deliciously
She bow'd into the heavens her timid head.
Slowly she rose, as though she would have
    fled,
While to his lady meek the Carian turn'd,
To mark if her dark eyes had yet discern'd
This beauty in its birth — Despair! despair!
He saw her body fading gaunt and spare
In the cold moonshine. Straight he seized
    her wrist;
It melted from his grasp; her hand he kiss'd,
And, horror! kiss'd his own — he was alone.
Her steed a little higher soar'd, and then
Dropt hawk-wise to the earth.

                      There lies a den,
Beyond the seeming confines of the space
Made for the soul to wander in and trace
Its own existence, of remotest glooms.
Dark regions are around it, where the tombs
Of buried griefs the spirit sees, but scarce
One hour doth linger weeping, for the pierce
Of new-born woe it feels more inly smart;
And in these regions many a venom'd dart
At random flies; they are the proper home
Of every ill: the man is yet to come
Who hath not journey'd in this native hell.
But few have ever felt how calm and well
Sleep may be had in that deep den of all.
There anguish does not sting, nor pleasure
    pall;

Woe-hurricanes beat ever at the gate.
Yet all is still within and desolate.
Beset with plainful gusts, within ye hear
No sound so loud as when on curtain'd bier
The death-watch tick is stifled. Enter none
Who strive therefore; on the sudden it is won.
Just when the sufferer begins to burn,
Then it is free to him; and from an urn,
Still fed by melting ice, he takes a draught —
Young Semele such richness never quaft
In her maternal longing. Happy gloom!
Dark Paradise! where pale becomes the
    bloom
Of health by due; where silence dreariest
Is most articulate; where hopes infest;
Where those eyes are the brightest far that
    keep
Their lids shut longest in a dreamless sleep.
O happy spirit-home! O wondrous soul!
Pregnant with such a den to save the whole
In thine own depth. Hail, gentle Carian!
For, never since thy griefs and woes began,
Hast thou felt so content: a grievous feud
Hath led thee to this Cave of Quietude.
Ay, his lull'd soul was there, although up-
    borne
With dangerous speed: and so he did not
    mourn
Because he knew not whither he was going.
So happy was he, not the aerial blowing
Of trumpets at clear parley from the east

Could rouse from that fine relish, that high
    feast.
They stung the feather'd horse; with fierce
    alarm
He flapped towards the sound. Alas! no
    charm
Could lift Endymion's head, or he had view'd
A skyey mask, a pinion'd multitude, —
And silvery was its passing: voices sweet
Warbling the while as if to lull and greet
The wanderer in his path. Thus warbled they,
While past the vision went in bright array.

   'Who, who from Dian's feast would be
     away?
For all the golden bowers of the day
Are empty left? Who, who away would be
From Cynthia's wedding and festivity?
Not Hesperus: lo! upon his silver wings
He leans away for highest heaven and sings,
Snapping his lucid fingers merrily! —
Ah, Zephyrus! art here, and Flora too?
Ye tender bibbers of the rain and dew,
Young playmates of the rose and daffodil,
Be careful, ere ye enter in, to fill
            Your baskets high
With fennel green, and balm, and golden
    pines,
Savory, latter-mint, and columbines,
Cool parsley, basil sweet, and sunny thyme;
Yea, every flower and leaf of every clime,
All gather'd in the dewy morning: hie

Away! fly, fly! —
Crystalline brother of the belt of heaven,
Aquarius! to whom king Jove has given
Two liquid pulse streams 'stead of feather'd
    wings,
Two fanlike fountains, — thine illuminings
        For Dian play:
Dissolve the frozen purity of air;
Let thy white shoulders silvery and bare
Show cold through watery pinions; make
    more bright
The Star-Queen's crescent on her marriage
    night:
        Haste, haste away! —
Castor has tamed the planet Lion, see!
And of the Bear has Pollux mastery:
A third is in the race! who is the third,
Speeding away swift as the eagle bird?
        The ramping Centaur!
The Lion's mane's on end: the Bear how
    fierce!
The Centaur's arrow ready seems to pierce
Some enemy: far forth his bow is bent
Into the blue of heaven. He'll be shent,
        Pale unrelentor,
When he shall hear the wedding lutes
    a-playing. —
Andromeda! sweet woman! why delaying
So timidly among the stars: come hither!
Join this bright throng, and nimbly follow
    whither
        They all are going.

Danae's Son, before Jove newly bow'd,
Has wept for thee, calling to Jove aloud.
Thee, gentle lady, did he disenthral:
Ye shall for ever live and love, for all
                    Thy tears are flowing. —
By Daphne's fright, behold Apollo!' —

                                        More
Endymion heard not: down his steed him
    bore
Prone to the green head of a misty hill.

    His first touch of the earth went nigh to
        kill.
'Alas!' said he, 'were I but always borne
Through dangerous winds, but had my
    footsteps worn
A path in hell, for ever would I bless
Horrors which nourish an uneasiness
For my own sullen conquering: to him
Who lives beyond earth's boundary, grief is
    dim,
Sorrow is but a shadow: now I see
The grass; I feel the solid ground — Ah, me!
It is thy voice — divinest! Where? — who?
    who
Left thee so quiet on this bed of dew?
Behold upon this happy earth we are;
Let us aye love each other; let us fare
On forest-fruits, and never, never go
Among the abodes of mortals here below,
Or be by phantoms duped. O destiny!

Into a labyrinth now my soul would fly,
But with thy beauty will I deaden it.
Where didst thou melt to? By thee will I sit
For ever: let our fate stop here — a kid
I on this spot will offer: Pan will bid
Us live in peace, in love and peace among
His forest wildernesses. I have clung
To nothing, loved a nothing, nothing seen
Or felt but a great dream! O I have been
Presumptuous against love, against the sky,
Against all elements, against the tie
Of mortals each to each, against the blooms
Of flowers, rush of rivers, and the tombs
Of heroes gone! Against his proper glory
Has my own soul conspired: so my story
Will I to children utter, and repent.
There never lived a mortal man, who bent
His appetite beyond his natural sphere,
But starved and died. My sweetest Indian, here,
Here will I kneel, for thou redeemèd hast
My life from too thin breathing: gone and past
Are cloudy phantasms. Caverns lone, farewell!
And air of visions, and the monstrous swell
Of visionary seas! No, never more
Shall airy voices cheat me to the shore
Of tangled wonder, breathless and aghast.
Adieu, my daintiest Dream! although so vast
My love is still for thee. The hour may come
When we shall meet in pure elysium.

On earth I may not love thee, and therefore
Doves will I offer up, and sweetest store
All through the teeming year: so thou wilt
    shine
On me, and on this damsel fair of mine,
And bless our simple lives. My Indian bliss!
My river-lily bud! one human kiss!
One sigh of real breath — one gentle squeeze,
Warm as a dove's nest among summer trees,
And warm with dew at ooze from living
    blood!
Whither didst melt? Ah, what of that! — all
    good
We'll talk about — no more of dreaming.
    — Now,
Where shall our dwelling be? Under the brow
Of some steep mossy hill, where ivy dun
Would hide us up, although spring leaves
    were none;
And where dark yew-trees, as we rustle
    through,
Will drop their scarlet-berry cups of dew?
O thou wouldst joy to live in such a place!
Dusk for our loves, yet light enough to grace
Those gentle limbs on mossy bed reclined:
For by one step the blue sky shouldst thou
    find,
And by another, in deep dell below,
See, through the trees, a little river go
All in its mid-day gold and glimmering.
Honey from out the gnarled hive I'll bring,

And apples, wan with sweetness, gather
    thee, —
Cresses that grow where no man may them
    see,
And sorrel untorn by the dew-claw'd stag:
Pipes will I fashion of the syrinx flag,
That thou mayst always know whither I
    roam,
When it shall please thee in our quiet home
To listen and think of love. Still let me speak;
Still let me dive into the joy I seek, —
For yet the past doth prison me. The rill,
Thou haply mayst delight in, will I fill
With fairy fishes from the mountain tarn,
And thou shalt feed them from the squirrel's
    barn.
Its bottom will I strew with amber shells,
And pebbles blue from deep enchanted wells.
Its sides I'll plant with dew-sweet eglantine,
And honeysuckles full of clear bee-wine.
I will entice this crystal rill to trace
Love's silver name upon the meadow's face.
I'll kneel to Vesta, for a flame of fire;
And to God Phœbus, for a golden lyre;
To Empress Dian, for a hunting-spear,
To Vesper, for a taper silver-clear,
That I may see thy beauty through the night;
To Flora, and a nightingale shall light
Tame on thy finger; to the River-gods,
And they shall bring thee taper fishing-rods
Of gold, and lines of Naiads' long bright
    tress,

Heaven shield thee for thine utter loveliness!
Thy mossy footstool shall the altar be
'Fore which I'll bend, bending, dear love, to
    thee:
Those lips shall be my Delphos, and shall
    speak
Laws to my footsteps, colour to my cheek,
Trembling or stedfastness to this same voice,
And of three sweetest pleasurings the choice:
And that affectionate light, those diamond
    things,
Those eyes, those passions, those supreme
    pearl springs,
Shall be my grief, or twinkle me to pleasure.
Say, is not bliss within our perfect seizure?
O that I could not doubt!'

                   The mountaineer
Thus strove by fancies vain and crude to clear
His brier'd path to some tranquillity.
It gave bright gladness to his lady's eye,
And yet the tears she wept were tears of sor-
    row;
Answering thus, just as the golden morrow
Beam'd upward from the valleys of the east:
'O that the flutter of this heart had ceased,
Or the sweet name of love had pass'd away!
Young feather'd tyrant! by a swift decay
Wilt thou devote this body to the earth:
And I do think that at my very birth
I lisp'd thy blooming titles inwardly;

For at the first, first dawn and thought of
    thee,
With uplift hands I bless'd the stars of
    heaven.
Art thou not cruel? Ever have I striven
To think thee kind, but ah, it will not do!
When yet a child, I heard that kisses drew
Favour from thee, and so I kisses gave
To the void air, bidding them find out love:
But when I came to feel how far above
All fancy, pride, and fickle maidenhood,
All earthly pleasure, all imagined good,
Was the warm tremble of a devout kiss, —
Even then, that moment, at the thought of
    this,
Fainting I fell into a bed of flowers,
And languish'd there three days. Ye milder
    powers,
Am I not cruelly wrong'd? Believe, believe
Me, dear Endymion, were I to weave
With my own fancies garlands of sweet life,
Thou shouldst be one of all. Ah, bitter strife!
I may not be thy love: I am forbidden —
Indeed I am — thwarted, affrighted, chid-
    den,
By things I trembled at, and gorgon wrath.
Twice hast thou ask'd whither I went: hence-
    forth
Ask me no more! I may not utter it,
Nor may I be thy love. We might commit
Ourselves at once to vengeance; we might
    die;

251

We might embrace and die: voluptuous
   thought!
Enlarge not to my hunger, or I'm caught
In trammels of perverse deliciousness.
No, no, that shall not be: thee will I bless,
And bid a long adieu.'

The Carian
No word return'd: both lovelorn, silent, wan,
Into the valleys green together went.
Far wandering, they were perforce content
To sit beneath a fair lone beechen tree;
Nor at each other gazed, but heavily
Pored on its hazel cirque of shedded leaves.

   Endymion! unhappy! it nigh grieves
Me to behold thee thus in last extreme:
Ensky'd ere this, but truly that I deem
Truth the best music in a first-born song.
Thy lute-voiced brother will I sing ere long,
And thou shalt aid — hast thou not aided
   me?
Yes, moonlight Emperor! felicity
Has been thy meed for many thousand years;
Yet often have I, on the brink of tears,
Mourn'd as if yet thou wert a forester; —
Forgetting the old tale.

He did not stir
His eyes from the dead leaves, or one small
   pulse
Of joy he might have felt. The spirit culls

Unfaded amaranth, when wild it strays
Through the old garden-ground of boyish
    days.
A little onward ran the very stream
By which he took his first soft poppy dream;
And on the very bark 'gainst which he leant
A crescent he had carved, and round it spent
His skill in little stars. The teeming tree
Had swoll'n and green'd the pious charac-
    tery,
But not ta'en out. Why, there was not a slope
Up which he had not fear'd the antelope;
And not a tree, beneath whose rooty shade
He had not with his tamed leopards play'd;
Nor could an arrow light, or javelin,
Fly in the air where his had never been —
And yet he knew it not.

                    O treachery!
Why does his lady smile, pleasing her eye
With all his sorrowing? He sees her not.
But who so stares on him? His sister sure!
Peona of the woods! — Can she endure? —
Impossible — how dearly they embrace!
His lady smiles; delight is in her face;
It is no treachery.

                    'Dear brother mine!
Endymion, weep not so! Why shouldst thou
    pine
When all great Latmos so exalt will be?
Thank the great gods, and look not bitterly;

And speak not one pale word, and sigh no
  more.
Sure I will not believe thou hast such store
Of grief, to last thee to my kiss again.
Thou surely canst not bear a mind in pain,
Come hand in hand with one so beautiful.
Be happy both of you! for I will pull
The flowers of autumn for your coronals.
Pan's holy priest for young Endymion calls;
And when he is restored, thou, fairest dame,
Shalt be our queen. Now, is it not a shame
To see ye thus, — not very, very sad?
Perhaps ye are too happy to be glad:
O feel as if it were a common day;
Free-voiced as one who never was away.
No tongue shall ask, whence come ye? but ye
  shall
Be gods of your own rest imperial.
Not even I, for one whole month, will pry
Into the hours that have pass'd us by,
Since in my arbour I did sing to thee.
O Hermes! on this very night will be
A hymning up to Cynthia, queen of light;
For the soothsayers old saw yesternight
Good visions in the air, — whence will befall,
As say these sages, health perpetual
To shepherds and their flocks; and further-
  more
In Dian's face they read the gentle lore:
Therefore for her these vesper-carols are.
Our friends will all be there from nigh and
  far.

Many upon thy death have ditties made;
And many, even now, their foreheads shade
With cypress, on a day of sacrifice.
New singing for our maids shalt thou devise,
And pluck the sorrow from our huntsmen's
    brows,
Tell me, my lady-queen, how to espouse
This wayward brother to his rightful joys!
His eyes are on thee bent, as thou didst poise
His fate most goddess-like. Help me, I pray,
To lure — Endymion, dear brother, say
What ails thee?' He could bear no more, and
    so
Bent his soul fiercely like a spiritual bow,
And twang'd it inwardly, and calmly said:
'I would have thee my only friend, sweet
    maid!
My only visitor! not ignorant though,
That those deceptions which for pleasure go
'Mong men, are pleasures real as real may
    be:
But there are higher ones I may not see,
If impiously an earthly realm I take.
Since I saw thee, I have been wide awake
Night after night, and day by day, until
Of the empyrean I have drunk my fill.
Let it content thee, Sister, seeing me
More happy than betides mortality.
A hermit young, I'll live in mossy cave,
Where thou alone shalt come to me, and lave
Thy spirit in the wonders I shall tell.

Through me the shepherd realm shall prosper
    well;
For to thy tongue will I all health confide.
And for my sake, let this young maid abide
With thee as a dear sister. Thou alone,
Peona, mayst return to me. I own
This may sound strangely: but when, dearest
    girl,
Thou seest it for my happiness, no pearl
Will trespass down those cheeks. Companion
    fair!
Wilt be content to dwell with her, to share
This sister's love with me?' Like one resign'd
And bent by circumstance, and thereby blind
In self-commitment, thus, that meek un-
    known:
'Ay, but a buzzing by my ears has flown,
Of jubilee to Dian: — truth I heard!
Well then, I see there is no little bird,
Tender soever, but is Jove's own care.
Long have I sought for rest, and unaware,
Behold I find it! so exalted too!
So after my own heart! I knew, I knew
There was a place untenanted in it:
In that same void white Chastity shall sit,
And monitor me nightly to lone slumber.
With sanest lips I vow me to the number
Of Dian's sisterhood; and, kind lady,
With thy good help, this very night shall see
My future days to her fane consecrate.'

As feels a dreamer what doth most create

His own particular fright, so these three felt.
Or like one who, in after ages, knelt
To Lucifer or Baal, when he'd pine
After a little sleep: or when in mine
Far under-ground, a sleeper meets his friends
Who know him not. Each diligently bends
Towards common thoughts and things for
    very fear;
Striving their ghastly malady to cheer,
By thinking it a thing of yes and no,
That housewives talk of. But the spirit-blow
Was struck, and all were dreamers. At the
    last
Endymion said: 'Are not our fates all cast?
Why stand we here? Adieu, ye tender pair!
Adieu!' Whereat those maidens, with wild
    stare,
Walk'd dizzily away. Pained and hot
His eyes went after them, until they got
Near to a cypress grove, whose deadly maw,
In one swift moment, would what then he
    saw
Engulph for ever. 'Stay!' he cried, 'ah, stay!
Turn, damsels! hist! one word I have to say:
Sweet Indian, I would see thee once again.
It is a thing I dote on: so I'd fain,
Peona, ye should hand in hand repair
Into those holy groves, that silent are
Behind great Dian's temple. I'll be yon,
At vesper's earliest twinkle — they are
    gone —

But once, once, once again —' At this he prest
His hands against his face, and then did rest
His head upon a mossy hillock green,
And so remain'd as he a corpse had been
All the long day; save when he scantly lifted
His eyes abroad, to see how shadows shifted
With the slow move of time, — sluggish and weary
Until the poplar tops, in journey dreary,
Had reach'd the river's brim. Then up he rose,
And, slowly as that very river flows,
Walk'd towards the temple-grove with this lament:
'Why such a golden eve? The breeze is sent
Careful and soft, that not a leaf may fall
Before the serene father of them all
Bows down his summer head below the west.
Now am I of breath, speech, and speed possest,
But at the setting I must bid adieu
To her for the last time. Night will strew
On the damp grass myriads of lingering leaves,
And with them shall I die; nor much it grieves
To die, when summer dies on the cold sward.
Why, I have been a butterfly, a lord
Of flowers, garlands, love-knots, silly posies,
Groves, meadows, melodies, and arbour-roses;
My kingdom's at its death, and just it is

That I should die with it: so in all this
We miscall grief, bale, sorrow, heart-break,
   woe,
What is there to plain of? By Titan's foe
I am but rightly served.' So saying, he
Tripp'd lightly on, in sort of deathful glee;
Laughing at the clear stream and setting sun,
As though they jests had been: nor had he
   done
His laugh at nature's holy countenance,
Until that grove appear'd, as if perchance,
And then his tongue with sober seemlihed
Gave utterance as he enter'd: 'Ha! I said,
"King of the butterflies"; but by this gloom,
And by old Rhadamanthus' tongue of doom,
This dusk religion, pomp of solitude,
And the Promethean clay by thief endued,
By old Saturnus' forelock, by his head
Shook with eternal palsy, I did wed
Myself to things of light from infancy;
And thus to be cast out, thus lorn to die,
Is sure enough to make a mortal man
Grow impious.' So he inwardly began
On things for which no wording can be found
Deeper and deeper sinking, until drown'd
Beyond the reach of music: for the choir
Of Cynthia he heard not, though rough brier
Nor muffling thicket interposed to dull
The vesper hymn, far swollen, soft and full,
Through the dark pillars of those sylvan
   aisles.
He saw not the two maidens, nor their smiles,

Wan as primroses gather'd at midnight
By chilly-finger'd spring. Unhappy wight!
'Endymion!' said Peona, 'we are here!
What wouldst thou ere we all are laid on
    bier?'
Then he embraced her, and his lady's hand
Press'd, saying: 'Sister, I would have com-
    mand,
If it were heaven's will, on our sad fate.'
At which that dark-eyed stranger stood elate
And said, in a new voice, but sweet as love,
To Endymion's amaze: 'By Cupid's dove,
And so thou shalt? and by the lily truth
Of my own breast thou shalt, belovèd youth!'
And as she spake, into her face there came,
Light, as reflected from a silver flame:
Her long black hair swell'd ampler, in display
Full golden: in her eyes a brighter day
Dawn'd blue, and full of love. Ay, he beheld
Phœbe, his passion! joyous she upheld
Her lucid bow, continuing thus: 'Drear, drear
Has our delaying been; but foolish fear
Withheld me first; and then decrees of fate:
And then 'twas fit that from this mortal state
Thou shouldst, my love, by some unlook'd-
    for change
Be spiritualized. Peona, we shall range
These forests, and to thee they safe shall be
As was thy cradle; hither shalt thou flee
To meet us many a time.' Next Cynthia
    bright
Peona kiss'd, and bless'd with fair good night:

Her brother kiss'd her too, and knelt adown
Before his goddess, in a blissful swoon.
She gave her fair hands to him, and behold,
Before three swiftest kisses he had told,
They vanish'd far away! — Peona went
Home through the gloomy wood in wonder-
    ment.

■ ■ ■ ■

LAMIA, ISABELLA, THE EVE OF ST. AGNES, AND OTHER POEMS
1820

■ ■ ■ ■

ADVERTISEMENT

If any apology be thought necessary for the ap-
pearance of the unfinished poem of HYPERION,
the publishers beg to state that they alone are
responsible, as it was printed at their particular
request, and contrary to the wish of the author.
The poem was intended to have been of equal
length with ENDYMION, but the reception given
to that work discouraged the author from pro-
ceeding.

Fleet-Street, 26 June, 1820

Lamia

PART I

Upon a time, before the faery broods
Drove Nymph and Satyr from the prosper-
  ous woods,
Before King Oberon's bright diadem,
Sceptre, and mantle, clasp'd with dewy gem,
Frighted away the Dryads and the Fauns
From rushes green, and brakes, and
  cowslipp'd lawns,
The ever-smitten Hermes empty left
His golden throne, bent warm on amorous
  theft:
From high Olympus had he stolen light,
On this side of Jove's clouds, to escape the
  sight
Of his great summoner, and made retreat
Into a forest on the shores of Crete.
For somewhere in that sacred island dwelt
A nymph to whom all hoofèd Satyrs knelt;

At whose white feet the languid Tritons
    pour'd
Pearls, while on land they wither'd and
    adored.
Fast by the springs where she to bathe was
    wont,
And in those meads where sometime she
    might haunt,
Were strewn rich gifts, unknown to any
    Muse,
Though Fancy's casket were unlock'd to
    choose.
Ah, what a world of love was at her feet!
So Hermes thought, and a celestial heat
Burn'd from his winged heels to either ear,
That from a whiteness as the lily clear,
Blush'd into roses 'mid his golden hair,
Fallen in jealous curls about his shoulders
    bare.
From vale to vale, from wood to wood, he
    flew,
Breathing upon the flowers his passion new,
And wound with many a river to its head,
To find where this sweet nymph prepared her
    secret bed
In vain; the sweet nymph might nowhere be
    found,
And so he rested on the lonely ground,
Pensive, and full of painful jealousies
Of the Wood-Gods, and even the very trees.
There as he stood he heard a mournful voice,
Such as once heard, in gentle heart, destroys

All pain but pity: thus the lone voice spake:
'When from this wreathèd tomb shall I
    awake?
When move in a sweet body fit for life,
And love, and pleasure, and the ruddy strife
Of hearts and lips? Ah, miserable me!'
The God, dove-footed, glided silently
Round bush and tree, soft-brushing in his
    speed
The taller grasses and full-flowering weed,
Until he found a palpitating snake,
Bright, and cirque-couchant in a dusky brake.

   She was a gordian shape of dazzling hue,
Vermilion-spotted, golden, green, and blue;
Striped like a zebra, freckled like a pard,
Eyed like a peacock, and all crimson-barr'd;
And full of silver moons, that, as she
    breathed,
Dissolved, or brighter shone, or inter-
    wreathed
Their lustres with the gloomier tapestries —
So rainbow-sided, touch'd with miseries,
She seem'd at once, some penanced lady elf,
Some demon's mistress, or the demon's self.
Upon her crest she wore a wannish fire
Sprinkled with stars, like Ariadne's tiar:
Her head was serpent, but ah, bitter-sweet!
She had a woman's mouth with all its pearls
    complete;
And for her eyes: what could such eyes do
    there

But weep, and weep, that they were born so
    fair?
As Proserpine still weeps for her Sicilian air.
Her throat was serpent, but the words she
    spake
Came, as through bubbling honey, for Love's
    sake,
And thus; while Hermes on his pinions lay,
Like a stoop'd falcon ere he takes his prey:

'Fair Hermes, crown'd with feathers, flut-
    tering light,
I had a splendid dream of thee last night:
I saw thee sitting, on a throne of gold,
Among the Gods, upon Olympus old,
The only sad one; for thou didst not hear
The soft lute-finger'd Muses chaunting clear,
Nor even Apollo when he sang alone,
Deaf to his throbbing throat's long, long
    melodious moan.
I dreamt I saw thee, robed in purple flakes,
Break amorous through the clouds, as morn-
    ing breaks,
And swiftly as a bright Phœbean dart
Strike for the Cretan isle; and here thou art!
Too gentle Hermes, hast thou found the
    maid?'
Whereat the star of Lethe not delay'd
His rosy eloquence, and thus inquired:
'Thou smooth-lipp'd serpent, surely high in-
    spired!

Thou beauteous wreath, with melancholy
   eyes,
Possess whatever bliss thou canst devise,
Telling me only where my nymph is fled —
Where she doth breathe!' 'Bright planet, thou
   hast said,'
Return'd the snake, 'but seal with oaths, fair
   God!'
'I swear,' said Hermes, 'by my serpent rod,
And by thine eyes, and by thy starry crown!'
Light flew his earnest words, among the blos-
   soms blown.
Then thus again the brilliance feminine:
'Too frail of heart! for this lost nymph of
   thine,
Free as the air, invisibly, she strays
About these thornless wilds; her pleasant
   days
She tastes unseen; unseen her nimble feet
Leave traces in the grass and flowers sweet:
From weary tendrils and bow'd branches
   green
She plucks the fruit unseen, she bathes un-
   seen:
And by my power is her beauty veil'd
To keep it unaffronted, unassail'd
By the love-glances of unlovely eyes,
Of Satyrs, Fauns, and blear'd Silenus' sighs.
Pale grew her immortality, for woe
Of all these lovers, and she grievèd so
I took compassion on her, bade her steep
Her hair in weïrd syrops, that would keep

271

Her loveliness invisible, yet free
To wander as she loves, in liberty.
Thou shalt behold her, Hermes, thou alone
If thou wilt, as thou swearest, grant my boon.'
Then, once again, the charmèd God began
An oath, and through the serpent's ears it
    ran
Warm, tremulous, devout, psalterian.
Ravish'd, she lifted her Circean head,
Blush'd a live damask, and swift-lisping said,
'I was a woman, let me have once more
A woman's shape, and charming as before.
I love a youth of Corinth — O the bliss!
Give me my woman's form, and place me
    where he is.
Stoop, Hermes, let me breathe upon thy
    brow,
And thou shalt see thy sweet nymph even
    now.'
The God on half-shut feathers sank serene,
She breathed upon his eyes, and swift was
    seen
Of both the guarded nymph near-smiling on
    the green.
It was no dream; or say a dream it was,
Real are the dreams of Gods, and smoothly
    pass
Their pleasures in a long immortal dream.
One warm, flush'd moment, hovering, it
    might seem,
Dash'd by the wood-nymph's beauty, so he
    burn'd;

Then, lighting on the printless verdure, turn'd
To the swoon'd serpent, and with languid arm,
Delicate, put to proof the lithe Caducean charm.
So done, upon the nymph his eyes he bent
Full of adoring tears and blandishment,
And towards her stept: she, like a moon in wane,
Faded before him, cower'd, nor could re-strain
Her fearful sobs, self-folding like a flower
That faints into itself at evening hour:
But the God fostering her chillèd hand,
She felt the warmth, her eyelids open'd bland,
And, like new flowers at morning song of bees,
Bloom'd, and gave up her honey to the lees.
Into the green-recessèd woods they flew;
Nor grew they pale, as mortal lovers do.

Left to herself, the serpent now began
To change; her elfin blood in madness ran;
Her mouth foam'd, and the grass, therewith besprent,
Wither'd at dew so sweet and virulent;
Her eyes in torture fix'd and anguish drear,
Hot, glazed, and wide, with lid-lashes all sear,
Flash'd phosphor and sharp sparks, without one cooling tear.

The colours all inflamed throughout her
    train,
She writhed about, convulsed with scarlet
    pain:
A deep volcanian yellow took the place,
Of all her milder-moonèd body's grace;
And, as the lava ravishes the mead,
Spoilt all her silver mail, and golden brede:
Made gloom of all her frecklings, streaks and
    bars,
Eclipsed her crescents, and lick'd up her
    stars:
So that, in moments few, she was undrest
Of all her sapphires, greens, and amethyst,
And rubious-argent: of all these bereft,
Nothing but pain and ugliness were left.
Still shone her crown; that vanish'd, also she
Melted and disappear'd as suddenly;
And in the air, her new voice luting soft,
Cried, 'Lycius! gentle Lycius!' — Borne aloft
With the bright mists about the mountains
    hoar
These words dissolved: Crete's forests heard
    no more.

   Whither fled Lamia, now a lady bright,
A full-born beauty new and exquisite?
She fled into that valley they pass o'er
Who go to Corinth from Cenchreas' shore;
And rested at the foot of those wild hills,
The rugged founts of the Peræan rills,
And of that other ridge whose barren back

Stretches, with all its mist and cloudy rack,
South-westward to Cleone. There she stood,
About a young bird's flutter from a wood,
Fair, on a sloping green of mossy tread,
By a clear pool, wherein she passioned
To see herself escaped from so sore ills,
While her robes flaunted with the daffodils.

Ah, happy Lycius! — for she was a maid
More beautiful than ever twisted braid,
Or sigh'd, or blush'd, or on spring-flower'd
   lea
Spread a green kirtle to the minstrelsy:
A virgin purest lipp'd, yet in the lore
Of love deep learned to the red heart's core:
Not one hour old, yet of sciential brain
To unperplex bliss from its neighbour pain;
Define their pettish limits, and estrange
Their points of contact, and swift counter-
   change;
Intrigue with the specious chaos, and dispart
Its most ambiguous atoms with sure art;
As though in Cupid's college she had spent
Sweet days a lovely graduate, still unshent,
And kept his rosy terms in idle languishment.

Why this fair creature chose so fairily
By the wayside to linger, we shall see;
But first 'tis fit to tell how she could muse
And dream, when in the serpent prison-
   house,
Of all she list, strange or magnificent:

275

How, ever, where she will'd her spirit went;
Whether to faint Elysium, or where
Down through tress-lifting waves the Nereids
   fair
Wind into Thetis' bower by many a pearly
   stair;
Or where God Bacchus drains his cups di-
   vine,
Stretch'd out, at ease, beneath a glutinous
   pine;
Or where in Pluto's gardens palatine
Mulciber's columns gleam in far piazzian
   line.
And sometimes into cities she would send
Her dream, with feast and rioting to blend;
And once, while among mortals dreaming
   thus,
She saw the young Corinthian Lycius
Charioting foremost in the envious race,
Like a young Jove with calm uneager face,
And fell into a swooning love of him.
Now on the moth-time of that evening dim
He would return that way, as well she knew,
To Corinth from the shore; for freshly blew
The eastern soft wind, and his galley now
Grated the quay-stones with her brazen prow
In port Cenchreas, from Egina isle
Fresh anchor'd; whither he had been awhile
To sacrifice to Jove, whose temple there
Waits with high marble doors for blood and
   incense rare.
Jove heard his vows, and better'd his desire;

For by some freakful chance he made retire
From his companions, and set forth to walk,
Perhaps grown wearied of their Corinth talk:
Over the solitary hills he fared,
Thoughtless at first, but ere eve's star
    appear'd
His phantasy was lost, where reason fades,
In the calm'd twilight of Platonic shades.
Lamia beheld him coming, near, more
    near —
Close to her passing, in indifference drear,
His silent sandals swept the mossy green;
So neighbour'd to him, and yet so unseen,
She stood: he pass'd, shut up in mysteries,
His mind wrapp'd like his mantle, while her
    eyes
Follow'd his steps, and her neck regal white
Turn'd — syllabling thus: 'Ah, Lycius bright!
And will you leave me on the hills alone?
Lycius, look back! and be some pity shown.'
He did; not with cold wonder, fearingly,
But Orpheus-like at an Eurydice;
For so delicious were the words she sung,
It seem'd he had loved them a whole sum-
    mer long.
And soon his eyes had drunk her beauty up,
Leaving no drop in the bewildering cup,
And still the cup was full, — while he, afraid
Lest she should vanish ere his lip had paid
Due adoration, thus began to adore;
Her soft look growing coy, she saw his chain
    so sure:

'Leave thee alone! Look back! Ah, Goddess,
    see
Whether my eyes can ever turn from thee!
For pity do not this sad heart belie —
Even as thou vanishest so I shall die.
Stay! though a Naiad of the rivers, stay!
To thy far wishes will thy streams obey:
Stay! though the greenest woods be thy do-
    main,
Alone they can drink up the morning rain;
Though a descended Pleiad, will not one
Of thine harmonious sisters keep in tune
Thy spheres, and as thy silver proxy shine?
So sweetly to these ravish'd ears of mine
Came thy sweet greeting, that if thou
    shouldst fade,
Thy memory will waste me to a shade.
For pity do not melt!' — 'If I should stay,'
Said Lamia, 'here, upon this floor of clay,
And pain my steps upon these flowers too
    rough,
What canst thou say or do of charm enough
To dull the nice remembrance of my home?
Thou canst not ask me with thee here to
    roam
Over these hills and vales, where no joy is, —
Empty of immortality and bliss!
Thou art a scholar, Lycius, and must know
That finer spirits cannot breathe below
In human climes, and live. Alas! poor youth,
What taste of purer air hast thou to soothe
My essence? What serener palaces,

278

Where I may all my many senses please
And by mysterious sleights a hundred thirsts
  appease?
It cannot be — Adieu!' So said, she rose
Tiptoe, with white arms spread. He, sick to
  lose
The amorous promise of her lone complain,
Swoon'd, murmuring of love, and pale with
  pain.
The cruel lady, without any show
Of sorrow for her tender favourite's woe,
But rather, if her eyes could brighter be,
With brighter eyes and slow amenity,
Put her new lips to his, and gave afresh
The life she had so tangled in her mesh:
And as he from one trance was wakening
Into another, she began to sing,
Happy in beauty, life, and love, and every-
  thing,
A song of love, too sweet for earthly lyres,
While, like held breath, the stars drew in their
  panting fires.
And then she whisper'd in such trembling
  tone
As those who, safe together met alone
For the first time through many anguish'd
  days,
Use other speech than looks; bidding him
  raise
His drooping head, and clear his soul of
  doubt,
For that she was a woman, and without

Any more subtle fluid in her veins
Than throbbing blood, and that the self-same
  pains
Inhabited her frail-strung heart as his.
And next she wonder'd how his eyes could
  miss
Her face so long in Corinth, where, she said,
She dwelt but half retired, and there had led
Days happy as the gold coin could invent
Without the aid of love; yet in content,
Till she saw him, as once she pass'd him by
Where 'gainst a column he leant thoughtfully
At Venus' temple porch, 'mid baskets heap'd
Of amorous herbs and flowers, newly reap'd
Late on that eve, as 'twas the night before
The Adonian feast; whereof she saw no more,
But wept alone those days, for why should
  she adore?
Lycius from death awoke into amaze
To see her still, and singing so sweet lays;
Then from amaze into delight he fell
To hear her whisper woman's lore so well;
And every word she spake enticed him on
To unperplex'd delight and pleasure known.
Let the mad poets say whate'er they please
Of the sweets of Fairies, Peris, Goddesses,
There is not such a treat among them all,
Haunters of cavern, lake, and waterfall,
As a real woman, lineal indeed
From Pyrrha's pebbles or old Adam's seed.
Thus gentle Lamia judged, and judged
  aright,

That Lycius could not love in half a fright,
So threw the goddess off, and won his heart
More pleasantly by playing woman's part,
With no more awe than what her beauty gave,
That, while it smote, still guaranteed to save.
Lycius to all made eloquent reply,
Marrying to every word a twin-born sigh;
And last, pointing to Corinth, ask'd her
    sweet,
If 'twas too far that night for her soft feet.
The way was short, for Lamia's eagerness
Made, by a spell, the triple league decrease
To a few paces; not at all surmised
By blinded Lycius. So, in her comprised,
They pass'd the city gates, he knew not how,
So noiseless, and he never thought to know.

  As men talk in a dream, so Corinth all,
Throughout her palaces imperial,
And all her populous streets and temples
    lewd,
Mutter'd, like tempest in the distance brew'd,
To the wide-spreaded night above her tow-
    ers.
Men, women, rich and poor, in the cool
    hours,
Shuffled their sandals o'er the pavement
    white,
Companion'd or alone; while many a light
Flared, here and there, from wealthy festivals,
And threw their moving shadows on the
    walls,

Or found them cluster'd in the corniced
    shade
Of some arch'd temple door or dusky colon-
    nade.

Muffling his face, of greeting friends in fear,
Her finger he press'd hard, as one came near
With curl'd grey beard, sharp eyes, and
    smooth bald crown,
Slow-stepp'd, and robed in philosophic
    gown:
Lycius shrank closer, as they met and past,
Into his mantle, adding wings to haste,
While hurried Lamia trembled. 'Ah!' said he,
'Why do you shudder, love, so ruefully?
Why does your tender palm dissolve in
    dew?' —
'I'm wearied,' said fair Lamia: 'tell me who
Is that old man? I cannot bring to mind
His features: — Lycius! wherefore did you
    blind
Yourself from his quick eyes?' Lycius replied,
' 'Tis Apollonius sage, my trusty guide
And good instructor; but to-night he seems
The ghost of folly haunting my sweet
    dreams.'

While yet he spake they had arrived before
A pillar'd porch, with lofty portal door,
Where hung a silver lamp, whose phosphor
    glow
Reflected in the slabbèd steps below,

Mild as a star in water; for so new
And so unsullied was the marble hue,
So through the crystal polish, liquid fine,
Ran the dark veins, that none but feet divine
Could e'er have touch'd there. Sounds Æo-
    lian
Breathed from the hinges, as the ample span
Of the wide doors disclosed a place unknown
Some time to any, but those two alone,
And a few Persian mutes, who that same year
Were seen about the markets: none knew
    where
They could inhabit; the most curious
Were foil'd, who watch'd to trace them to
    their house:
And but the flitter-wingèd verse must tell,
For truth's sake, what woe afterwards befell,
'Twould humour many a heart to leave them
    thus
Shut from the busy world of more incredu-
    lous.

PART II

Love in a hut, with water and a crust,
Is — Love, forgive us! — cinders, ashes, dust;
Love in a palace is perhaps at last
More grievous torment than a hermit's
    fast: —
That is a doubtful tale from faery land,
Hard for the non-elect to understand.
Had Lycius lived to hand his story down,
He might have given the moral a fresh frown,

Or clench'd it quite: but too short was their
  bliss
To breed distrust and hate, that make the
  soft voice hiss.
Beside, there, nightly, with terrific glare,
Love, jealous grown of so complete a pair,
Hover'd and buzz'd his wings, with fearful
  roar,
Above the lintel of their chamber door,
And down the passage cast a glow upon the
  floor.

   For all this came a ruin: side by side
They were enthronèd, in the even tide,
Upon a couch, near to a curtaining
Whose airy texture, from a golden string,
Floated into the room, and let appear
Unveil'd the summer heaven, blue and clear,
Betwixt two marble shafts: — there they re-
  posed,
Where use had made it sweet, with eyelids
  closed,
Saving a tithe which love still open kept,
That they might see each other while they
  almost slept;
When from the slope side of a suburb hill,
Deafening the swallow's twitter, came a thrill
Of trumpets. Lycius started — the sounds
  fled,
But left a thought, a buzzing in his head.
For the first time, since first he harbour'd in
That purple-linèd palace of sweet sin,

His spirit pass'd beyond its golden bourn
Into the noisy world almost forsworn.
The lady, ever watchful, penetrant,
Saw this with pain, so arguing a want
Of something more, more than her empery
Of joys; and she began to moan and sigh
Because he mused beyond her, knowing well,
That but a moment's thought is passion's
    passing bell.
'Why do you sigh, fair creature?' whisper'd
    he:
'Why do you think?' return'd she tenderly:
'You have deserted me; where am I now?
Not in your heart while care weighs on your
    brow:
No, no, you have dismiss'd me, and I go,
From your breast houseless: ay, it must be
    so.'
He answer'd, bending to her open eyes,
Where he was mirror'd small in paradise, —
'My silver planet, both of eve and morn!
Why will you plead yourself so sad forlorn,
While I am striving how to fill my heart
With deeper crimson and a double smart?
How to entangle, trammel up, and snare
Your soul in mine, and labyrinth you there,
Like the hid scent in an unbudded rose?
Ay, a sweet kiss — you see your mighty woes.
My thoughts! shall I unveil them? Listen
    then.
What mortal hath a prize, that other men
May be confounded and abash'd withal,

But lets it sometimes pace abroad majestical,
And triumph, as in thee I should rejoice
Amid the hoarse alarm of Corinth's voice.
Let my foes choke, and my friends shout afar,
While through the throngèd streets your bridal car
Wheels round its dazzling spokes.' — The lady's cheek
Trembled; she nothing said, but, pale and meek,
Arose and knelt before him, wept a rain
Of sorrows at his words; at last with pain
Beseeching him, the while his hand she wrung,
To change his purpose. He thereat was stung,
Perverse, with stronger fancy to reclaim
Her wild and timid nature to his aim;
Besides, for all his love, in self despite,
Against his better self, he took delight
Luxurious in her sorrows, soft and new.
His passion, cruel grown, took on a hue
Fierce and sanguineous as 'twas possible
In one whose brow had no dark veins to swell.
Fine was the mitigated fury, like
Apollo's presence when in act to strike
The serpent — Ha, the serpent! certes, she
Was none. She burnt, she loved the tyranny,
And, all subdued, consented to the hour
When to the bridal he shall lead his paramour.

Whispering in midnight silence, said the
   youth,
'Sure some sweet name thou hast, though,
   by my truth,
I have not ask'd it, ever thinking thee
Not mortal, but of heavenly progeny,
As still I do. Hast any mortal name,
Fit appellation for this dazzling frame?
Or friends or kinsfolk on the citied earth,
To share our marriage feast and nuptial
   mirth?'
'I have no friends,' said Lamia, 'no, not one;
My presence in wide Corinth hardly known.
My parents' bones are in their dusty urns
Sepulchred, where no kindled incense burns,
Seeing all their luckless race are dead save
   me,
And I neglect the holy rite for thee.
Even as you list invite your many guests;
But if, as now it seems, your vision rests
With any pleasure on me, do not bid
Old Apollonius — from him keep me hid.'
Lycius, perplex'd at words so blind and
   blank,
Made close inquiry; from whose touch she
   shrank,
Feigning a sleep; and he to the dull shade
Of deep sleep in a moment was betray'd.

  It was the custom then to bring away
The bride from home at blushing shut of day,
Veil'd, in a chariot, heralded along

By strewn flowers, torches, and a marriage
  song,
With other pageants: but this fair unknown
Had not a friend. So being left alone
(Lycius was gone to summon all his kin),
And knowing surely she could never win
His foolish heart from its mad pompousness,
She set herself, high-thoughted, how to dress
The misery in fit magnificence.
She did so, but 'tis doubtful how and whence
Came and who were her subtle servitors.
About the halls, and to and from the doors,
There was a noise of wings, till in short space
The glowing banquet-room shone with wide-
  archèd grace;
A haunting music, sole perhaps and lone
Supportress of the faery-roof, made moan
Throughout, as fearful the whole charm
  might fade,
Fresh carvèd cedar, mimicking a glade
Of palm and plantain, met from either side,
High in the midst, in honour of the bride:
Two palms and then two plantains, and so
  on,
From either side their stems branch'd one to
  one
All down the aislèd place; and beneath all
There ran a stream of lamps straight on from
  wall to wall.
So canopied, lay an untasted feast
Teeming with odours. Lamia, regal drest,
Silently paced about, and as she went,

In pale contented sort of discontent,
Mission'd her viewless servants to enrich
The fretted splendour of each nook and
    niche,
Between the tree-stems, marbled plain at
    first,
Came jasper panels; then anon there burst
Forth creeping imagery of slighter trees,
And with the larger wove in small intricacies.
Approving all, she faded at self-will,
And shut the chamber up, close, hush'd and
    still,
Complete and ready for the revels rude,
When dreadful guests would come to spoil
    her solitude.

  The day appear'd, and all the gossip rout.
O senseless Lycius! Madman! wherefore flout
The silent-blessing fate, warm cloister'd
    hours,
And show to common eyes these secret bow-
    ers?
The herd approach'd; each guest, with busy
    brain,
Arriving at the portal, gazed amain,
And enter'd marvelling: for they knew the
    street,
Remember'd it from childhood all complete
Without a gap, yet ne'er before had seen
That royal porch, that high-built fair de-
    mesne;

So in they hurried all, mazed, curious and
    keen;
Save one, who look'd thereon with eye severe,
And with calm-planted steps walk'd in aus-
    tere;
'Twas Apollonius: something too he laugh'd,
As though some knotty problem, that had
    daft
His patient thought, had now begun to thaw
And solve and melt: 'twas just as he foresaw.

He met within the murmurous vestibule
His young disciple. ' 'Tis no common rule,
Lycius,' said he, 'for uninvited guest
To force himself upon you, and infest
With an unbidden presence the bright throng
Of younger friends; yet must I do this wrong,
And you forgive me.' Lycius blush'd, and led
The old man through the inner doors broad-
    spread;
With reconciling words and courteous mien
Turning into sweet milk the sophist's spleen.

Of wealthy lustre was the banquet-room,
Fill'd with pervading brilliance and perfume:
Before each lucid panel fuming stood
A censer fed with myrrh and spicèd wood,
Each by a sacred tripod held aloft,
Whose slender feet wide-swerved upon the
    soft
Wool-woofèd carpets: fifty wreaths of smoke
From fifty censers their light voyage took

To the high roof, still mimick'd as they rose
Along the mirror'd walls by twin-clouds
     odorous.
Twelve spherèd tables, by silk seats in-
     sphered,
High as the level of a man's breast rear'd
On libbard's paws, upheld the heavy gold
Of cups and goblets, and the store thrice told
Of Ceres' horn, and, in huge vessels, wine
Came from the gloomy tun with merry shine.
Thus loaded with a feast the tables stood,
Each shrining in the midst the image of a
     God.

   When in an antechamber every guest
Had felt the cold full sponge to pleasure
     press'd
By minist'ring slaves upon his hands and feet,
And fragrant oils with ceremony meet
Pour'd on his hair, they all moved to the feast
In white robes, and themselves in order
     placed
Around the silken couches, wondering
Whence all this mighty cost and blaze of
     wealth could spring.

   Soft went the music the soft air along,
While fluent Greek a vowel'd under-song
Kept up among the guests, discoursing low
At first, for scarcely was the wine at flow;
But when the happy vintage touch'd their
     brains,

Louder they talk, and louder come the strains
Of powerful instruments: — the gorgeous
  dyes,
The space, the splendour of the draperies,
The roof of awful richness, nectarous cheer,
Beautiful slaves, and Lamia's self, appear.
Now, when the wine has done its rosy deed
And every soul from human trammels freed,
No more so strange; for merry wine, sweet
  wine,
Will make Elysian shades not too fair, too di-
  vine.
Soon was God Bacchus at meridian height;
Flush'd were their cheeks, and bright eyes
  double bright;
Garlands of every green and every scent
From vales deflower'd or forest-trees branch-
  rent,
In baskets of bright osier'd gold were
  brought,
High as the handles heap'd, to suit the
  thought
Of every guest; that each, as he did please,
Might fancy-fit his brows, silk-pillow'd at his
  ease.

  What wreath for Lamia? What for Lycius?
What for the sage, old Apollonius?
Upon her aching forehead be there hung
The leaves of willow and of adder's tongue;
And for the youth, quick, let us strip for him
The thyrsus, that his watching eyes may swim

Into forgetfulness; and, for the sage,
Let spear-grass and the spiteful thistle wage
War on his temples. Do not all charms fly
At the mere touch of cold philosophy?
There was an awful rainbow once in heaven:
We know her woof, her texture; she is given
In the dull catalogue of common things.
Philosophy will clip an Angel's wings,
Conquer all mysteries by rule and line,
Empty the haunted air and gnomed mine —
Unweave a rainbow, as it erewhile made
The tender-person'd Lamia melt into a
    shade.

By her glad Lycius sitting, in chief place,
Scarce saw in all the room another face,
Till, checking his love trance, a cup he took
Full brimm'd, and opposite sent forth a look
'Cross the broad table, to beseech a glance
From his old teacher's wrinkled countenance,
And pledge him. The bald-head philosopher
Had fix'd his eye, without a twinkle or a stir,
Full on the alarmèd beauty of the bride,
Brow-beating her fair form and troubling her
    sweet pride.
Lycius then press'd her hand, with devout
    touch,
As pale it lay upon the rosy couch:
'Twas icy, and the cold ran through his veins;
Then sudden it grew hot, and all the pains
Of an unnatural heat shot to his heart.
'Lamia, what means this? Wherefore dost

thou start?
Know'st thou that man?' Poor Lamia
    answer'd not.
He gazed into her eyes, and not a jot
Own'd they the lovelorn piteous appeal:
More, more he gazed: his human senses reel:
Some hungry spell that loveliness absorbs;
There was no recognition in those orbs.
'Lamia!' he cried — and no soft-toned reply.
The many heard, and the loud revelry
Grew hush; the stately music no more
    breathes;
The myrtle sicken'd in a thousand wreaths.
By faint degrees, voice, lute, and pleasure
    ceased;
A deadly silence step by step increased
Until it seem'd a horrid presence there,
And not a man but felt the terror in his hair.
'Lamia!' he shriek'd; and nothing but the
    shriek
With its sad echo did the silence break.
'Begone, foul dream!' he cried, gazing again
In the bride's face, where now no azure vein
Wander'd on fair-spaced temples, no soft
    bloom
Misted the cheek, no passion to illume
The deep-recessèd vision: — all was blight:
Lamia, no longer fair, there sat, a deadly
    white.
'Shut, shut those juggling eyes, thou ruthless
    man!

Turn them aside, wretch! or the righteous
    ban
Of all the Gods, whose dreadful images
Here represent their shadowy presences,
May pierce them on the sudden with the
    thorn
Of painful blindness; leaving thee forlorn,
In trembling dotage to the feeblest fright
Of conscience, for their long-offended might,
For all thine impious proud-heart sophistries,
Unlawful magic, and enticing lies.
Corinthians! look upon that grey-beard
    wretch!
Mark how, possess'd, his lashless eyelids
    stretch
Around his demon eyes! Corinthians, see!
My sweet bride withers at their potency.'
'Fool!' said the sophist, in an under-tone
Gruff with contempt; which a death-nighing
    moan
From Lycius answer'd, as, heart-struck and
    lost,
He sank supine beside the aching ghost.
'Fool! Fool!' repeated he, while his eyes still
Relented not, nor moved: 'from every ill
Of life have I preserved thee to this day,
And shall I see thee made a serpent's prey?'
Then Lamia breathed death-breath; the
    sophist's eye,
Like a sharp spear, went through her utterly,
Keen, cruel, perceant, stinging: she, as well
As her weak hand could any meaning tell,

Motion'd him to be silent; vainly so;
He look'd and look'd again a level — No!
'A serpent!' echoed he. No sooner said,
Than with a frightful scream she vanishèd;
And Lycius' arms were empty of delight,
As were his limbs of life, from that same
    night.
On the high couch he lay — his friends came
    round —
Supported him; no pulse or breath they
    found,
And in its marriage robe the heavy body
    wound.

Isabella; or, The Pot of Basil

A Story from Boccaccio

Fair Isabel, poor simple Isabel!
  Lorenzo, a young palmer in Love's eye!
They could not in the self-same mansion
    dwell
  Without some stir of heart, some malady;
They could not sit at meals but feel how well
  It soothèd each to be the other by;
They could not, sure, beneath the same roof
    sleep,
But to each other dream, and nightly weep.

With every morn their love grew tenderer,
  With every eve deeper and tenderer still;
He might not in house, field, or garden stir,

But her full shape would all his seeing fill;
And his continual voice was pleasanter
  To her, than noise of trees or hidden rill;
Her lute-string gave an echo of his name,
She spoilt her half-done broidery with the
    same.

He knew whose gentle hand was at the latch,
  Before the door had given her to his eyes;
And from her chamber-window he would
    catch
  Her beauty farther than the falcon spies;
And constant as her vespers would he watch,
  Because her face was turn'd to the same
    skies;
And with sick longing all the night outwear,
To hear her morning step upon the stair.

A whole long month of May in this sad plight
  Made their cheeks paler by the break of
    June:
'To-morrow will I bow to my delight,
  To-morrow will I ask my lady's boon.' —
'O may I never see another night,
  Lorenzo, if thy lips breathe not love's
    tune.' —
So spake they to their pillows; but, alas,
Honeyless days and days did he let pass;

Until sweet Isabella's untouch'd cheek
  Fell sick within the rose's just domain,
Fell thin as a young mother's, who doth seek

By every lull to cool her infant's pain:
'How ill she is!' said he, 'I may not speak
  And yet I will, and tell my love all plain:
If looks speak love-laws, I will drink her tears,
And at the least 'twill startle off her cares.'

So said he one fair morning, and all day
  His heart beat awfully against his side;
And to his heart he inwardly did pray
  For power to speak; but still the ruddy tide
Stifled his voice, and pulsed resolve away —
  Fever'd his high conceit of such a bride,
Yet brought him to the meekness of a child:
Alas! when passion is both meek and wild!

So once more he had waked and anguishèd
  A dreary night of love and misery,
If Isabel's quick eye had not been wed
  To every symbol on his forehead high;
She saw it waxing very pale and dead,
  And straight all flush'd; so, lispèd tenderly,
'Lorenzo!' — here she ceased her timid quest,
But in her tone and look he read the rest.

'O Isabella! I can half perceive
  That I may speak my grief into thine ear;
If thou didst ever anything believe,
  Believe how I love thee, believe how near
My soul is to its doom: I would not grieve
  Thy hand by unwelcome pressing, would
    not fear
Thine eyes by gazing; but I cannot live

Another night, and not my passion shrive.

'Love: thou art leading me from wintry cold,
  Lady! thou leadest me to summer clime,
And I must taste the blossoms that unfold
  In its ripe warmth this gracious morning
    time.'
So said, his erewhile timid lips grew bold,
  And poesied with hers in dewy rhyme:
Great bliss was with them, and great happi-
  ness
Grew, like a lusty flower in June's caress.

Parting they seem'd to tread upon the air,
  Twin roses by the zephyr blown apart
Only to meet again more close, and share
  The inward fragrance of each other's heart.
She, to her chamber gone, a ditty fair
  Sang, of delicious love and honey'd dart;
He with light steps went up a western hill,
And bade the sun farewell, and joy'd his fill.

All close they met again, before the dusk
  Had taken from the stars its pleasant veil,
All close they met, all eves, before the dusk
  Had taken from the stars its pleasant veil,
Close in a bower of hyacinth and musk,
  Unknown of any, free from whispering tale.
Ah! better had it been for ever so,
Than idle ears should pleasure in their woe.

Were they unhappy then? — It cannot be —

Too many tears for lovers have been shed,
Too many sighs give we to them in fee,
　Too much of pity after they are dead,
Too many doleful stories do we see,
　Whose matter in bright gold were best be
　read;
Except in such a page where Theseus' spouse
Over the pathless waves towards him bows.

But for the general award of love,
　The little sweet doth kill much bitterness;
Though Dido silent is in under-grove,
　And Isabella's was a great distress,
Though young Lorenzo in warm Indian clove
　Was not embalm'd, this truth is not the
　less —
Even bees, the little almsmen of spring-
　bowers,
Know there is richest juice in poison-flowers.

With her two brothers this fair lady dwelt,
　Enrichèd from ancestral merchandise,
And for them many a weary hand did swelt
　In torchèd mines and noisy factories,
And many once proud-quiver'd loins did
　melt
　In blood from stinging whip; with hollow
　eyes
Many all day in dazzling river stood,
To take the rich-ored driftings of the flood.

For them the Ceylon diver held his breath,

And went all naked to the hungry shark;
For them his ears gush'd blood; for them in
     death
The seal on the cold ice with piteous bark
Lay full of darts; for them alone did seethe
     A thousand men in troubles wide and dark:
Half-ignorant, they turn'd an easy wheel,
That set sharp racks at work, to pinch and
     peel.

Why were they proud? Because their marble
     founts
     Gush'd with more pride than do a wretch's
     tears?
Why were they proud? Because fair orange-
     mounts
     Were of more soft ascent than lazar stairs!
Why were they proud? Because red-lined ac-
     counts
     Were richer than the songs of Grecian
     years?
Why were they proud? again we ask aloud,
Why in the name of Glory were they proud?

Yet were these Florentines as self-retired
     In hungry pride and gainful cowardice,
As two close Hebrews in that land inspired,
     Paled in and vineyarded from beggar-spies;
The hawks of ship-mast forests — the un-
     tired
     And pannier'd mules for ducats and old
     lies —

Quick cat's-paws on the generous
    stray-away, —
Great wits in Spanish, Tuscan, and Malay.

How was it these same ledger-men could spy
    Fair Isabella in her downy nest?
How could they find out in Lorenzo's eye
    A straying from his toil? Hot Egypt's pest
Into their vision covetous and sly!
    How could these money-bags see east and
        west?
Yet so they did — and every dealer fair
Must see behind, as doth the hunted hare.

O eloquent and famed Boccaccio!
    Of thee we now should ask forgiving boon,
And of thy spicy myrtles as they blow,
    And of thy roses amorous of the moon,
And of thy lilies, that do paler grow
    Now they can no more hear thy ghittern's
        tune,
For venturing syllables that ill beseem
The quiet glooms of such a piteous theme.

Grant thou a pardon here, and then the tale
    Shall move on soberly, as it is meet;
There is no other crime, no mad assail
    To make old prose in modern rhyme more
        sweet;
But it is done — succeed the verse or fail —
    To honour thee, and thy gone spirit greet;
To stead thee as a verse in English tongue,

An echo of thee in the north-wind sung.

These brethren having found by many signs
  What love Lorenzo for their sister had,
And how she loved him too, each unconfines
  His bitter thoughts to other, well-nigh mad
That he, the servant of their trade designs,
  Should in their sister's love be blithe and
    glad,
When 'twas their plan to coax her by degrees
To some high noble and his olive-trees.

And many a jealous conference had they,
  And many times they bit their lips alone,
Before they fix'd upon a surest way
  To make the youngster for his crime atone;
And at the last, these men of cruel clay
  Cut Mercy with a sharp knife to the bone;
For they resolvèd in some forest dim
To kill Lorenzo, and there bury him.

So, on a pleasant morning, as he leant
  Into the sun-rise, o'er the balustrade
Of the garden-terrace, towards him they bent
  Their footing through the dews; and to him
    said,
'You seem there in the quiet of content,
  Lorenzo, and we are most loth to invade
Calm speculation; but if you are wise,
Bestride your steed while cold is in the skies.

'To-day we purpose, ay, this hour we mount

To spur three leagues towards the Apen-
    nine;
Come down, we pray thee, ere the hot sun
    count
    His dewy rosary on the eglantine.'
Lorenzo, courteously as he was wont,
    Bow'd a fair greeting to these serpents'
    whine,
And went in haste, to get in readiness,
With belt, and spur, and bracing huntsman's
    dress.

And as he to the court-yard pass'd along,
    Each third step did he pause, and listen'd
    oft
If he could hear his lady's matin-song,
    Or the light whisper of her footstep soft;
And as he thus over his passion hung,
    He heard a laugh full musical aloft;
When, looking up, he saw her features bright
Smile through an in-door lattice, all delight.

'Love, Isabel!' said he, 'I was in pain
    Lest I should miss to bid thee a good mor-
    row:
Ah! what if I should lose thee, when so fain
    I am to stifle all the heavy sorrow
Of a poor three hours' absence? but we'll
    gain
    Out of the amorous dark what day doth
    borrow.
Good bye! I'll soon be back.' — 'Good bye!'

said she:
And as he went she chanted merrily.

So the two brothers and their murder'd man
  Rode past fair Florence, to where Arno's
    stream
Gurgles through straiten'd banks, and still
    doth fan
  Itself with dancing bulrush, and the bream
Keeps head against the freshets. Sick and wan
  The brothers' faces in the ford did seem,
Lorenzo's flush with love. — They pass'd the
    water
Into a forest quiet for the slaughter.

There was Lorenzo slain and buried in,
  There in that forest did his great love cease;
Ah! when a soul doth thus its freedom win,
  It aches in loneliness — is ill at peace
As the break-covert blood-hounds of such
    sin:
  They dipp'd their swords in the water, and
    did tease
Their horses homeward, with convulsèd spur,
Each richer by his being a murderer.

They told their sister how, with sudden
    speed,
  Lorenzo had ta'en ship for foreign lands,
Because of some great urgency and need
  In their affairs, requiring trusty hands.
Poor girl! put on thy stifling widow's weed,

And 'scape at once from Hope's accursèd
  bands;
To-day thou wilt not see him, nor to-morrow,
And the next day will be a day of sorrow.

She weeps alone for pleasures not to be;
  Sorely she wept until the night came on,
And then, instead of love, O misery!
  She brooded o'er the luxury alone:
His image in the dusk she seem'd to see,
  And to the silence made a gentle moan,
Spreading her perfect arms upon the air,
And on her couch low murmuring, 'Where?
  O where?'

But Selfishness, Love's cousin, held not long
  Its fiery vigil in her single breast;
She fretted for the golden hour, and hung
  Upon the time with feverish unrest —
Not long; for soon into her heart a throng
  Of higher occupants, a richer zest,
Came tragic; passion not to be subdued,
And sorrow for her love in travels rude.

In the mid days of autumn, on their eves
  The breath of Winter comes from far away,
And the sick west continually bereaves
  Of some gold tinge, and plays a roundelay
Of death among the bushes and the leaves,
  To make all bare before he dares to stray
From his north cavern. So sweet Isabel
By gradual decay from beauty fell,

Because Lorenzo came not. Oftentimes
  She ask'd her brothers, with an eye all pale
Striving to be itself, what dungeon climes
  Could keep him off so long? They spake a
    tale
Time after time, to quiet her. Their crimes
  Came on them, like a smoke from Hin-
    nom's vale;
And every night in dreams they groan'd
    aloud,
To see their sister in her snowy shroud.

And she had died in drowsy ignorance,
  But for a thing more deadly dark than all;
It came like a fierce potion, drunk by chance,
  Which saves a sick man from the feather'd
    pall
For some few gasping moments; like a lance,
  Waking an Indian from his cloudy hall
With cruel pierce, and bringing him again
Sense of the gnawing fire at heart and brain.

It was a vision. In the drowsy gloom,
  The dull of midnight, at her couch's foot
Lorenzo stood, and wept: the forest tomb
  Had marr'd his glossy hair which once
    could shoot
Lustre into the sun, and put cold doom
  Upon his lips, and taken the soft lute
From his lorn voice, and past his loamèd ears
Had made a miry channel for his tears.

Strange sound it was, when the pale shadow
  spake,
  For there was striving, in its piteous tongue,
To speak as when on earth it was awake,
  And Isabella on its music hung:
Languor there was in it, and tremulous shake,
  As in a palsied Druid's harp unstrung;
And through it moan'd a ghostly under-song,
Like hoarse night-gusts sepulchral brièrs
  among.

Its eyes, though wild, were still all dewy
  bright
  With love, and kept all phantom fear aloof
From the poor girl by magic of their light,
  The while it did unthread the horrid woof
Of the late darken'd time — the murderous
  spite
  Of pride and avarice — the dark pine roof
In the forest — and the sodden turfèd dell,
Where, without any word, from stabs he fell.

Saying moreover, 'Isabel, my sweet!
  Red whortle-berries droop above my head,
And a large flint-stone weighs upon my feet;
  Around me beeches and high chestnuts
  shed
Their leaves and prickly nuts; a sheep-fold
  bleat
  Comes from beyond the river to my bed:
Go, shed one tear upon my heather-bloom,
And it shall comfort me within the tomb.

'I am a shadow now, alas! alas!
  Upon the skirts of human nature dwelling
Alone: I chant alone the holy mass,
  While little sounds of life are round my
    knelling,
And glossy bees at noon do fieldward pass,
  And many a chapel bell the hour is telling,
Paining me through: those sounds grow
    strange to me,
And thou art distant in Humanity.

'I know what was, I feel full well what is,
  And I should rage, if spirits could go mad;
Though I forget the taste of earthly bliss,
  That paleness warms my grave, as though I
    had
A seraph chosen from the bright abyss
  To be my spouse; thy paleness makes me
    glad;
Thy beauty grows upon me, and I feel
A greater love through all my essence steal.'

The Spirit mourn'd 'Adieu!' — dissolved,
    and left
  The atom darkness in a slow turmoil;
As when of healthful midnight sleep bereft,
  Thinking on rugged hours and fruitless toil,
We put our eyes into a pillowy cleft,
  And see the spangly gloom froth up and
    boil:
It made sad Isabella's eyelids ache,
And in the dawn she started up awake;

'Ha! ha!' said she, 'I knew not this hard life,
  I thought the worst was simple misery;
I thought some Fate with pleasure or with
    strife
  Portion'd us — happy days, or else to die;
But there is crime — a brother's bloody knife!
  Sweet Spirit, thou hast school'd my infancy:
I'll visit thee for this, and kiss thine eyes,
And greet thee morn and even in the skies.'

When the full morning came, she had devised
  How she might secret to the forest hie;
How she might find the clay, so dearly prized,
  And sing to it one latest lullaby;
How her short absence might be unsurmised,
  While she the inmost of the dream would
    try.
Resolved, she took with her an aged nurse,
And went into that dismal forest-hearse.

See, as they creep along the river side,
  How she doth whisper to that aged dame,
And, after looking round the champaign
    wide,
  Shows her a knife. — 'What feverous hectic
    flame
Burns in thee, child? — what good can thee
    betide
  That thou shouldst smile again?' — The
    evening came,
And they had found Lorenzo's earthy bed;
The flint was there, the berries at his head.

Who hath not loiter'd in a green church-
   yard,
  And let his spirit, like a demon mole,
Work through the clayey soil and gravel hard,
  To see skull, coffin'd bones, and funeral
   stole;
Pitying each form that hungry Death had
   marr'd,
  And filling it once more with human soul?
Ah! this is holiday to what was felt
When Isabella by Lorenzo knelt.

She gazed into the fresh-thrown mould, as
   though
  One glance did fully all its secrets tell;
Clearly she saw, as other eyes would know
  Pale limbs at bottom of a crystal well;
Upon the murderous spot she seem'd to
   grow,
  Like to a native lily of the dell:
Then with her knife, all sudden, she began
To dig more fervently than misers can.

Soon she turn'd up a soilèd glove, whereon
  Her silk had play'd in purple phantasies;
She kiss'd it with a lip more chill than stone,
  And put it in her bosom, where it dries
And freezes utterly unto the bone
  Those dainties made to still an infant's
   cries:
Then 'gan she work again; nor stay'd her
   care,

But to throw back at times her veiling hair.

That old nurse stood beside her wondering,
  Until her heart felt pity to the core
At sight of such a dismal labouring,
  And so she kneelèd, with her locks all hoar,
And put her lean hands to the horrid thing:
  Three hours they labour'd at this travail
    sore;
At last they felt the kernel of the grave,
And Isabella did not stamp and rave.

Ah! wherefore all this wormy circumstance?
  Why linger at the yawning tomb so long?
O for the gentleness of old Romance,
  The simple plaining of a minstrel's song!
Fair reader, at the old tale take a glance,
  For here, in truth, it doth not well belong
To speak: — O turn thee to the very tale,
And taste the music of that vision pale.

With duller steel than the Persèan sword
  They cut away no formless monster's head,
But one, whose gentleness did well accord
  With death, as life. The ancient harps have
    said,
Love never dies, but lives, immortal Lord:
  If Love impersonate was ever dead,
Pale Isabella kiss'd it, and low moan'd.
'Twas love; cold, — dead indeed, but not
    dethroned.

In anxious secrecy they took it home,
  And then the prize was all for Isabel:
She calm'd its wild hair with a golden comb
  And all around each eye's sepulchral cell
Pointed each fringèd lash; the smearèd loam
  With tears, as chilly as a dripping well,
She drench'd away: and still she comb'd, and
    kept
Sighing all day — and still she kiss'd, and
    wept.

Then in a silken scarf — sweet with the dews
  Of precious flowers pluck'd in Araby,
And divine liquids come with odorous ooze
  Through the cold serpent-pipe
    refreshfully, —
She wrapp'd it up; and for its tomb did
    choose
  A garden-pot, wherein she laid it by,
And cover'd it with mould, and o'er it set
Sweet Basil, which her tears kept ever wet.

And she forgot the stars, the moon, and sun,
  And she forgot the blue above the trees,
And she forgot the dells where waters run,
  And she forgot the chilly autumn breeze;
She had no knowledge when the day was
    done,
  And the new morn she saw not: but in
    peace
Hung over her sweet Basil evermore,
And moisten'd it with tears unto the core.

And so she ever fed it with thin tears,
  Whence thick, and green, and beautiful it
    grew,
So that it smelt more balmy than its peers
  Of Basil-tufts in Florence; for it drew
Nurture besides, and life, from human fears,
  From the fast mouldering head there shut
    from view;
So that the jewel, safely casketed,
Came forth, and in perfumèd leafits spread.

O Melancholy, linger here awhile!
  O Music, Music, breathe despondingly!
O Echo, Echo, from some sombre isle,
  Unknown, Lethean, sigh to us — O sigh!
Spirits in grief, lift up your heads, and smile;
  Lift up your heads, sweet Spirits, heavily,
And make a pale light in your cypress glooms,
Tinting with silver wan your marble tombs.

Moan hither, all ye syllables of woe,
  From the deep throat of sad Melpomene!
Through bronzèd lyre in tragic order go,
  And touch the strings into a mystery;
Sound mournfully upon the winds and low;
  For simple Isabel is soon to be
Among the dead: She withers, like a palm
Cut by an Indian for its juicy balm.

O leave the palm to wither by itself,
  Let not quick Winter chill its dying
    hour! —

It may not be — those Baälites of pelf,
  Her brethren, noted the continual shower
From her dead eyes; and many a curious elf,
  Among her kindred, wonder'd that such
    dower
Of youth and beauty should be thrown aside
By one mark'd out to be a Noble's bride.

And, furthermore, her brethren wonder'd
    much
  Why she sat drooping by the Basil green,
And why it flourish'd, as by magic touch;
  Greatly they wonder'd what the thing might
    mean:
They could not surely give belief, that such
  A very nothing would have power to wean
Her from her own fair youth, and pleasures
    gay,
And even remembrance of her love's delay.

Therefore they watch'd a time when they
    might sift
  This hidden whim; and long they watch'd
    in vain;
For seldom did she go to chapel-shrift,
  And seldom felt she any hunger-pain:
And when she left, she hurried back, as swift
  As bird on wing to breast its eggs again:
And, patient as a hen-bird, sat her there
Beside her Basil, weeping through her hair.

Yet they contrived to steal the Basil-pot,

And to examine it in secret place:
The thing was vile with green and livid spot,
  And yet they knew it was Lorenzo's face:
The guerdon of their murder they had got,
  And so left Florence in a moment's space,
Never to turn again. — Away they went,
With blood upon their heads, to banishment.

O Melancholy, turn thine eyes away!
  O Music, Music, breathe despondingly
O Echo, Echo, on some other day,
  From isles Lethean, sigh to us — O sigh!
Spirits of grief, sing not your 'Well-a-way!'
  For Isabel, sweet Isabel, will die;
Will die a death too lone and incomplete,
Now they have ta'en away her Basil sweet.

Piteous she look'd on dead and senseless
    things,
  Asking for her lost Basil amorously:
And with melodious chuckle in the strings
  Of her lorn voice, she oftentimes would cry
After the Pilgrim in his wanderings,
  To ask him where her Basil was; and why
'Twas hid from her: 'For cruel 'tis,' said she,
'To steal my Basil-pot away from me.'

And so she pined, and so she died forlorn,
  Imploring for her Basil to the last.
No heart was there in Florence but did
    mourn
  In pity of her love, so overcast.

And a sad ditty of this story borne
  From mouth to mouth through all the
    country pass'd:
Still is the burthen sung — 'O cruelty,
To steal my Basil-pot away from me!'

The Eve of St. Agnes

St. Agnes' Eve — Ah, bitter chill it was!
The owl, for all his feathers, was a-cold;
The hare limp'd trembling through the
  frozen grass,
And silent was the flock in woolly fold:
Numb were the Beadsman's fingers while
  he told
His rosary, and while his frosted breath,
Like pious incense from a censer old,
Seem'd taking flight for heaven, without a
  death,
Past the sweet Virgin's picture, while his
  prayer he saith.

His prayer he saith, this patient, holy man:
Then takes his lamp, and riseth from his
  knees,
And back returneth, meagre, barefoot, wan,
Along the chapel aisle by slow degrees:
The sculptured dead, on each side, seem to
  freeze,
Emprison'd in black, purgatorial rails:
Knights, ladies, praying in dumb orat'ries,
He passeth by, and his weak spirit fails

To think how they may ache in icy hoods
   and mails.

Northward he turneth through a little door,
And scarce three steps, ere Music's golden
   tongue
Flatter'd to tears this aged man and poor.
But no — already had his death-bell rung;
The joys of all his life were said and sung;
His was harsh penance on St. Agnes' Eve:
Another way he went, and soon among
Rough ashes sat he for his soul's reprieve,
And all night kept awake, for sinners' sake to
   grieve.

That ancient Beadsman heard the prelude
   soft;
And so it chanced, for many a door was
   wide,
From hurry to and fro. Soon, up aloft,
The silver, snarling trumpets 'gan to chide:
The level chambers, ready with their pride,
Were glowing to receive a thousand guests:
The carvèd angels, ever eager-eyed,
Stared, where upon their heads the cornice
   rests,
With hair blown back, and wings put cross-
   wise on their breasts.

At length burst in the argent revelry,
With plume, tiara, and all rich array,
Numerous as shadows haunting fairily

The brain new-stuff'd, in youth, with
    triumphs gay
Of old romance. These let us wish away,
And turn, sole-thoughted, to one Lady
    there,
Whose heart had brooded, all that wintry
    day,
On love, and wing'd St. Agnes' saintly care,
As she had heard old dames full many times
    declare.

They told her how, upon St. Agnes' Eve,
Young virgins might have visions of delight,
And soft adorings from their loves receive
Upon the honey'd middle of the night,
If ceremonies due they did aright;
As, supperless to bed they must retire,
And couch supine their beauties, lily white;
Nor look behind, nor sideways, but require
Of Heaven with upward eyes for all that they
    desire.

Full of this whim was thoughtful Madeline:
The music, yearning like a God in pain,
She scarcely heard: her maiden eyes divine,
Fix'd on the floor, saw many a sweeping
    train
Pass by — she heeded not at all: in vain
Came many a tiptoe, amorous cavalier,
And back retired; not cool'd by high dis-
    dain,
But she saw not: her heart was otherwhere;

She sigh'd for Agnes' dreams, the sweetest of
    the year.

    She danced along with vague, regardless
        eyes,
    Anxious her lips, her breathing quick and
        short:
    The hallow'd hour was near at hand: she
        sighs
    Amid the timbrels, and the throng'd resort
    Of whisperers in anger, or in sport;
    'Mid looks of love, defiance, hate, and
        scorn,
    Hoodwink'd with faery fancy; all amort,
    Save to St. Agnes and her lambs unshorn,
And all the bliss to be before to-morrow
    morn.

    So, purposing each moment to retire,
    She linger'd still. Meantime, across the
        moors
    Had come young Porphyro, with heart on
        fire
    For Madeline. Beside the portal doors,
    Buttress'd from moonlight, stands he, and
        implores
    All saints to give him sight of Madeline,
    But for one moment in the tedious hours,
    That he might gaze and worship all unseen;
Perchance speak, kneel, touch, kiss — in
    sooth such things have been.

He ventures in: let no buzz'd whisper tell,
All eyes be muffled, or a hundred swords
Will storm his heart, Love's feverous cita-
  del:
For him, those chambers held barbarian
  hordes,
Hyena foemen, and hot-blooded lords,
Whose very dogs would execrations howl
Against his lineage; not one breast affords
Him any mercy in that mansion foul,
Save one old beldame, weak in body and in
  soul.

Ah, happy chance! the aged creature came,
Shuffling along with ivory-headed wand,
To where he stood, hid from the torch's
  flame,
Behind a broad hall pillar, far beyond
The sound of merriment and chorus bland.
He startled her: but soon she knew his face,
And grasp'd his fingers in her palsied hand,
Saying, 'Mercy, Porphyro! hie thee from
  this place;
They are all here to-night, the whole blood-
  thirsty race!

'Get hence! get hence! there's dwarfish
  Hildebrand:
He had a fever late, and in the fit
He cursèd thee and thine, both house and
  land:

Then there's that old Lord Maurice, not a
    whit
More tame for his grey hairs — Alas me!
    flit!
Flit like a ghost away.' — 'Ah, Gossip dear,
We're safe enough; here in this arm-chair
    sit,
And tell me how' — 'Good Saints! not
    here, not here;
Follow me, child, or else these stones will be
    thy bier.'

He follow'd through a lowly archèd way,
Brushing the cobwebs with his lofty plume;
And as she mutter'd 'Well-a — well-a-day!'
He found him in a little moonlight room,
Pale, latticed, chill, and silent as a tomb.
'Now tell me where is Madeline,' said he,
'O tell me, Angela, by the holy loom
Which none but secret sisterhood may see,
When they St. Agnes' wool are weaving
    piously.'

'St. Agnes! Ah! it is St. Agnes' Eve —
Yet men will murder upon holy days.
Thou must hold water in a witch's sieve,
And be liege-lord of all the Elves and Fays
To venture so: it fills me with amaze
To see thee, Porphyro! — St. Agnes' Eve!
God's help! my lady fair the conjurer plays
This very night: good angels her deceive!

But let me laugh awhile, I've mickle time to
    grieve.'

Feebly she laugheth in the languid moon,
While Porphyro upon her face doth look,
Like puzzled urchin on an aged crone
Who keepeth closed a wondrous riddle-
    book,
As spectacled she sits in chimney nook.
But soon his eyes grew brilliant, when she
    told
His lady's purpose; and he scarce could
    brook
Tears, at the thought of those enchant-
    ments cold,
And Madeline asleep in lap of legends old.

Sudden a thought came like a full-blown
    rose,
Flushing his brow, and in his painèd heart
Made purple riot: then doth he propose
A stratagem, that makes the beldame start:
'A cruel man and impious thou art!
Sweet lady! let her pray, and sleep, and
    dream
Alone with her good angels, far apart
From wicked men like thee. Go, go! — I
    deem
Thou canst not surely be the same that thou
    didst seem.'

'I will not harm her, by all saints I swear!'

Quoth Porphyro: 'O may I ne'er find grace
When my weak voice shall whisper its last
  prayer,
If one of her soft ringlets I displace,
Or look with ruffian passion in her face.
Good Angela, believe me, by these tears;
Or I will, even in a moment's space,
Awake, with horrid shout, my foemen's
  ears,
And beard them, though they be more fang'd
  than wolves and bears.'

'Ah! why wilt thou affright a feeble soul?
A poor, weak, palsy-stricken, churchyard
  thing,
Whose passing-bell may ere the midnight
  toll;
Whose prayers for thee, each morn and
  evening,
Were never miss'd.' Thus plaining, doth she
  bring
A gentler speech from burning Porphyro;
So woeful, and of such deep sorrowing,
That Angela gives promise she will do
Whatever he shall wish, betide her weal or
  woe.

Which was, to lead him, in close secrecy,
Even to Madeline's chamber, and there
  hide
Him in a closet, of such privacy
That he might see her beauty unespied,

And win perhaps that night a peerless bride,
While legion'd fairies paced the coverlet,
And pale enchantment held her sleepy-
  eyed.
Never on such a night have lovers met,
Since Merlin paid his Demon all the mon-
  strous debt.

'It shall be as thou wishest,' said the Dame:
'All cates and dainties shall be storèd there
Quickly on this feast-night: by the tambour
  frame
Her own lute thou wilt see: no time to
  spare,
For I am slow and feeble, and scarce dare
On such a catering trust my dizzy head.
Wait here, my child, with patience; kneel in
  prayer
The while. Ah! thou must needs the lady
  wed,
Or may I never leave my grave among the
  dead.'

So saying, she hobbled off with busy fear.
The lover's endless minutes slowly pass'd;
The dame return'd, and whisper'd in his
  ear
To follow her; with aged eyes aghast
From fright of dim espial. Safe at last
Through many a dusky gallery, they gain
The maiden's chamber, silken, hush'd, and
  chaste;

Where Porphyro took covert, pleased
  amain.
His poor guide hurried back with agues in
  her brain.

Her faltering hand upon the balustrade,
Old Angela was feeling for the stair,
When Madeline, St. Agnes' charmèd maid,
Rose, like a mission'd spirit, unaware:
With silver taper's light, and pious care,
She turn'd, and down the aged gossip led
To a safe level matting. Now prepare,
Young Porphyro, for gazing on that bed;
She comes, she comes again, like ring-dove
  fray'd and fled.

Out went the taper as she hurried in;
Its little smoke, in pallid moonshine, died:
She closed the door, she panted, all akin
To spirits of the air, and visions wide:
No utter'd syllable, or, woe betide!
But to her heart, her heart was voluble,
Paining with eloquence her balmy side;
As though a tongueless nightingale should
  swell
Her throat in vain, and die, heart-stifled, in
  her dell.

A casement high and triple-arch'd there
  was,
All garlanded with carven imageries,

Of fruits and flowers, and bunches of knot-
    grass,
And diamonded with panes of quaint de-
    vice,
Innumerable of stains and splendid dyes,
As are the tiger-moth's deep-damask'd
    wings;
And in the midst, 'mong thousand herald-
    ries,
And twilight saints, and dim emblazonings,
A shielded scutcheon blush'd with blood of
    queens and kings.

Full on this casement shone the wintry
    moon,
And threw warm gules on Madeline's fair
    breast,
As down she knelt for Heaven's grace and
    boon;
Rose-bloom fell on her hands, together
    prest,
And on her silver cross soft amethyst,
And on her hair a glory, like a saint:
She seem'd a splendid angel, newly drest,
Save wings, for heaven: — Porphyro grew
    faint:
She knelt, so pure a thing, so free from
    mortal taint.

Anon his heart revives: her vespers done,
Of all its wreathèd pearls her hair she frees;
Unclasps her warmèd jewels one by one;

Loosens her fragrant boddice; by degrees
Her rich attire creeps rustling to her knees:
Half-hidden, like a mermaid in sea-weed,
Pensive awhile she dreams awake, and sees,
In fancy, fair St. Agnes in her bed,
But dares not look behind, or all the charm
    is fled.

Soon, trembling in her soft and chilly nest,
In sort of wakeful swoon, perplex'd she lay,
Until the poppied warmth of sleep
    oppress'd
Her soothèd limbs, and soul fatigued away;
Flown, like a thought, until the morrow-
    day;
Blissfully haven'd both from joy and pain;
Clasp'd like a missal where swart Paynims
    pray;
Blinded alike from sunshine and from rain,
As though a rose should shut, and be a bud
    again.

Stolen to this paradise, and so entranced,
Porphyro gazed upon her empty dress,
And listen'd to her breathing, if it chanced
To wake into a slumberous tenderness;
Which when he heard, that minute did he
    bless,
And breath'd himself: then from the closet
    crept,
Noiseless as fear in a wide wilderness,
And over the hush'd carpet, silent, stept,

And 'tween the curtains peep'd, where, lo!
  — how fast she slept!

  Then by the bed-side, where the faded
    moon
  Made a dim, silver twilight, soft he set
  A table, and, half anguish'd, threw thereon
  A cloth of woven crimson, gold, and jet: —
  O for some drowsy Morphean amulet!
  The boisterous, midnight, festive clarion,
  The kettle-drum, and far-heard clarionet,
  Affray his ears, though but in dying
    tone: —
The hall-door shuts again, and all the noise
  is gone.

  And still she slept an azure-lidded sleep,
  In blanchèd linen, smooth, and lavender'd,
  While he from forth the closet brought a
    heap
  Of candied apple, quince, and plum, and
    gourd;
  With jellies soother than the creamy curd,
  And lucent syrops, tinct with cinnamon;
  Manna and dates, in argosy transferr'd
  From Fez; and spicèd dainties, every one,
From silken Samarcand to cedar'd Lebanon.

  These delicates he heap'd with glowing
    hand
  On golden dishes and in baskets bright
  Of wreathèd silver: sumptuous they stand

In the retired quiet of the night,
Filling the chilly room with perfume
  light. —
'And now, my love, my seraph fair, awake!
Thou art my heaven, and I thine eremite:
Open thine eyes, for meek St. Agnes' sake,
Or I shall drowse beside thee, so my soul
  doth ache.'

Thus whispering, his warm, unnervèd arm
Sank in her pillow. Shaded was her dream
By the dusk curtains: — 'twas a midnight
  charm
Impossible to melt as icèd stream:
The lustrous salvers in the moonlight
  gleam;
Broad golden fringe upon the carpet lies:
It seem'd he never, never could redeem
From such a stedfast spell his lady's eyes;
So mused awhile, entoil'd in woofèd phanta-
  sies.

Awakening up, he took her hollow lute, —
Tumultuous, — and, in chords that tender-
  est be,
He play'd an ancient ditty, long since mute,
In Provence call'd 'La belle dame sans
  mercy':
Close to her ear touching the melody; —
Wherewith disturb'd, she utter'd a soft
  moan:

330

He ceased — she panted quick — and suddenly
Her blue affrayèd eyes wide open shone:
Upon his knees he sank, pale as smooth-
  sculptured stone.

Her eyes were open, but she still beheld,
Now wide awake, the vision of her sleep:
There was a painful change, that nigh
  expell'd
The blisses of her dream so pure and deep.
At which fair Madeline began to weep,
And moan forth witless words with many a
  sigh,
While still her gaze on Porphyro would
  keep;
Who knelt, with joinèd hands and piteous
  eye,
Fearing to move or speak, she look'd so
  dreamingly.

'Ah, Porphyro!' said she, 'but even now
Thy voice was at sweet tremble in mine ear,
Made tunable with every sweetest vow;
And those sad eyes were spiritual and clear:
How changed thou art! how pallid, chill,
  and drear!
Give me that voice again, my Porphyro,
Those looks immortal, those complainings
  dear!
O leave me not in this eternal woe,

For if thou diest, my Love, I know not where
   to go.'

Beyond a mortal man impassion'd far
At these voluptuous accents, he arose,
Ethereal, flush'd, and like a throbbing star
Seen 'mid the sapphire heaven's deep re-
   pose;
Into her dream he melted, as the rose
Blendeth its odour with the violet, —
Solution sweet: meantime the frost-wind
   blows
Like Love's alarum pattering the sharp sleet
Against the window-panes; St. Agnes' moon
   hath set.

'Tis dark: quick pattereth the flaw-blown
   sleet,
'This is no dream, my bride, my Madeline!'
'Tis dark: the icèd gusts still rave and beat:
'No dream, alas! alas! and woe is mine!
Porphyro will leave me here to fade and
   pine.
Cruel! what traitor could thee hither bring?
I curse not, for my heart is lost in thine,
Though thou forsakest a deceivèd thing; —
A dove forlorn and lost with sick unprunèd
   wing.'

'My Madeline! sweet dreamer! lovely bride!
Say, may I be for aye thy vassal blest?
Thy beauty's shield, heart-shaped and

332

vermeil-dyed?
Ah, silver shrine, here will I take my rest
After so many hours of toil and quest,
A famish'd pilgrim, — saved by miracle.
Though I have found, I will not rob thy
    nest,
Saving of thy sweet self; if thou think'st well
To trust, fair Madeline, to no rude infidel.

'Hark! 'tis an elfin storm from faery land,
Of haggard seeming, but a boon indeed:
Arise — arise! the morning is at hand; —
The bloated wassailers will never heed: —
Let us away, my love, with happy speed;
There are no ears to hear, or eyes to see, —
Drown'd all in Rhenish and the sleepy
    mead.
Awake! arise! my love, and fearless be,
For o'er the southern moors I have a home
    for thee.'

She hurried at his words, beset with fears,
For there were sleeping dragons all around,
At glaring watch, perhaps, with ready
    spears.
Down the wide stairs a darkling way they
    found;
In all the house was heard no human
    sound.
A chain-droop'd lamp was flickering by
    each door;

The arras, rich with horsemen, hawk, and
  hound,
Flutter'd in the besieging wind's uproar;
And the long carpets rose along the gusty
  floor.

They glide, like phantoms, into the wide
  hall;
Like phantoms to the iron porch they glide,
Where lay the Porter, in uneasy sprawl,
With a huge empty flagon by his side:
The wakeful bloodhound rose, and shook
  his hide,
But his sagacious eye an inmate owns:
By one, and one, the bolts full easy
  slide: —
The chains lie silent on the footworn
  stones;
The key turns, and the door upon its hinges
  groans.

And they are gone: ay, ages long ago
These lovers fled away into the storm.
That night the Baron dreamt of many a
  woe,
And all his warrior-guests with shade and
  form
Of witch, and demon, and large coffin-
  worm,
Were long be-nightmared. Angela the old
Died palsy-twitch'd, with meagre face de-
  form;

The Beadsman, after thousand aves told,
For aye unsought-for slept among his ashes
    cold.

Ode to a Nightingale

My heart aches, and a drowsy numbness
    pains
    My sense, as though of hemlock I had
    drunk,
Or emptied some dull opiate to the drains
    One minute past, and Lethe-wards had
    sunk:
'Tis not through envy of thy happy lot,
    But being too happy in thy happiness, —
        That thou, light-wingèd Dryad of the
        trees,
            In some melodious plot
    Of beechen green, and shadows number-
    less,
        Singest of summer in full-throated ease.

O for a draught of vintage, that hath been
    Cool'd a long age in the deep-delvèd earth,
Tasting of Flora and the country green,
    Dance, and Provençal song, and sunburnt
    mirth!
O for a beaker full of the warm South,
    Full of the true, the blushful Hippocrene,
        With beaded bubbles winking at the
        brim,
            And purple-stainèd mouth;

That I might drink and leave the world
  unseen,
And with thee fade away into the forest dim:

Fade far away, dissolve, and quite forget
  What thou among the leaves hast never
  known,
The weariness, the fever, and the fret
  Here, where men sit and hear each other
  groan;
Where palsy shakes a few, sad, last grey hairs,
  Where youth grows pale, and spectre-thin,
  and dies;
    Where but to think is to be full of sorrow
      And leaden-eyed despairs;
  Where Beauty cannot keep her lustrous
  eyes,
Or new Love pine at them beyond to-
  morrow.

Away! away! for I will fly to thee,
  Not charioted by Bacchus and his pards,
But on the viewless wings of Poesy,
  Though the dull brain perplexes and re-
  tards:
Already with thee! tender is the night,
  And haply the Queen-Moon is on her
  throne,
    Cluster'd around by all her starry Fays;
      But here there is no light,
  Save what from heaven is with the breezes
  blown

Through verdurous glooms and winding
  mossy ways.

I cannot see what flowers are at my feet,
  Nor what soft incense hangs upon the
  boughs,
But, in embalmèd darkness, guess each sweet
  Wherewith the seasonable month endows
The grass, the thicket, and the fruit-tree wild;
  White hawthorn, and the pastoral eglantine;
    Fast-fading violets cover'd up in leaves;
      And mid-May's eldest child,
  The coming musk-rose, full of dewy wine,
The murmurous haunt of flies on summer
  eves.

Darkling I listen; and for many a time
  I have been half in love with easeful Death,
Call'd him soft names in many a musèd
  rhyme,
  To take into the air my quiet breath;
Now more than ever seems it rich to die,
  To cease upon the midnight with no pain,
    While thou art pouring forth thy soul
    abroad
      In such an ecstasy!
  Still wouldst thou sing, and I have ears in
  vain —
To thy high requiem become a sod.

Thou wast not born for death, immortal
  Bird!

No hungry generations tread thee down;
The voice I hear this passing night was heard
  In ancient days by emperor and clown:
Perhaps the self-same song that found a path
  Through the sad heart of Ruth, when sick
    for home,
      She stood in tears amid the alien corn;
        The same that oft-times hath
  Charm'd magic casements, opening on the
    foam
Of perilous seas, in faery lands forlorn.

Forlorn! the very word is like a bell
  To toll me back from thee to my sole self.
Adieu! the fancy cannot cheat so well
  As she is famed to do, deceiving elf,
Adieu! adieu! thy plaintive anthem fades
  Past the near meadows, over the still
    stream,
      Up the hill-side; and now 'tis buried deep
        In the next valley-glades:
  Was it a vision, or a waking dream?
Fled is that music: — do I wake or sleep?

Ode on a Grecian Urn

Thou still unravish'd bride of quietness!
  Thou foster-child of Silence and slow Time,
Sylvan historian, who canst thus express
  A flowery tale more sweetly than our
    rhyme:
What leaf-fringed legend haunts about thy
  shape

Of deities or mortals, or of both,
  In Tempe or the dales of Arcady?
What men or gods are these? What maidens
  loth?
What mad pursuit? What struggle to escape?
  What pipes and timbrels? What wild ec-
  stasy?

Heard melodies are sweet, but those unheard
  Are sweeter: therefore, ye soft pipes, play
  on;
Not to the sensual ear, but, more endear'd,
  Pipe to the spirit ditties of no tone:
Fair youth, beneath the trees, thou canst not
  leave
  Thy song, nor ever can those trees be bare;
  Bold Lover, never, never canst thou kiss,
Though winning near the goal — yet, do not
  grieve;
  She cannot fade, though thou hast not
  thy bliss,
  For ever wilt thou love, and she be fair!

Ah, happy, happy boughs! that cannot shed
  Your leaves, nor ever bid the Spring adieu;
And, happy melodist, unwearièd,
  For ever piping songs for ever new;
More happy love! more happy, happy love!
  For ever warm and still to be enjoy'd,
  For ever panting and for ever young;
All breathing human passion far above,

That leaves a heart high sorrowful and
  cloy'd,
    A burning forehead, and a parching
    tongue.

Who are these coming to the sacrifice?
  To what green altar, O mysterious priest,
Lead'st thou that heifer lowing at the skies,
  And all her silken flanks with garlands
  drest?
What little town by river or sea-shore,
  Or mountain-built with peaceful citadel,
    Is emptied of its folk, this pious morn?
And, little town, thy streets for evermore
  Will silent be; and not a soul to tell
    Why thou art desolate, can e'er return.

O Attic shape! Fair attitude! with brede
  Of marble men and maidens overwrought,
With forest branches and the trodden weed;
  Thou, silent form, dost tease us out of
  thought
As doth eternity: Cold Pastoral!
  When old age shall this generation waste,
    Thou shalt remain, in midst of other woe
Than ours, a friend to man, to whom thou
  say'st,
'Beauty is truth, truth beauty, — that is all
  Ye know on earth, and all ye need to
  know.'

O goddess! hear these tuneless numbers,
    wrung
  By sweet enforcement and remembrance
    dear,
And pardon that thy secrets should be sung,
  Even into thine own soft-conchèd ear:
Surely I dreamt to-day, or did I see
  The wingèd Psyche with awaken'd eyes?
I wander'd in a forest thoughtlessly,
  And, on the sudden, fainting with surprise,
Saw two fair creatures, couchèd side by side
  In deepest grass, beneath the whisp'ring
    roof
  Of leaves and trembled blossoms, where
    there ran
        A brooklet, scarce espied:

'Mid hush'd, cool-rooted flowers fragrant-
    eyed,
  Blue, silver-white, and budded Tyrian,
They lay calm-breathing on the bedded grass;
  Their arms embracèd, and their pinions
    too;
  Their lips touch'd not, but had not bade
    adieu
As if disjoinèd by soft-handed slumber,
And ready still past kisses to outnumber
  At tender eye-dawn of aurorean love:
        The wingèd boy I knew;

But who wast thou, O happy, happy dove?
      His Psyche true!

O latest-born and loveliest vision far
  Of all Olympus' faded hierarchy!
Fairer than Phœbe's sapphire-region'd star,
  Or Vesper, amorous glow-worm of the sky;
Fairer than these, though temple thou hast
    none,
    Nor altar heap'd with flowers;
Nor virgin-choir to make delicious moan
    Upon the midnight hours;
No voice, no lute, no pipe, no incense sweet
  From chain-swung censer teeming;
No shrine, no grove, no oracle, no heat
  Of pale-mouth'd prophet dreaming.

O brightest! though too late for antique vows,
  Too, too late for the fond believing lyre,
When holy were the haunted forest boughs,
  Holy the air, the water, and the fire;
Yet even in these days so far retired
  From happy pieties, thy lucent fans,
  Fluttering among the faint Olympians
I see, and sing, by my own eyes inspired.
  So let me be thy choir, and make a moan
      Upon the midnight hours!
Thy voice, thy lute, thy pipe, thy incense
    sweet
  From swingèd censer teeming:
Thy shrine, thy grove, thy oracle, thy heat
  Of pale-mouth'd prophet dreaming.

Yes, I will be thy priest, and build a fane
   In some untrodden region of my mind,
Where branchèd thoughts, new grown with pleasant
         pain,
   Instead of pines shall murmur in the wind:
Far, far around shall those dark-cluster'd trees
   Fledge the wild-ridgèd mountains steep by steep;
And there by zephyrs, streams, and birds, and bees,
   The moss-lain Dryads shall be lull'd to sleep;
And in the midst of this wide quietness
   A rosy sanctuary will I dress
With the wreath'd trellis of a working brain,
   With buds, and bells, and stars without a name.
With all the gardener Fancy e'er could feign,
   Who breeding flowers, will never breed the same:
And there shall be for thee all soft delight
   That shadowy thought can win,
A bright torch, and a casement ope at night,
   To let the warm Love in!

Fancy

Ever let the Fancy roam,
Pleasure never is at home:
At a touch sweet Pleasure melteth,
Like to bubbles when rain pelteth;

Then let wingèd Fancy wander
Through the thought still spread beyond her:
Open wide the mind's cage door,
She'll dart forth, and cloudward soar,
O sweet Fancy! let her loose;
Summer's joys are spoilt by use,
And the enjoying of the Spring
Fades as does its blossoming:
Autumn's red-lipp'd fruitage too,
Blushing through the mist and dew,
Cloys with tasting: What do then?
Sit thee by the ingle, when
The sear faggot blazes bright,
Spirit of a winter's night;
When the soundless earth is muffled,
And the cakèd snow is shuffled
From the ploughboy's heavy shoon;
When the Night doth meet the Noon
In a dark conspiracy
To banish Even from her sky.
Sit thee there, and send abroad,
With a mind self-overawed,
Fancy, high-commission'd: — send her!
She has vassals to attend her:
She will bring, in spite of frost,
Beauties that the earth hath lost;
She will bring thee, all together,
All delights of summer weather;
All the buds and bells of May,
From dewy sward or thorny spray;
All the heapèd Autumn's wealth,
With a still, mysterious stealth:

She will mix these pleasures up
Like three fit wines in a cup,
And thou shalt quaff it: — thou shalt hear
Distant harvest-carols clear;
Rustle of the reapèd corn;
Sweet birds antheming the morn:
And, in the same moment — hark!
'Tis the early April lark,
Or the rooks, with busy caw,
Foraging for sticks and straw.
Thou shalt, at one glance, behold
The daisy and the marigold;
White-plumed lilies, and the first
Hedge-grown primrose that hath burst;
Shaded hyacinth, alway
Sapphire queen of the mid-May;
And every leaf, and every flower
Pearlèd with the self-same shower.
Thou shalt see the field-mouse peep
Meagre from its cellèd sleep;
And the snake all winter-thin
Cast on sunny bank its skin!
Freckled nest eggs thou shalt see
Hatching in the hawthorn-tree,
When the hen-bird's wing doth rest
Quiet on her mossy nest;
Then the hurry and alarm
When the beehive casts its swarm;
Acorns ripe down-pattering
While the autumn breezes sing.

Oh, sweet Fancy! let her loose;

Every thing is spoilt by use:
Where's the cheek that doth not fade,
Too much gazed at? Where's the maid
Whose lip mature is ever new?
Where's the eye, however blue,
Doth not weary? Where's the face
One would meet in every place?
Where's the voice, however soft,
One would hear so very oft?
At a touch sweet Pleasure melteth
Like to bubbles when rain pelteth.
Let, then, wingèd Fancy find
Thee a mistress to thy mind:
Dulcet-eyed as Ceres' daughter,
Ere the God of Torment taught her
How to frown and how to chide;
With a waist and with a side
White as Hebe's, when her zone
Slipt its golden clasp, and down
Fell her kirtle to her feet,
While she held the goblet sweet,
And Jove grew languid. — Break the mesh
Of the Fancy's silken leash;
Quickly break her prison-string,
And such joys as these she'll bring. —
Let the wingèd Fancy roam,
Pleasure never is at home.

Ode

Bards of Passion and of Mirth,
Ye have left your souls on earth!
Have ye souls in heaven too,

Double-lived in regions new?
Yes, and those of heaven commune
With the spheres of sun and moon:
With the noise of fountains wondrous,
And the parle of voices thund'rous;
With the whisper of heaven's trees
And one another, in soft ease
Seated on Elysian lawns
Browsed by none but Dian's fawns;
Underneath large blue-bells tented,
Where the daisies are rose-scented,
And the rose herself has got
Perfume which on earth is not;
Where the nightingale doth sing
Not a senseless, trancèd thing,
But divine, melodious truth,
Philosophic numbers smooth;
Tales and golden histories
Of heaven and its mysteries.

   Thus ye live on high, and then
On the earth ye live again;
And the souls ye left behind you
Teach us, here, the way to find you,
Where your other souls are joying,
Never slumber'd, never cloying.
Here, your earth-born souls still speak
To mortals, of their little week;
Of their sorrows and delights;
Of their passions and their spites;
Of their glory and their shame;
What does strengthen, and what maim.

Thus ye teach us, every day,
Wisdom, though fled far away.

Bards of Passion and of Mirth,
Ye have left your souls on earth!
Ye have souls in heaven too,
Double-lived in regions new!

Souls of poets dead and gone,
What Elysium have ye known,
Happy field or mossy cavern,
Choicer than the Mermaid Tavern?
Have ye tippled drink more fine
Than mine host's Canary wine?
Or are fruits of Paradise
Sweeter than those dainty pies
Of venison? O generous food!
Drest as though bold Robin Hood
Would, with his maid Marian,
Sup and bowse from horn and can.

I have heard that on a day
Mine host's sign-board flew away,
Nobody knew whither, till
An astrologer's old quill
To a sheepskin gave the story,
Said he saw you in your glory,
Underneath a new old sign
Sipping beverage divine,
And pledging with contented smack
The Mermaid in the Zodiac.

Souls of poets dead and gone,
What Elysium have ye known,
Happy field or mossy cavern,
Choicer than the Mermaid Tavern?

Robin Hood

To a Friend

No! those days are gone away,
And their hours are old and grey,
And their minutes buried all
Under the down-trodden pall
Of the leaves of many years:
Many times have winter's shears,
Frozen North, and chilling East,
Sounded tempests to the feast
Of the forest's whispering fleeces,
Since men knew nor rent nor leases.

No, the bugle sounds no more,
And the twanging bow no more;
Silent is the ivory shrill
Past the heath and up the hill;
There is no mid-forest laugh,
Where lone Echo gives the half
To some wight, amazed to hear
Jesting, deep in forest drear.

On the fairest time of June
You may go, with sun or moon,
Or the seven stars to light you,
Or the polar ray to right you;
But you never may behold
Little John, or Robin bold:
Never one, of all the clan,
Thrumming on an empty can

Some old hunting ditty, while
He doth his green way beguile
To fair hostess Merriment,
Down beside the pasture Trent;
For he left the merry tale,
Messenger for spicy ale.

Gone, the merry morris din;
Gone, the song of Gamelyn;
Gone, the tough-belted outlaw
Idling in the 'grené shawe';
All are gone away and past!
And if Robin should be cast
Sudden from his turfèd grave,
And if Marian should have
Once again her forest days,
She would weep, and he would craze;
He would swear, for all his oaks,
Fall'n beneath the dockyard strokes,
Have rotted on the briny seas;
She would weep that her wild bees
Sang not to her — strange! that honey
Can't be got without hard money!

So it is; yet let us sing
Honour to the old bow-string!
Honour to the bugle-horn!
Honour to the woods unshorn!
Honour to the Lincoln green!
Honour to the archer keen!
Honour to tight little John,
And the horse he rode upon!

Honour to bold Robin Hood,
Sleeping in the underwood:
Honour to Maid Marian,
And to all the Sherwood clan!
Though their days have hurried by
Let us two a burden try.

To Autumn

Season of mists and mellow fruitfulness!
  Close bosom-friend of the maturing sun;
Conspiring with him how to load and bless
  With fruit the vines that round the thatch-
    eaves run;
To bend with apples the moss'd cottage-
    trees,
  And fill all fruit with ripeness to the core;
    To swell the gourd, and plump the hazel
      shells
  With a sweet kernel; to set budding more,
And still more, later flowers for the bees,
Until they think warm days will never cease,
    For Summer has o'er-brimm'd their
      clammy cells.

Who hath not seen thee oft amid thy store?
  Sometimes whoever seeks abroad may find
Thee sitting careless on a granary floor,
  Thy hair soft-lifted by the winnowing wind;
Or on a half-reap'd furrow sound asleep,
  Drowsed with the fumes of poppies, while
    thy hook
    Spares the next swath and all its twinèd

flowers;
And sometimes like a gleaner thou dost keep
  Steady thy laden head across a brook;
  Or by a cider-press, with patient look,
    Thou watchest the last oozings, hours by
    hours.

Where are the songs of Spring? Ay, where
  are they?
  Think not of them, thou hast thy music too,
    While barrèd clouds bloom the soft-
    dying day,
And touch the stubble-plains with rosy hue;
  Then in a wailful choir the small gnats
  mourn
  Among the river sallows, borne aloft
    Or sinking as the light wind lives or dies;
And full-grown lambs loud bleat from hilly
  bourn;
  Hedge-crickets sing; and now with treble
  soft
  The redbreast whistles from a garden-croft,
    And gathering swallows twitter in the
    skies.

Ode on Melancholy

No, no! go not to Lethe, neither twist
  Wolf's-bane, tight-rooted, for its poisonous
  wine;
Nor suffer thy pale forehead to be kiss'd
  By nightshade, ruby grape of Proserpine;
Make not your rosary of yew-berries,

Nor let the beetle, nor the death-moth be
  Your mournful Psyche, nor the downy
    owl
A partner in your sorrow's mysteries;
  For shade to shade will come too drowsily,
    And drown the wakeful anguish of the
    soul.

But when the melancholy fit shall fall
  Sudden from heaven like a weeping cloud,
That fosters the droop-headed flowers all,
  And hides the green hill in an April shroud;
Then glut thy sorrow on a morning rose,
  Or on the rainbow of the salt sand-wave,
    Or on the wealth of globèd peonies;
Or if thy mistress some rich anger shows,
  Emprison her soft hand, and let her rave,
    And feed deep, deep upon her peerless
    eyes.

She dwells with Beauty — Beauty that must
    die;
  And Joy, whose hand is ever at his lips
Bidding adieu; and aching Pleasure nigh,
  Turning to poison while the bee-mouth
    sips:
Ay, in the very temple of Delight
  Veil'd Melancholy has her sovran shrine,
    Though seen of none save him whose
    strenuous tongue
  Can burst Joy's grape against his palate
    fine:

His soul shall taste the sadness of her might,
  And be among her cloudy trophies hung.

Hyperion

BOOK I

Deep in the shady sadness of a vale
Far sunken from the healthy breath of morn,
Far from the fiery noon, and eve's one star,
Sat grey-hair'd Saturn, quiet as a stone,
Still as the silence round about his lair;
Forest on forest hung about his head
Like cloud on cloud. No stir of air was there,
Not so much life as on a summer's day
Robs not one light seed from the feather'd
    grass,
But where the dead leaf fell, there did it rest.
A stream went voiceless by, still deadened
    more
By reason of his fallen divinity,
Spreading a shade: the Naiad 'mid her reeds
Press'd her cold finger closer to her lips.

  Along the margin-sand large foot-marks
    went,
No further than to where his feet had stray'd,
And slept there since. Upon the sodden
    ground
His old right hand lay nerveless, listless, dead,
Unsceptred; and his realmless eyes were
    closed;

355

While his bow'd head seem'd list'ning to the
    Earth,
His ancient mother, for some comfort yet.

  It seem'd no force could wake him from
    his place;
But there came one, who with a kindred hand
Touch'd his wide shoulders, after bending
    low
With reverence, though to one who knew it
    not.
She was a Goddess of the infant world;
By her in stature the tall Amazon
Had stood a pigmy's height: she would have
    ta'en
Achilles by the hair and bent his neck;
Or with a finger stay'd Ixion's wheel.
Her face was large as that of Memphian
    sphinx,
Pedestal'd haply in a palace-court,
When sages look'd to Egypt for their lore.
But oh! how unlike marble was that face:
How beautiful, if sorrow had not made
Sorrow more beautiful than Beauty's self.
There was a listening fear in her regard,
As if calamity had but begun;
As if the vanward clouds of evil days
Had spent their malice, and the sullen rear
Was with its stored thunder labouring up.
One hand she press'd upon that aching spot
Where beats the human heart, as if just there,
Though an immortal, she felt cruel pain:

The other upon Saturn's bended neck
She laid, and to the level of his ear
Leaning with parted lips, some words she
  spake
In solemn tenour and deep organ tone:
Some mourning words, which in our feeble
  tongue
Would come in these like accents; O how frail
To that large utterance of the early Gods!
'Saturn, look up! — though wherefore, poor
  old King?
I have no comfort for thee, no not one:
I cannot say, "O wherefore sleepest thou?"
For heaven is parted from thee, and the earth
Knows thee not, thus afflicted, for a God;
And ocean too, with all its solemn noise,
Has from thy sceptre pass'd; and all the air
Is emptied of thine hoary majesty.
Thy thunder, conscious of the new com-
  mand,
Rumbles reluctant o'er our fallen house;
And thy sharp lightning in unpractised hands
Scorches and burns our once serene domain.
O aching time! O moments big as years!
All as ye pass swell out the monstrous truth,
And press it so upon our weary griefs
That unbelief has not a space to breathe.
Saturn, sleep on: — O thoughtless, why did I
Thus violate thy slumbrous solitude?
Why should I ope thy melancholy eyes?
Saturn, sleep on! while at thy feet I weep.'

As when, upon a trancèd summer-night,
Those green-robed senators of mighty
      woods,
Tall oaks, branch-charmèd by the earnest
      stars,
Dream, and so dream all night without a stir,
Save from one gradual solitary gust
Which comes upon the silence, and dies off,
As if the ebbing air had but one wave:
So came these words and went; the while in
      tears
She touch'd her fair large forehead to the
      ground,
Just where her falling hair might be outspread
A soft and silken mat for Saturn's feet.
One moon, with alteration slow, had shed
Her silver seasons four upon the night,
And still these two were postured motion-
      less,
Like natural sculpture in cathedral cavern;
The frozen God still couchant on the earth,
And the sad Goddess weeping at his feet:
Until at length old Saturn lifted up
His faded eyes, and saw his kingdom gone,
And all the gloom and sorrow of the place,
And that fair kneeling Goddess; and then
      spake,
As with a palsied tongue, and while his beard
Shook horrid with such aspen-malady:
'O tender spouse of gold Hyperion,
Thea, I feel thee ere I see thy face;
Look up, and let me see our doom in it;

Look up, and tell me, if this feeble shape
Is Saturn's; tell me, if thou hear'st the voice
Of Saturn; tell me, if this wrinkling brow,
Naked and bare of its great diadem,
Peers like the front of Saturn? Who had
    power
To make me desolate? whence came the
    strength?
How was it nurtured to such bursting forth,
While Fate seem'd strangled in my nervous
    grasp?
But it is so; and I am smother'd up,
And buried from all godlike exercise
Of influence benign on planets pale,
Of admonitions to the winds and seas,
Of peaceful sway above man's harvesting,
And all those acts which Deity supreme
Doth ease its heart of love in. I am gone
Away from my own bosom: I have left
My strong identity, my real self,
Somewhere between the throne, and where I
    sit
Here on this spot of earth. Search, Thea,
    search,
Open thine eyes eterne, and sphere them
    round
Upon all space: space starr'd, and lorn of
    light,
Space region'd with life-air; and barren void;
Spaces of fire, and all the yawn of hell.
Search, Thea, search! and tell me if thou seest
A certain shape or shadow, making way

With wings or chariot fierce to repossess
A heaven he lost erewhile: it must — it must
Be of ripe progress — Saturn must be King!
Yes, there must be a golden victory;
There must be Gods thrown down, and
    trumpets blown
Of triumph calm, and hymns of festival
Upon the gold clouds metropolitan,
Voices of soft proclaim, and silver stir
Of strings in hollow shells; and there shall be
Beautiful things made new, for the surprise
Of the sky-children; I will give command:
Thea! Thea! Thea! where is Saturn?'

  This passion lifted him upon his feet,
And made his hands to struggle in the air,
His Druid locks to shake and ooze with
    sweat,
His eyes to fever out, his voice to cease.
He stood, and heard not Thea's sobbing
    deep;
A little time, and then again he snatch'd
Utterance thus: 'But cannot I create?
Cannot I form? Cannot I fashion forth
Another world, another universe,
To overbear and crumble this to nought?
Where is another chaos? Where?' That word
Found way unto Olympus, and made quake
The rebel three. Thea was startled up,
And in her bearing was a sort of hope,
As thus she quick-voiced spake, yet full of
    awe.

'This cheers our fallen house: come to our
    friends,
O Saturn! come away, and give them heart;
I know the covert, for thence came I hither.'
Thus brief, then with beseeching eyes she
    went
With backward footing through the shade a
    space:
He follow'd, and she turn'd to lead the way
Through aged boughs, that yielded like the
    mist
Which eagles cleave, upmounting from their
    nest.

   Meanwhile in other realms big tears were
    shed,
More sorrow like to this, and such like woe,
Too huge for mortal tongue or pen of scribe:
The Titans fierce, self-hid or prison-bound,
Groan'd for the old allegiance once more,
And listen'd in sharp pain for Saturn's voice.
But one of the whole mammoth-brood still
    kept
His sovereignty, and rule, and majesty;
Blazing Hyperion on his orbèd fire
Still sat, still snuff'd the incense, teeming up
From man to the sun's God, yet unsecure:
For as among us mortals omens drear
Fright and perplex, so also shudder'd he,
Not at dog's howl, or gloom-bird's hated
    screech,
Or the familiar visiting of one

Upon the first toll of his passing-bell,
Or prophesyings of the midnight lamp;
But horrors, portion'd to a giant nerve,
Oft made Hyperion ache. His palace bright,
Bastion'd with pyramids of glowing gold,
And touched with shade of bronzèd obelisks,
Glared a blood-red through all its thousand
    courts,
Arches, and domes, and fiery galleries;
And all its curtains of Aurorian clouds
Flush'd angerly: while sometimes eagle's
    wings,
Unseen before by Gods or wondering men,
Darken'd the place; and neighing steeds were
    heard,
Not heard before by Gods or wondering
    men.
Also, when he would taste the spicy wreaths
Of incense, breathed aloft from sacred hills,
Instead of sweets, his ample palate took
Savour of poisonous brass and metal sick:
And so, when harbour'd in the sleepy west,
After the full completion of fair day,
For rest divine upon exalted couch,
And slumber in the arms of melody,
He paced away the pleasant hours of ease
With stride colossal, on from hall to hall;
While far within each aisle and deep recess,
His wingèd minions in close clusters stood,
Amazed and full of fear; like anxious men
Who on wide plains gather in panting troops,

When earthquakes jar their battlements and
    towers.
Even now, while Saturn, roused from icy
    trance,
Went step for step with Thea through the
    woods,
Hyperion, leaving twilight in the rear,
Came slope upon the threshold of the west;
Then, as was wont, his palace-door flew ope
In smoothest silence, save what solemn tubes,
Blown by the serious Zephyrs, gave of sweet
And wandering sounds, slow-breathèd melo-
    dies;
And like a rose in vermeil tint and shape,
In fragrance soft, and coolness to the eye,
That inlet to severe magnificence
Stood full blown, for the God to enter in.

  He enter'd, but he enter'd full of wrath;
His flaming robes streamed out beyond his
    heels,
And gave a roar, as if of earthly fire,
That scared away the meek ethereal Hours
And made their dove-wings tremble. On he
    flared
From stately nave to nave, from vault to vault,
Through bowers of fragrant and enwreathèd
    light,
And diamond-pavèd lustrous long arcades,
Until he reached the great main cupola;
There standing fierce beneath, he stampt his
    foot,

And from the basements deep to the high
    towers
Jarr'd his own golden region; and before
The quavering thunder thereupon had
    ceased,
His voice leapt out, despite of godlike curb,
To this result: 'O dreams of day and night!
O monstrous forms! O effigies of pain!
O spectres busy in a cold, cold gloom!
O lank-ear'd Phantoms of black-weeded
    pools!
Why do I know ye? why have I seen ye? why
Is my eternal essence thus distraught
To see and to behold these horrors new?
Saturn is fallen, am I too to fall?
Am I to leave this haven of my rest,
This cradle of my glory, this soft clime,
This calm luxuriance of blissful light,
These crystalline pavilions, and pure fanes,
Of all my lucent empire? It is left
Deserted, void, nor any haunt of mine.
The blaze, the splendour, and the symmetry,
I cannot see — but darkness, death and dark-
    ness.
Even here, into my centre of repose,
The shady visions come to domineer,
Insult, and blind, and stifle up my pomp —
Fall! — No, by Tellus and her briny robes!
Over the fiery frontier of my realms
I will advance a terrible right arm
Shall scare that infant thunderer, rebel Jove,
And bid old Saturn take his throne again.'

He spake, and ceased, the while a heavier
  threat
Held struggle with his throat, but came not
  forth;
For as in theatres of crowded men
Hubbub increases more they call out 'Hush!'
So at Hyperion's words the Phantoms pale
Bestirr'd themselves, thrice horrible and cold;
And from the mirror'd level where he stood
A mist arose, as from a scummy marsh.
At this, through all his bulk an agony
Crept gradual, from the feet unto the crown,
Like a lithe serpent vast and muscular
Making slow way, with head and neck con-
  vulsed
From over-strainèd might. Released, he fled
To the eastern gates, and full six dewy hours
Before the dawn in season due should blush,
He breathed fierce breath against the sleepy
  portals,
Clear'd them of heavy vapours, burst them
  wide
Suddenly on the ocean's chilly streams.
The planet orb of fire, whereon he rode
Each day from east to west the heavens
  through,
Spun round in sable curtaining of clouds;
Not therefore veilèd quite, blindfold and hid,
But ever and anon the glancing spheres,
Circles, and arcs, and broad-belting colure,
Glow'd through, and wrought upon the muf-
  fling dark

Sweet-shapèd lightnings from the nadir deep
Up to the zenith — hieroglyphics old,
Which sages and keen-eyed astrologers
Then living on the earth, with labouring
    thought
Won from the gaze of many centuries:
Now lost, save what we find on remnants
    huge
Of stone, or marble swart; their import gone,
Their wisdom long since fled. Two wings this
    orb
Possess'd for glory, two fair argent wings,
Ever exalted at the God's approach:
And now, from forth the gloom their plumes
    immense
Rose, one by one, till all outspreaded were;
While still the dazzling globe maintain'd
    eclipse,
Awaiting for Hyperion's command.
Fain would he have commanded, fain took
    throne
And bid the day begin, if but for change.
He might not: — No, though a primeval God
The sacred seasons might not be disturb'd,
Therefore the operations of the dawn
Stay'd in their birth, even as here 'tis told.
Those silver wings expanded sisterly,
Eager to sail their orb; the porches wide
Open'd upon the dusk demesnes of night;
And the bright Titan, phrenzied with new
    woes,
Unused to bend, by hard compulsion bent

His spirit to the sorrow of the time;
And all along a dismal rack of clouds,
Upon the boundaries of day and night,
He stretch'd himself in grief and radiance
    faint.
There as he lay, the Heaven with its stars
Look'd down on him with pity, and the voice
Of Cœlus, from the universal space,
Thus whisper'd low and solemn in his ear:
'O brightest of my children dear, earth-born
And sky-engender'd, Son of Mysteries
All unrevealèd even to the powers
Which met at thy creating! at whose joys
And palpitations sweet, and pleasures soft,
I, Cœlus, wonder how they came and
    whence;
And at the fruits thereof what shapes they
    be,
Distinct, and visible; symbols divine,
Manifestations of that beauteous life
Diffused unseen throughout eternal space;
Of these new-form'd art thou, oh brightest
    child!
Of these, thy brethren and the Goddesses!
There is sad feud among ye, and rebellion
Of son against his sire. I saw him fall,
I saw my first-born tumbled from his throne!
To me his arms were spread, to me his voice
Found way from forth the thunders round
    his head!
Pale wox I, and in vapours hid my face.
Art thou, too, near such doom? vague fear

there is:
For I have seen my sons most unlike Gods.
Divine ye were created, and divine
In sad demeanour, solemn, undisturb'd,
Unruffled, like high Gods, ye lived and ruled:
Now I behold in you fear, hope, and wrath;
Actions of rage and passions; even as
I see them, on the mortal world beneath,
In men who die. — This is the grief, O Son!
Sad sign of ruin, sudden dismay, and fall!
Yet do thou strive; as thou art capable,
As thou canst move about, an evident God,
And canst oppose to each malignant hour
Ethereal presence: — I am but a voice;
My life is but the life of winds and tides,
No more than winds and tides can I avail: —
But thou canst. — Be thou therefore in the
    van
Of circumstance; yea, seize the arrow's barb
Before the tense string murmur. — To the
    earth!
For there thou wilt find Saturn, and his woes.
Meantime I will keep watch on thy bright
    sun,
And of thy seasons be a careful nurse.' —
Ere half this region-whisper had come down
Hyperion arose, and on the stars
Lifted his curvèd lids, and kept them wide
Until it ceased; and still he kept them wide:
And still they were the same bright, patient
    stars.
Then with a slow incline of his broad breast,

Like to a diver in the pearly seas,
Forward he stoop'd over the airy shore,
And plunged all noiseless into the deep night.

BOOK II

Just at the self-same beat of Time's wide
  wings
Hyperion slid into the rustled air,
And Saturn gain'd with Thea that sad place
Where Cybele and the bruised Titans
  mourn'd.
It was a den where no insulting light
Could glimmer on their tears; where their
  own groans
They felt, but heard not, for the solid roar
Of thunderous waterfalls and torrents hoarse,
Pouring a constant bulk, uncertain where.
Crag jutting forth to crag, and rocks that
  seem'd
Ever as if just rising from a sleep,
Forehead to forehead held their monstrous
  horns;
And thus in thousand hugest phantasies
Made a fit roofing to this nest of woe.
Instead of thrones, hard flint they sat upon,
Couches of rugged stone, and slaty ridge
Stubborn'd with iron. All were not as-
  sembled:
Some chain'd in torture, and some wander-
  ing.
Cœus, and Gyges, and Briareüs,
Typhon and Dolor, and Porphyrion,

With many more, the brawniest in assault,
Were pent in regions of laborious breath;
Dungeon'd in opaque element, to keep
Their clenchèd teeth still clench'd, and all
  their limbs
Lock'd up like veins of metal, crampt and
  screw'd;
Without a motion, save of their big hearts
Heaving in pain, and horribly convulsed
With sanguine feverous boiling gurge of
  pulse.
Mnemosyne was straying in the world;
Far from her moon had Phœbe wanderèd;
And many else were free to roam abroad,
But for the main, here found they covert
  drear.
Scarce images of life, one here, one there,
Lay vast and edgeways; like a dismal cirque
Of Druid stones, upon a forlorn moor,
When the chill rain begins at shut of eve,
In dull November, and their chancel vault,
The heaven itself, is blinded throughout
  night.
Each one kept shroud, nor to his neighbour
  gave
Or word or look, or action of despair.
Creüs was one; his ponderous iron mace
Lay by him, and a shatter'd rib of rock
Told of his rage, ere he thus sank and pined.
Iapetus another; in his grasp,
A serpent's plashy neck; its barbèd tongue

Squeezed from the gorge, and all its uncurl'd
    length
Dead: and because the creature could not
    spit
Its poison in the eyes of conquering Jove.
Next Cottus: prone he lay, chin uppermost,
As though in pain; for still upon the flint
He ground severe his skull, with open mouth
And eyes at horrid working. Nearest him
Asia, born of most enormous Caf,
Who cost her mother Tellus keener pangs,
Though feminine, than any of her sons:
More thought than woe was in her dusky
    face,
For she was prophesying of her glory;
And in her wide imagination stood
Palm-shaded temples, and high rival fanes
By Oxus or in Ganges' sacred isles.
Even as Hope upon her anchor leans,
So leant she, not so fair, upon a tusk
Shed from the broadest of her elephants.
Above her, on a crag's uneasy shelve,
Upon his elbow raised, all prostrate else,
Shadow'd Enceladus; once tame and mild
As grazing ox unworried in the meads;
Now tiger-passion'd, lion-thoughted, wroth,
He meditated, plotted, and even now
Was hurling mountains in that second war,
Not long delay'd, that scared the younger
    Gods
To hide themselves in forms of beast and
    bird.

Not far hence Atlas; and beside him prone
Phorcus, the sire of Gorgons. Neighbour'd
    close
Oceanus, and Tethys, in whose lap
Sobbed Clymene among her tangled hair.
In midst of all lay Themis, at the feet
Of Ops the queen all clouded round from
    sight;
No shape distinguishable, more than when
Thick night confounds the pine-tops with
    the clouds;
And many else whose names may not be told.
For when the muse's wings are air-ward
    spread,
Who shall delay her flight? And she must
    chaunt
Of Saturn, and his guide, who now had
    climb'd
With damp and slippery footing from a depth
More horrid still. Above a sombre cliff
Their heads appear'd, and up their stature
    grew
Till on the level height their steps found ease;
Then Thea spread abroad her trembling arms
Upon the precincts of this nest of pain,
And sidelong fix'd her eye on Saturn's face:
There saw she direst strife; the supreme God
At war with all the frailty of grief,
Of rage, of fear, anxiety, revenge,
Remorse, spleen, hope, but most of all de-
    spair.

Against these plagues he strove in vain; for
  Fate
Had pour'd a mortal oil upon his head,
A disanointing poison: so that Thea,
Affrighted, kept her still, and let him pass
First onwards in, among the fallen tribe.

  As with us mortal men, the laden heart
Is persecuted more, and fever'd more,
When it is nighing to the mournful house
Where other hearts are sick of the same
  bruise;
So Saturn, as he walk'd into the midst,
Felt faint, and would have sunk among the
  rest,
But that he met Enceladus's eye,
Whose mightiness, and awe of him, at once
Came like an inspiration; and he shouted,
'Titans, behold your God!' at which some
  groan'd;
Some started on their feet; some also
  shouted,
Some wept, some wail'd — all bowed with
  reverence;
And Ops, uplifting her black folded veil,
Show'd her pale cheeks, and all her forehead
  wan,
Her eyebrows thin and jet, and hollow eyes.
There is a roaring in the bleak-grown pines
When Winter lifts his voice; there is a noise
Among immortals when a God gives sign,
With hushing finger, how he means to load

His tongue with the full weight of utterless
    thought,
With thunder, and with music, and with
    pomp:
Such noise is like the roar of bleak-grown
    pines,
Which, when it ceases in this mountain'd
    world,
No other sound succeeds; but ceasing here,
Among these fallen, Saturn's voice therefrom
Grew up like organ, that begins anew
Its strain, when other harmonies, stopt short,
Leave the dinn'd air vibrating silverly.
Thus grew it up: 'Not in my own sad breast,
Which is its own great judge and searcher
    out,
Can I find reason why ye should be thus:
Not in the legends of the first of days,
Studied from that old spirit-leavèd book
Which starry Uranus with finger bright
Saved from the shores of darkness, when the
    waves
Low-ebb'd still hid it up in shallow gloom;
And the which book ye know I ever kept
For my firm-basèd footstool: — Ah, infirm!
Not there, nor in sign, symbol, or portent
Of element, earth, water, air, and fire, —
At war, at peace, or inter-quarrelling
One against one, or two, or three, or all,
Each several one against the other three,
As fire with air loud warring when rain-floods
Drown both, and press them both against

earth's face,
Where, finding sulphur, a quadruple wrath
Unhinges the poor world; — not in that strife,
Wherefrom I take strange lore, and read it
    deep,
Can I find reason why ye should be thus:
No, nowhere can unriddle, though I search,
And pore on Nature's universal scroll
Even to swooning, why ye, Divinities,
The first-born of all shaped and palpable
    Gods,
Should cower beneath what, in comparison,
Is untremendous might. Yet ye are here,
O'erwhelm'd and spurn'd, and batter'd, ye
    are here!
O Titans, shall I say, "Arise!" — Ye groan:
Shall I say "Crouch!" — Ye groan. What can
    I then?
O Heaven wide! O unseen parent dear!
What can I? Tell me, all ye brethren Gods,
How we can war, how engine our great wrath!
O speak your counsel now, for Saturn's ear
Is all a-hunger'd. Thou, Oceanus,
Ponderest high and deep; and in thy face
I see, astonied, that severe content
Which comes of thought and musing: give us
    help!'

So ended Saturn; and the God of the Sea,
Sophist and sage, from no Athenian grove,
But cogitation in his watery shades,
Arose, with locks not oozy, and began,

In murmurs, which his first-endeavouring
 tongue
Caught infant-like from the far-foamèd
 sands.
'O ye, whom wrath consumes! who, passion-
 stung,
Writhe at defeat, and nurse your agonies!
Shut up your senses, stifle up your ears,
My voice is not a bellows unto ire.
Yet listen, ye who will, whilst I bring proof
How ye, perforce, must be content to stoop:
And in the proof much comfort will I give,
If ye will take that comfort in its truth.
We fall by course of Nature's law, not force
Of thunder, or of Jove. Great Saturn, thou
Hast sifted well the atom-universe;
But for this reason, that thou art the King,
And only blind from sheer supremacy,
One avenue was shaded from thine eyes,
Through which I wander'd to eternal truth.
And first, as thou wast not the first of pow-
 ers,
So art thou not the last; it cannot be.
Thou art not the beginning nor the end.
From chaos and parental darkness came
Light, the first fruits of that intestine broil,
That sullen ferment, which for wondrous
 ends
Was ripening in itself. The ripe hour came,
And with it light, and light, engendering
Upon its own producer, forthwith touch'd
The whole enormous matter into life.

Upon that very hour, our parentage,
The Heavens and the Earth, were manifest:
Then thou first-born, and we the giant-race,
Found ourselves ruling new and beauteous
    realms.
Now comes the pain of truth, to whom 'tis
    pain;
O folly! for to bear all naked truths,
And to envisage circumstance, all calm,
That is the top of sovereignty. Mark well!
As Heaven and Earth are fairer, fairer far
Than Chaos and blank Darkness, though
    once chief;
And as we show beyond that Heaven and
    Earth
In form and shape compact and beautiful,
In will, in action free, companionship,
And thousand other signs of purer life;
So on our heels a fresh perfection treads,
A power more strong in beauty, born of us
And fated to excel us, as we pass
In glory that old Darkness: nor are we
Thereby more conquer'd than by us the rule
Of shapeless Chaos. Say, doth the dull soil
Quarrel with the proud forests it hath fed,
And feedeth still, more comely than itself?
Can it deny the chiefdom of green groves?
Or shall the tree be envious of the dove
Because it cooeth, and hath snowy wings
To wander wherewithal and find its joys?
We are such forest-trees, and our fair boughs
Have bred forth, not pale solitary doves,

377

But eagles golden-feather'd, who do tower
Above us in their beauty, and must reign
In right thereof, for 'tis the eternal law
That first in beauty should be first in might;
Yea, by that law, another race may drive
Our conquerors to mourn as we do now.
Have ye beheld the young God of the Seas,
My dispossessor? Have ye seen his face?
Have ye beheld his chariot, foam'd along
By noble wingèd creatures he hath made?
I saw him on the calmèd waters scud,
With such a glow of beauty in his eyes,
That it enforced me to bid sad farewell
To all my empire: farewell sad I took,
And hither came, to see how dolorous fate
Had wrought upon ye; and how I might best
Give consolation in this woe extreme,
Receive the truth, and let it be your balm.'

  Whether through posed conviction, or dis-
      dain,
They guarded silence, when Oceanus
Left murmuring, what deepest thought can
      tell?
But so it was, none answer'd for a space,
Save one whom none regarded, Clymene:
And yet she answer'd not, only complain'd,
With hectic lips, and eyes up-looking mild,
Thus wording timidly among the fierce:
'O Father! I am here the simplest voice,
And all my knowledge is that joy is gone,

And this thing woe crept in among our
hearts,
There to remain for ever, as I fear:
I would not bode of evil, if I thought
So weak a creature could turn off the help
Which by just right should come of mighty
Gods;
Yet let me tell my sorrow, let me tell
Of what I heard, and how it made me weep,
And know that we had parted from all hope.
I stood upon a shore, a pleasant shore,
Where a sweet clime was breathèd from a
land
Of fragrance, quietness, and trees, and flow-
ers.
Full of calm joy it was, as I of grief;
Too full of joy and soft delicious warmth;
So that I felt a movement in my heart
To chide, and to reproach that solitude
With songs of misery, music of our woes;
And sat me down, and took a mouthèd shell
And murmur'd into it, and made melody —
O melody no more! for while I sang,
And with poor skill let pass into the breeze
The dull shell's echo, from a bowery strand
Just opposite, an island of the sea,
There came enchantment with the shifting
wind,
That did both drown and keep alive my ears.
I threw my shell away upon the sand,
And a wave fill'd it, as my sense was fill'd
With that new blissful golden melody.

A living death was in each gush of sounds,
Each family of rapturous hurried notes,
That fell, one after one, yet all at once,
Like pearl beads dropping sudden from their
    string:
And then another, then another strain,
Each like a dove leaving its olive perch,
With music wing'd instead of silent plumes,
To hover round my head, and make me sick
Of joy and grief at once. Grief overcame,
And I was stopping up my frantic ears,
When, past all hindrance of my trembling
    hands,
A voice came, sweeter, sweeter than all tune,
And still it cried, "Apollo! young Apollo!
The morning-bright Apollo! young Apollo!"
I fled, it follow'd me, and cried "Apollo!"
O Father, and O Brethren! had ye felt
Those pains of mine; O Saturn, hadst thou
    felt,
Ye would not call this too indulgèd tongue
Presumptuous, in thus venturing to be
    heard!'

    So far her voice flow'd on, like timorous
    brook
That, lingering along a pebbled coast,
Doth fear to meet the sea: but sea it met,
And shudder'd; for the overwhelming voice
Of huge Enceladus swallow'd it in wrath:
The ponderous syllables, like sullen waves
In the half-glutted hollows of reef-rocks,

Came booming thus, while still upon his arm
He lean'd; not rising, from supreme con-
    tempt.
'Or shall we listen to the over-wise,
Or to the over-foolish giant, Gods?
Not thunderbolt on thunderbolt, till all
That rebel Jove's whole armoury were spent,
Not world on world upon these shoulders
    piled,
Could agonise me more than baby-words
In midst of this dethronement horrible.
Speak! roar! shout! yell! ye sleepy Titans all.
Do ye forget the blows, the buffets vile?
Are ye not smitten by a youngling arm?
Dost thou forget, sham Monarch of the
    Waves,
Thy scalding in the seas? What! have I roused
Your spleens with so few simple words as
    these?
O joy! for now I see ye are not lost:
O joy! for now I see a thousand eyes
Wide glaring for revenge!' — As this he said,
He lifted up his stature vast, and stood,
Still without intermission speaking thus:
'Now ye are flames, I'll tell ye how to burn,
And purge the ether of our enemies:
How to feed fierce the crooked stings of fire,
And singe away the swollen clouds of Jove,
Stifling that puny essence in its tent,
O let him feel the evil he hath done!
For though I scorn Oceanus's lore,

Much pain have I for more than loss of
    realms:
The days of peace and slumberous calm are
    fled;
Those days, all innocent of scathing war,
When all the fair Existences of heaven
Came open-eyed to guess what we would
    speak: —
That was before our brows were taught to
    frown,
Before our lips knew else but solemn sounds;
That was before we knew the wingèd thing,
Victory, might be lost, or might be won.
And be ye mindful that Hyperion,
Our brightest brother, still is undisgraced —
Hyperion, lo! his radiance is here!'

    All eyes were on Enceladus's face,
And they beheld, while still Hyperion's name
Flew from his lips up to the vaulted rocks,
A pallid gleam across his features stern:
Not savage, for he saw full many a God
Wroth as himself. He look'd upon them all,
And in each face he saw a gleam of light,
But splendider in Saturn's, whose hoar locks
Shone like the bubbling foam about a keel
When the prow sweeps into a midnight cove.
In pale and silver silence they remain'd,
Till suddenly a splendour, like the morn,
Pervaded all the beetling gloomy steeps,
All the sad spaces of oblivion,
And every gulf, and every chasm old,

And every height, and every sullen depth,
Voiceless, or hoarse with loud tormented
   streams:
And all the everlasting cataracts,
And all the headlong torrents far and near,
Mantled before in darkness and huge shade,
Now saw the light and made it terrible.
It was Hyperion: — a granite peak
His bright feet touch'd, and there he stay'd
   to view
The misery his brilliance had betray'd
To the most hateful seeing of itself.
Golden his hair of short Numidian curl,
Regal his shape majestic, a vast shade
In midst of his own brightness, like the bulk
Of Memnon's image at the set of sun
To one who travels from the dusking East:
Sighs, too, as mournful as that Memnon's
   harp
He utter'd, while his hands contemplative
He press'd together, and in silence stood.
Despondence seized again the fallen Gods
At sight of the dejected King of Day,
And many hid their faces from the light:
But fierce Enceladus sent forth his eyes
Among the brotherhood; and, at their glare,
Uprose Iäpetus, and Creüs too,
And Phorcus, sea-born, and together strode
To where he tower'd on his eminence.
There those four shouted forth old Saturn's
   name.
Hyperion from the peak loud answer'd,

'Saturn!'
Saturn sat near the Mother of the Gods,
In whose face was no joy, though all the Gods
Gave from their hollow throat the name of
  'Saturn!'

BOOK III

Thus, in alternate uproar and sad peace,
Amazèd were those Titans utterly.
O leave them, Muse! O leave them to their
  woes;
For thou art weak to sing such tumults dire:
A solitary sorrow best befits
Thy lips, and antheming a lonely grief.
Leave them, O Muse! for thou anon wilt find
Many a fallen old Divinity
Wandering in vain about bewilder'd shores.
Meantime touch piously the Delphic harp,
And not a wind of heaven but will breathe
In aid soft warble from the Dorian flute;
For lo! 'tis for the Father of all verse.
Flush every thing that hath a vermeil hue,
Let the rose glow intense and warm the air,
And let the clouds of even and of morn
Float in voluptuous fleeces o'er the hills;
Let the red wine within the goblet boil,
Cold as a bubbling well; let faint-lipp'd shells,
On sands or in great deeps, vermilion turn
Through all their labyrinths; and let the maid
Blush keenly, as with some warm kiss sur-
  prised.
Chief isle of the embowered Cyclades,

384

Rejoice, O Delos, with thine olives green,
And poplars, and lawn-shading palms, and
  beech,
In which the Zephyr breathes the loudest
  song,
And hazels thick, dark-stemm'd beneath the
  shade:
Apollo is once more the golden theme!
Where was he, when the Giant of the Sun
Stood bright, amid the sorrow of his peers?
Together had he left his mother fair
And his twin-sister sleeping in their bower,
And in the morning twilight wander'd forth
Beside the osiers of a rivulet,
Full ankle-deep in lilies of the vale.
The nightingale had ceased, and a few stars
Were lingering in the heavens, while the
  thrush
Began calm-throated. Throughout all the isle
There was no covert, no retired cave,
Unhaunted by the murmurous noise of
  waves,
Though scarcely heard in many a green re-
  cess.
He listen'd, and he wept, and his bright tears
Went trickling down the golden bow he held.
Thus with half-shut suffusèd eyes he stood,
While from beneath some cumbrous boughs
  hard by
With solemn step an awful Goddess came,
And there was purport in her looks for him,
Which he with eager guess began to read

Perplex'd, the while melodiously he said:
'How cam'st thou over the unfooted sea?
Or hath that antique mien and robèd form
Moved in these vales invisible till now?
Sure I have heard those vestments sweeping
    o'er
The fallen leaves, when I have sat alone
In cool mid-forest. Surely I have traced
The rustle of those ample skirts about
These grassy solitudes, and seen the flowers
Lift up their heads, as still the whisper pass'd.
Goddess! I have beheld those eyes before,
And their eternal calm, and all that face,
Or I have dream'd.' — 'Yes,' said the supreme
    shape,
'Thou hast dream'd of me; and awaking up
Didst find a lyre all golden by thy side,
Whose strings touch'd by thy fingers, all the
    vast
Unwearied ear of the whole universe
Listen'd in pain and pleasure at the birth
Of such new tuneful wonder. Is 't not strange
That thou shouldst weep, so gifted? Tell me,
    youth,
What sorrow thou canst feel; for I am sad
When thou dost shed a tear: explain thy griefs
To one who in this lonely isle hath been
The watcher of thy sleep and hours of life,
From the young day when first thy infant
    hand
Pluck'd witless the weak flowers, till thine
    arm

Could bend that bow heroic to all times.
Show thy heart's secrets to an ancient Power
Who hath forsaken old and sacred thrones
For prophecies of thee, and for the sake
Of loveliness new-born.' — Apollo then,
With sudden scrutiny and gloomless eyes
Thus answer'd, while his white melodious
    throat
Throbb'd with the syllables: 'Mnemosyne!
Thy name is on my tongue, I know not how;
Why should I tell thee what thou so well
    seest?
Why should I strive to show what from my
    lips
Would come no mystery? For me, dark, dark,
And painful vile oblivion seals my eyes:
I strive to search wherefore I am so sad,
Until a melancholy numbs my limbs;
And then upon the grass I sit, and moan,
Like one who once had wings. O why
    should I
Feel cursed and thwarted, when the liegeless
    air
Yields to my step aspirant? why should I
Spurn the green turf as hateful to my feet?
Goddess benign! point forth some unknown
    thing.
Are there not other regions than this isle?
What are the stars? There is the sun, the sun!
And the most patient brilliance of the moon!
And stars by thousands! Point me out the
    way

To any one particular beauteous star,
And I will flit into it with my lyre,
And make its silvery splendour pant with
    bliss.
I have heard the cloudy thunder: where is
    power?
Whose hand, whose essence, what divinity
Makes this alarum in the elements,
While I here idle listen on the shores
In fearless yet in aching ignorance?
O tell me, lonely Goddess! by thy harp,
That waileth every morn and eventide,
Tell me why thus I rave about these groves.
Mute thou remainest — mute! yet I can read
A wondrous lesson in thy silent face:
Knowledge enormous makes a God of me.
Names, deeds, grey legends, dire events, re-
    bellions,
Majesties, sovran voices, agonies,
Creations and destroyings, all at once
Pour into the wide hollows of my brain,
And deify me, as if some blithe wine
Or bright elixir peerless I had drunk,
And so become immortal.' — Thus the God,
While his enkindled eyes, with level glance
Beneath his white soft temples, stedfast kept
Trembling with light upon Mnemosyne.
Soon wild commotions shook him, and made
    flush
All the immortal fairness of his limbs:
Most like the struggle at the gate of death;
Or liker still to one who should take leave

Of pale immortal death, and with a pang
As hot as death's is chill, with fierce convulse
Die into life: so young Apollo anguish'd;
His very hair, his golden tresses famed,
Kept undulation round his eager neck.
During the pain Mnemosyne upheld
Her arms as one who prophesied. At length
Apollo shriek'd; — and lo! from all his limbs
Celestial

. . .

■ ■ ■ ■

POSTHUMOUS AND
FUGITIVE POEMS

■ ■ ■ ■

On Peace

O Peace! and dost thou with thy presence
  bless
  The dwellings of this war-surrounded isle;
Soothing with placid brow our late distress,
  Making the triple kingdom brightly smile?
Joyful I hail thy presence; and I hail
  The sweet companions that await on thee;
Complete my joy — let not my first wish fail,
  Let the sweet mountain nymph thy favour-
    ite be,
With England's happiness proclaim Europa's
    liberty.
O Europe! let not sceptred tyrants see
  That thou must shelter in thy former state;
Keep thy chains burst, and boldly say thou
    art free;
  Give thy kings law — leave not uncurbed
    the great;
  So with the horrors past thou'lt win thy
    happier fate.

*Lines written on 29 May, the Anniversary of
Charles's Restoration, on hearing the Bells ringing*

Infatuate Britons, will you still proclaim
His memory, your direst, foulest shame?
      Nor patriots revere?
Ah! when I hear each traitorous lying bell,
'Tis gallant Sydney's, Russell's, Vane's sad
  knell,
      That pains my wounded ear.

Ode to Apollo

In thy western halls of gold,
  When thou sittest in thy state,
Bards, that erst sublimely told
  Heroic deeds, and sang of fate,
With fervour seize their adamantine lyres,
Whose chords are solid rays, and twinkle
  radiant fires.

Here Homer with his nervous arms
  Strikes the twanging harp of war,
And even the western splendour warms,
  While the trumpets sound afar:
But, what creates the most intense surprise,
His soul looks out through renovated eyes.

Then, through thy Temple wide, melodious
  swells
  The sweet majestic tone of Maro's lyre:
The soul delighted on each accent
  dwells, —

Enraptured dwells, — not daring to re-
    spire,
The while he tells of grief around a funeral
    pyre.

'Tis awful silence then again;
    Expectant stand the spheres;
    Breathless the laurell'd peers,
Nor move, till ends the lofty strain,
Nor move till Milton's tuneful thunders
    cease,
And leave once more the ravish'd heavens in
    peace.

Thou biddest Shakespeare wave his hand,
    And quickly forward spring
The Passions — a terrific band —
    And each vibrates the string
That with its tyrant temper best accords,
While from their Master's lips pour forth
    the inspiring words.

A silver trumpet Spenser blows,
    And, as its martial notes to silence flee,
From a virgin chorus flows
    A hymn in praise of spotless Chastity.
'Tis still! Wild warblings from the Æolian
    lyre
Enchantment softly breathe, and tremblingly
    expire.

Next thy Tasso's ardent numbers

Float along the pleasèd air,
Calling youth from idle slumbers,
   Rousing them from Pleasure's lair:
Then o'er the strings his fingers gently
   move,
And melt the soul to pity and to love.

But when *Thou* joinest with the Nine,
And all the powers of song combine,
   We listen here on earth:
The dying tones that fill the air,
And charm the ear of evening fair,
From thee, great God of Bards, receive their
   heavenly birth.

'As from the darkening gloom a silver dove'

As from the darkening gloom a silver dove
   Upsoars, and darts into the Eastern light,
   On pinions that naught moves but pure
   delight,
So fled thy soul into the realms above,
Regions of peace and everlasting love;
   Where happy spirits, crowned with circlets
   bright
   Of starry beam, and gloriously bedight,
Taste the high joy none but the blest can
   prove.
There thou or joinest the immortal quire
   In melodies that even Heaven fair
Fill with superior bliss, or, at desire
   Of the omnipotent Father, cleavest the air

On holy message sent — What pleasures
   higher?
   Wherefore does any grief our joy impair?

To Lord Byron

Byron! how sweetly sad thy melody!
   Attuning still the soul to tenderness,
   As if soft Pity, with unusual stress,
Had touched her plaintive lute, and thou,
   being by,
Hadst caught the tones, nor suffered them to
   die.
   O'ershading sorrow doth not make thee less
   Delightful: thou thy griefs dost dress
With a bright halo, shining beamily,
As when a cloud a golden moon doth veil,
   Its sides are tinged with a resplendent glow,
Through the dark robe oft amber rays prevail,
   And like fair veins in sable marble flow;
Still warble, dying swan! still tell the tale,
   The enchanting tale, the tale of pleasing
   woe.

'Fill for me a brimming bowl'

Fill for me a brimming bowl
And let me in it drown my soul:
But put therein some drug, designed
To banish Woman from my mind:
For I want not the stream inspiring
That heats the sense with lewd desiring,
But I want as deep a draught
As e'er from Lethe's waves was quaffed;

From my despairing breast to charm
The Image of the fairest form
That e'er my revelling eyes beheld,
That e'er my wandering fancy spelled.
'Tis vain! away I cannot chase
The melting softness of that face,
The beaminess of those bright eyes,
That breast — earth's only Paradise.
My sight will never more be blessed;
For all I see has lost its zest:
Nor with delight can I explore
The Classic page, the Muse's lore.
Had she but known how beat my heart,
And with one smile relieved its smart,
I should have felt a sweet relief,
I should have felt 'the joy of grief'.
Yet as a Tuscan 'mid the snow
Of Lapland thinks on sweet Arno,
Even so for ever shall she be
The Halo of my Memory.

To Chatterton

O Chatterton! how very sad thy fate!
  Dear child of sorrow — son of misery!
  How soon the film of death obscured that
    eye,
Whence Genius wildly flashed, and high de-
    bate.
How soon that voice, majestic and elate,
  Melted in dying murmurs! Oh! how nigh
  Was night to thy fair morning. Thou didst
    die

A half-blown flower which cold blasts amate.
But this is past: thou art among the stars
    Of highest Heaven: to the rolling spheres
Thou sweetly singest: naught thy hymning
        mars,
    Above the ingrate world and human fears.
On earth the good man base detraction bars
    From thy fair name, and waters it with
        tears.

To Emma

O come, dearest Emma! the rose is full
        blown,
And the riches of Flora are lavishly strown,
The air is all softness, and crystal the streams,
And the West is resplendently clothèd in
        beams.

We will hasten, my fair, to the opening glades,
The quaintly carved seats, and the freshen-
        ing shades,
Where the faeries are chanting their evening
        hymns,
And in the last sunbeam the sylph lightly
        swims.

And when thou art weary I'll find thee a bed
Of mosses and flowers to pillow thy head;
There, beauteous Emma, I'll sit at thy feet,
While my story of love I enraptured repeat.

So fondly I'll breathe, and so softly I'll sigh,

Thou wilt think that some amorous Zephyr
  is nigh —
Ah, no! — as I breathe, I will press thy fair
  knee,
And then thou wilt know that the sigh comes
  from me.

Then why, lovely girl, should we lose all these
  blisses?
That mortal's a fool who such happiness
  misses.
So smile acquiescence, and give me thy hand,
With love-looking eyes, and with voice
  sweetly bland.

'Give me Women, Wine, and Snuff'

Give me Women, Wine, and Snuff
Until I cry out, 'Hold, enough!'
You may do so sans objection
Till the day of resurrection;
For, bless my beard, they aye shall be
My belovèd Trinity.

On receiving a Laurel Crown from Leigh Hunt

Minutes are flying swiftly, and as yet
  Nothing unearthly has enticed my brain
  Into a delphic labyrinth — I would fain
Catch an immortal thought to pay the debt
I owe to the kind poet who has set
  Upon my ambitious head a glorious gain.
  Two bending laurel sprigs — 'tis nearly pain
To be conscious of such a coronet.

Still time is fleeting, and no dream arises
    Gorgeous as I would have it — only I see
A trampling down of what the world most
        prizes,
    Turbans and crowns, and blank regality;
And then I run into most wild surmises
    Of all the many glories that may be.

'Come hither all sweet maidens soberly'

Come hither all sweet maidens soberly,
    Down-looking aye, and with a chasten'd
        light
    Hid in the fringes of your eyelids white,
And meekly let your fair hands joinèd be,
As if so gentle that ye could not see,
    Untouch'd, a victim of your beauty bright
    Sinking away to his young spirit's night,
Sinking bewilder'd 'mid the dreary sea:
    'Tis young Leander toiling to his death;
    Nigh swooning, he doth purse his weary
        lips
For Hero's cheek, and smiles against her
        smile.
    O horrid dream! see how his body dips,
    Dead-heavy; arms and shoulders gleam
        awhile:
He's gone: up bubbles all his amorous breath!

Written in Disgust of Vulgar Superstition

The church bells toll a melancholy round,
    Calling the people to some other prayers,

401

Some other gloominess, more dreadful
  cares,
More hearkening to the sermon's horrid
  sound.
Surely the mind of man is closely bound
  In some blind spell: seeing that each one
  tears
  Himself from fireside joys and Lydian airs,
And converse high of those with glory
  crown'd.
Still, still they toll, and I should feel a damp,
  A chill as from a tomb, did I not know
That they are dying like an outburnt
    lamp, —
  That 'tis their sighing, wailing ere they go
  Into oblivion — that fresh flowers will grow,
And many glories of immortal stamp.

'O! how I love, on a fair summer's eve'

O! how I love, on a fair summer's eve,
  When streams of light pour down the
  golden west,
  And on the balmy zephyrs tranquil rest
The silver clouds, far — far away to leave
All meaner thoughts, and take a sweet re-
  prieve
  From little cares; to find, with easy quest,
  A fragrant wild, with Nature's beauty
  dressed,
And there into delight my soul deceive.
There warm my breast with patriotic lore,

Musing on Milton's fate — on Sidney's
bier —
  Till their stern forms before my mind
  arise:
Perhaps on the wing of Poesy upsoar,
  Full often dropping a delicious tear,
    When some melodious sorrow spells
    mine eyes.

To a Young Lady who sent me a Laurel Crown

Fresh morning gusts have blown away all
fear
  From my glad bosom: now from gloomi-
  ness
      I mount for ever — not an atom less
Than the proud laurel shall content my
bier.
  No! by the eternal stars! or why sit here
In the Sun's eye, and 'gainst my temples
press
      Apollo's very leaves, woven to bless
  By thy white fingers and thy spirit
  clear.
Lo! who dares say, 'Do this'? Who dares call
down
  My will from its high purpose? Who say,
  'Stand',
    Or 'Go'? This very moment I would
    frown
    On abject Caesars — not the stoutest
    band

Of mailèd heroes should tear off my
  crown:
  Yet would I kneel and kiss thy gentle
hand!

'After dark vapours have oppressed our plains'

  After dark vapours have oppressed our
  plains
  For a long dreary season, comes a day
  Born of the gentle South, and clears away
  From the sick heavens all unseemly stains.
    The anxious month, relieving from its
  pains,
  Takes as a long-lost right the feel of May,
    The eyelids with the passing coolness
  play,
  Like rose leaves with the drip of summer
  rains.
And calmest thoughts come round us — as
  of leaves
Budding — fruit ripening in stillness —
  autumn suns
    Smiling at eve upon the quiet sheaves
  —

Sweet Sappho's cheek — a sleeping infant's
  breath —
The gradual sand that through an hour-glass
  runs —
A woodland rivulet — a Poet's death.

Lines in a Letter to J. H. Reynolds, from Oxford
  The Gothic looks solemn —

The plain Doric column
Supports an old Bishop and crosier;
The mouldering arch,
Shaded o'er by a larch
Stands next door to Wilson the Hosier.

Vicè — that is, by turns —
O'er pale faces mourns
The black-tassled trencher and common hat;
The chantry boy sings,
The steeple bell rings,
And as for the Chancellor — *dominat.*

There are plenty of trees,
And plenty of ease,
And plenty of fat deer for parsons;
And when it is venison,
Short is the benison —
Then each on a leg or thigh fastens.

On the Sea

It keeps eternal whisperings around
  Desolate shores, and with its mighty swell
  Gluts twice ten thousand caverns; till the
    spell
Of Hecate leaves them their old shadowy
    sound.
Often 'tis in such gentle temper found
  That scarcely will the very smallest shell
  Be moved for days from whence it some-
    time fell,

When last the winds of heaven were un-
   bound.
O ye who have your eyeballs vext and tir'd,
  Feast them upon the wideness of the sea;
O ye whose ears are dinned with uproar rude
  Or fed too much with cloying melody —
Sit ye near some old cavern's mouth and
   brood
  Until ye start as if the sea nymphs quired.

To the Ladies who saw me Crowned

What is there in the universal Earth
  More lovely than a wreath from the bay
    tree?
  Haply a halo round the moon — a glee
Circling from three sweet pair of lips in
    mirth;
And haply you will say the dewy birth
  Of morning roses — ripplings tenderly
  Spread by the halcyon's breath upon the
    sea —
But these comparisons are nothing worth.
Then is there nothing in the world so fair?
  The silvery tears of April? Youth of May?
Or June that breathes out life for butterflies?
  No — none of these can from my favourite
    bear
Away the palm — yet shall it ever pay
  Due reverence to your most sovereign eyes.

Nebuchadnezzar's Dream

Before he went to feed with owls and bats
  Nebuchadnezzar had an ugly dream,
  Worse than an Hus'if's when she thinks her
    cream
Made a Naumachia for mice and rats.
So scared, he sent for that 'Good King of
    Cats'
  Young Daniel, who soon did pluck away
    the beam
  From out his eye, and said he did not deem
The sceptre worth a straw — his Cushions

407

old door-mats.
A horrid nightmare similar somewhat
  Of late has haunted a most motley crew,
    Most loggerheads and Chapmen — we
    are told
That any Daniel tho' he be a sot
  Can make the lying lips turn pale of hue
    By belching out 'ye are that head of
    Gold'.

'Haydon! forgive me that I cannot speak'

Haydon! forgive me that I cannot speak
  Definitively on these mighty things;
  Forgive me that I have not Eagle's
  wings —
That what I want I know not where to seek:
And think that I would not be over-meek
  In rolling out up-followed thunderings,
  Even to the steep of Heliconian springs,
Were I of ample strength for such a freak —
Think too, that all those numbers should be
    thine;
  Whose else? In this who touch thy vesture's
  hem?
For when men stared at what was most di-
  vine
  With browless idiotism — o'erwise
  phlegm —
Thou hadst beheld the Hesperian shine
  Of their star in the East, and gone to wor-
  ship them.

Hymn to Apollo

God of the golden bow,
  And of the golden lyre,
And of the golden hair,
  And of the golden fire,
    Charioteer
    Of the patient year,
  Where — where slept thine ire,
When like a blank idiot I put on thy wreath,
  Thy laurel, thy glory,
  The light of thy story,
Or was I a worm — too low crawling for
  death?
  O Delphic Apollo!

The Thunderer grasp'd and grasp'd,
  The Thunderer frown'd and frown'd;
  The eagle's feathery mane
    For wrath became stiffen'd — the sound
      Of breeding thunder
      Went drowsily under,
    Muttering to be unbound.
  O why didst thou pity, and for a worm
    Why touch thy soft lute
    Till the thunder was mute?
Why was I not crush'd — such a pitiful germ?
    O Delphic Apollo!

The Pleiades were up,
  Watching the silent air;
The seeds and roots in the Earth

Were swelling for summer fare;
   The Ocean, its neighbour,
   Was at his old labour,
When, who — who did dare
To tie, like a madman, thy plant round his
   brow,
   And grin and look proudly,
   And blaspheme so loudly,
And live for that honour, to stoop to thee
   now?
   O Delphic Apollo!

On seeing the Elgin Marbles

My spirit is too weak — mortality
   Weighs heavily on me like unwilling sleep,
   And each imagined pinnacle and steep
Of godlike hardship tells me I must die
Like a sick eagle looking at the sky.
   Yet 'tis a gentle luxury to weep
   That I have not the cloudy winds to keep
Fresh for the opening of the morning's eye.
Such dim-conceived glories of the brain
   Bring round the heart an undescribable
   feud;
So do these wonders a most dizzy pain
   That mingles Grecian grandeur with the
   rude
Wasting of old time — with a billowy
   main —
   A sun — a shadow of a magnitude.

On 'The Story of Rimini'

Who loves to peer up at the morning sun,
  With half-shut eyes and comfortable cheek,
  Let him, with this sweet tale, full often seek
For meadows where the little rivers run;
Who loves to linger with that brightest one
  Of Heaven — Hesperus — let him lowly
    speak
  These numbers to the night, and starlight
    meek,
Or moon, if that her hunting be begun.
He who knows these delights, and too is
    prone
  To moralise upon a smile or tear,
Will find at once a region of his own,
  A bower for his spirit, and will steer
To alleys, where the fir-tree drops its cone,
  Where robins hop, and fallen leaves are
    sear.

Written on a Blank Space at the End of Chaucer's 'The Floure and the Leafe'

This pleasant tale is like a little copse:
  The honeyed lines do freshly interlace
  To keep the reader in so sweet a place,
So that he here and there full-hearted stops;
And oftentimes he feels the dewy drops
  Come cool and suddenly against his face,
  And by the wandering melody may trace
Which way the tender-leggèd linnet hops.
Oh! what a power has white simplicity!
  What mighty power has this gentle story!

411

I that do ever feel athirst for glory
Could at this moment be content to lie
  Meekly upon the grass, as those whose sob-
  bings
  Were heard of none beside the mournful
  robins.

'In drear nighted December'

In drear nighted December,
  Too happy, happy tree,
Thy branches ne'er remember
  Their green felicity —
The north cannot undo them
With a sleety whistle through them,
Nor frozen thawings glue them
  From budding at the prime.

In drear nighted December,
  Too happy, happy brook,
Thy bubblings ne'er remember
  Apollo's summer look —
But with a sweet forgetting
They stay their crystal fretting,
Never, never petting
  About the frozen time.

Ah! would 'twere so with many
  A gentle girl and boy —
But were there ever any
  Writh'd not of passed joy?
    The feel of not to feel it,
When there is none to heal it,

Nor numbed sense to steel it,
  Was never said in rhyme.

'Unfelt, unheard, unseen'

Unfelt, unheard, unseen,
  I've left my little queen,
Her languid arms in silver slumber lying:
  Ah! through their nestling touch,
  Who — who could tell how much
There is for madness — cruel, or complying?

  Those faery lids how sleek!
  Those lips how moist! — they speak,
In ripest quiet, shadows of sweet sounds:
  Into my fancy's ear
  Melting a burden dear,
How 'Love doth know no fullness nor no
  bounds.'

  True! — tender monitors!
  I bend unto your laws:
This sweetest day for dalliance was born!
  So, without more ado,
  I'll feel my heaven anew,
For all the blushing of the hasty morn.

Stanzas

I

You say you love; but with a voice
  Chaster than a nun's, who singeth
The soft Vespers to herself

413

While the chime-bell ringeth —
   O love me truly!

II

You say you love; but with a smile
   Cold as sunrise in September,
As you were Saint Cupid's nun,
   And kept his weeks of Ember.
     O love me truly!

III

You say you love — but then your lips
   Coral tinted teach no blisses
More than coral in the sea —
   They never pout for kisses —
     O love me truly!

IV

You say you love; but then your hand
   No soft squeeze for squeeze returneth,
It is like a statue's, dead —
   While mine for passion burneth —
     O love me truly!

V

O breathe a word or two of fire!
   Smile, as if those words should burn me,
Squeeze as lovers should — O kiss
   And in thy heart inurn me!
     O love me truly!

Hither, hither, love —
  'Tis a shady mead —
Hither, hither, love,
  Let us feed and feed!

Hither, hither, sweet —
  'Tis a cowslip bed —
Hither, hither, sweet!
  'Tis with dew bespread!

Hither, hither, dear —
  By the breath of life —
Hither, hither, dear!
  Be the summer's wife!

Though one moment's pleasure
  In one moment flies,
Though the passion's treasure
  In one moment dies;

Yet it has not passed —
  Think how near, how near! —
And while it doth last,
  Think how dear, how dear!

Hither, hither, hither,
  Love this boon has sent —
If I die and wither
  I shall die content.

'Think not of it, sweet one, so —'

Think not of it, sweet one, so —
  Give it not a tear;
Sigh thou mayst, and bid it go
  Any, any where.

Do not look so sad, sweet one —
  Sad and fadingly;
Shed one drop, then it is gone,
  O 'twas born to die.

Still so pale? then, dearest, weep —
  Weep, I'll count the tears,
And each one shall be a bliss
  For thee in after years.

Brighter has it left thine eyes
  Than a sunny rill;
And thy whispering melodies
  Are tenderer still.

Yet — as all things mourn awhile
  At fleeting blisses,
E'en let us too! but be our dirge
  A dirge of kisses.

On sitting down to read 'King Lear' once again

O golden-tongued Romance with serene lute!
  Fair plumed Syren! Queen of far away!
  Leave melodizing on this wintry day,
Shut up thine olden pages, and be mute.
Adieu! for once again the fierce dispute,

416

Betwixt damnation and impassion'd clay
Must I burn through; once more humbly
  assay
The bitter-sweet of this Shakespearian fruit.
Chief Poet! and ye clouds of Albion,
  Begetters of our deep eternal theme,
When through the old oak forest I am gone,
  Let me not wander in a barren dream,
But when I am consumèd in the fire
Give me new Phœnix wings to fly at my
  desire.

To a Cat

Cat! who hast pass'd thy grand climacteric,
  How many mice and rats hast in thy days
  Destroy'd? — How many tit bits
  stolen? Gaze
With those bright languid segments green,
  and prick
Those velvet ears — but pr'ythee do not stick
  Thy latent talons in me — and upraise
  Thy gentle mew — and tell me all thy frays
Of fish and mice, and rats and tender chick.
Nay, look not down, nor lick thy dainty
  wrists —
  For all the wheezy asthma, — and for all
Thy tail's tip is nick'd off — and though the
  fists
  Of many a maid have given thee many a
  maul,
Still is that fur as soft as when the lists

In youth thou enter'dst on glass-bottled
  wall.

    'Hence Burgundy, Claret, and Port'
Hence Burgundy, Claret, and Port,
  Away with old Hock and Madeira,
Too earthly ye are for my sport;
  There's a beverage brighter and clearer.
Instead of a pitiful rummer,
My wine overbrims a whole summer;
  My bowl is the sky,
  And I drink at my eye,
  Till I feel in the brain
  A Delphian pain —
Then follow, my Caius! then follow:
  On the green of the hill
  We will drink our fill
  Of golden sunshine,
  Till our brains intertwine
With the glory and grace of Apollo!
  God of the Meridian
    And of the East and West,
  To thee my soul is flown,
    And my body is earthward press'd. —
It is an awful mission,
A terrible division;
And leaves a gulph austere
To be fill'd with worldly fear.
Aye, when the soul is fled
To high above our head,
Affrighted do we gaze
After its airy maze,

As doth a mother wild,
When her young infant child
Is in an eagle's claws —
And is not this the cause
Of madness? — God of Song,
Thou bearest me along
Through sights I scarce can bear:
O let me, let me share
With the hot lyre and thee,
The staid Philosophy.
Temper my lonely hours,
And let me see thy bowers
More unalarm'd!

Lines on seeing a Lock of Milton's Hair

Chief of organic numbers!
  Old Scholar of the Spheres!
Thy spirit never slumbers,
  But rolls about our ears,
For ever, and for ever!
O what a mad endeavour
    Worketh he,
Who to thy sacred and ennobled hearse
Would offer a burnt sacrifice of verse
    And melody.

How heavenward thou soundest,
  Live Temple of sweet noise,
And Discord unconfoundest,
  Giving Delight new joys,
And Pleasure nobler pinions!
O, where are thy dominions?

Lend thine ear
To a young delian oath, — aye, by thy soul,
By all that from thy mortal lips did roll,
And by the kernel of thine earthly love,
Beauty, in things on earth, and things above
        I swear!

    When every childish fashion
        Has vanish'd from my rhyme,
    Will I, grey-gone in passion,
        Leave to an after-time,
            Hymning and harmony
Of thee, and of thy works, and of thy life;
But vain is now the burning and the strife,
Pangs are in vain, until I grow high-rife
        With old Philosophy,
And mad with glimpses of futurity!

For many years my offering must be hush'd;
    When I do speak, I'll think upon this hour,
Because I feel my forehead hot and flush'd,
    Even at the simplest vassal of thy power, —
    A lock of thy bright hair, —
    Sudden it came,
And I was startled, when I caught thy name
        Coupled so unaware;
Yet, at the moment, temperate was my blood.
I thought I had beheld it from the flood.

'When I have fears that I may cease to be'

When I have fears that I may cease to be
   Before my pen has glean'd my teeming
   brain,
Before high-piled books, in charactery,
   Hold like rich garners the full ripen'd grain;
When I behold, upon the night's starr'd face,
   Huge cloudy symbols of a high romance,
And think that I may never live to trace
   Their shadows, with the magic hand of
   chance;
And when I feel, fair creature of an hour,
   That I shall never look upon thee more,
Never have relish in the faery power
   Of unreflecting love; — then on the shore
Of the wide world I stand alone, and think
Till love and fame to nothingness do sink.

To the Nile

Son of the old moon-mountains African!
   Chief of the Pyramid and Crocodile!
   We call thee fruitful, and, that very while,
A desert fills our seeing's inward span;
Nurse of swart nations since the world began,
   Art thou so fruitful? or dost thou beguile
   Such men to honour thee, who, worn with
   toil,
Rest for a space 'twixt Cairo and Decan?
O may dark fancies err! they surely do;
   'Tis ignorance that makes a barren waste
Of all beyond itself, thou dost bedew
   Green rushes like our rivers, and dost taste

The pleasant sun-rise, green isles hast thou
  too,
   And to the sea as happily dost haste.

To a Lady seen for a few Moments at Vauxhall

Time's sea hath been five years at its slow
  ebb,
   Long hours have to and fro let creep the
   sand,
Since I was tangled in thy beauty's web
   And snared by the ungloving of thine hand.
And yet I never look on midnight sky
   But I behold thine eyes' well-memory'd
   light;
I cannot look upon the rose's dye
   But to thy cheek my soul doth take its flight;
I cannot look on any budding flower
   But my fond ear, in fancy at thy lips
And hearkening for a love-sound, doth de-
  vour
   Its sweets in the wrong sense. Thou dost
   eclipse
Every delight with sweet remembering,
And grief unto my darling joys dost bring.

   'Spenser! a jealous honourer of thine'

Spenser! a jealous honourer of thine,
  A forester deep in thy midmost trees,
Did last eve ask my promise to refine
  Some English that might strive thine ear to
  please.
But, Elfin Poet, 'tis impossible

For an inhabitant of wintry earth
To rise like Phœbus with a golden quell,
 Fire-winged, and make a morning in his
   mirth.
It is impossible to escape from toil
 O' the sudden and receive thy spiriting:
The flower must drink the nature of the soil
 Before it can put forth its blossoming.
Be with me in the summer days and I
Will for thine honour and his pleasure try.

Answer to a Sonnet by J. H. Reynolds, ending —

                    'Dark eyes are dearer far
Than those that mock the hyacinthine bell.'

Blue! 'Tis the life of heaven, — the domain
 Of Cynthia, — the wide palace of the
   sun, —
The tent of Hesperus, and all his train, —
 The bosomer of clouds, gold, grey, and
   dun.
Blue! 'Tis the life of waters — ocean
 And all its vassal streams: pools numberless
May rage, and foam, and fret, but never can
 Subside, if not to dark-blue nativeness.
Blue! gentle cousin of the forest-green,
 Married to green in all the sweetest
   flowers —
Forget-me-not, — the blue-bell, — and, that
   queen
 Of secrecy, the violet: what strange powers

Hast thou, as a mere shadow! But how great,
When in an Eye thou art, alive with fate!

Apollo to the Graces

APOLLO

Which of the fairest three
To-day will ride with me?
My steeds are all pawing at the threshold of
the morn:
Which of the fairest three
To-day will ride with me
Across the gold Autumn's whole Kingdom
of corn?

THE GRACES *all answer*

I will, I — I — I —
O young Apollo let me fly
Along with thee,
I will — I — , I, I,
The many wonders see
I — I — I — I —
And thy lyre shall never have a slackened
string:
I, I, I, I,
Thro' the golden day will sing.

'O blush not so!'

I

O blush not so! O blush not so!
Or I shall think you knowing;
And if you smile the blushing while,

Then maidenheads are going.

II

There's a blush for won't, and a blush for
    shan't,
  And a blush for having done it:
There's a blush for thought and a blush for
    naught,
  And a blush for just begun it.

III

O sigh not so! O sigh not so!
  For it sounds of Eve's sweet pippin;
By these loosen'd lips you have tasted the
    pips
  And fought in an amorous nipping.

IV

Will you play once more at nice-cut-core,
  For it only will last our youth out,
And we have the prime of the kissing time,
  We have not one sweet tooth out.

V

There's a sigh for yes, and a sigh for no,
  And a sigh for I can't bear it!
O what can be done, shall we stay or run?
  O cut the sweet apple and share it!

'O thou whose face hath felt the Winter's wind'

O thou whose face hath felt the Winter's
  wind,

425

Whose eye has seen the snow-clouds hung in
    mist,
And the black elm tops 'mong the freezing
    stars!
To thee the spring will be a harvest time.
O thou whose only book has been the light
Of supreme darkness, which thou feddest on
Night after night, when Phœbus was away!
To thee the spring shall be a triple morn.
O fret not after knowledge. I have none,
And yet my song comes native with the
    warmth.
O fret not after knowledge! I have none.
And yet the evening listens. He who saddens
At thought of idleness cannot be idle,
And he's awake who thinks himself asleep.

The Human Seasons

Four Seasons fill the measure of the year;
    There are four seasons in the mind of man:
He has his lusty Spring, when fancy clear
    Takes in all beauty with an easy span:
He has his Summer, when luxuriously
    Spring's honey'd cud of youthful thought
    he loves
To ruminate, and by such dreaming high
    Is nearest unto Heaven: quiet coves
His soul has in its Autumn, when his wings
    He furleth close; contented so to look
On mists in idleness — to let fair things
    Pass by unheeded as a threshold brook.

He has his Winter too of pale misfeature,
Or else he would forego his mortal nature.

'Where be ye going, you Devon maid?'
Where be ye going, you Devon maid?
  And what have ye there in the basket?
Ye tight little fairy, just fresh from the dairy,
  Will ye give me some cream if I ask it?

I love your meads, and I love your flowers,
  And I love your junkets mainly,
But 'hind the door I love kissing more,
  O look not so disdainly.

I love your hills and I love your dales,
  And I love your flocks a-bleating —
But O, on the heather to lie together,
  With both our hearts a-beating!

I'll put your basket all safe in a nook,
  Your shawl I'll hang on a willow,
And we will sigh in the daisy's eye,
  And kiss on a grass-green pillow.

'For there's Bishop's Teign'

I

For there's Bishop's Teign
And King's Teign
And Coomb at the clear Teign head —
  Where close by the stream

You may have your cream
All spread upon barley bread.

II

There's Arch Brook
And there's Larch Brook
Both turning many a mill;
And cooling the drouth
Of the salmon's mouth,
And fattening his silver gill.

III

There is Wild Wood,
A mild hood
To the sheep on the lea o' the down,
Where the golden furze,
With its green, thin spurs,
Doth catch at the maiden's gown.

IV

There is Newton Marsh
With its spear grass harsh —
A pleasant summer level
Where the maidens sweet
Of the Market Street
Do meet in the dusk to revel.

V

There's the barton rich
With dyke and ditch
And hedge for the thrush to live in,
And the hollow tree

For the buzzing bee
And a bank for the wasp to hive in.

VI

And O, and O,
The daisies blow
And the primroses are wakened,
  And violet white
  Sits in silver plight,
And the green bud's as long as the spike end.

VII

Then who would go
Into dark Soho,
And chatter with dacked-haired critics,
  When he can stay
  For the new-mown hay,
And startle the dappled prickets?

To Homer

Standing aloof in giant ignorance,
  Of thee I hear and of the Cyclades,
As one who sits ashore and longs perchance
  To visit dolphin-coral in deep seas.
So thou wast blind! — but then the veil was
    rent;
  For Jove uncurtain'd Heaven to let thee
    live,
And Neptune made for thee a spumy tent,
  And Pan made sing for thee his forest-hive;
Ay, on the shores of darkness there is light,
  And precipices show untrodden green;

There is a budding morrow in midnight;
  There is a triple sight in blindness keen;
Such seeing hadst thou, as it once befell,
To Dian, Queen of Earth, and Heaven, and
  Hell.

To J. H. Reynolds from Teignmouth 25 March 1818

Dear Reynolds! as last night I lay in bed,
There came before my eyes that wonted
  thread
Of shapes, and shadows, and remembrances,
That every other minute vex and please:
Things all disjointed come from north and
  south, —
Two Witch's eyes above a Cherub's mouth,
Voltaire with casque and shield and haber-
  geon,
And Alexander with his nightcap on;
Old Socrates a-tying his cravat,
And Hazlitt playing with Miss Edgeworth's
  cat;
And Junius Brutus, pretty well so so,
Making the best of's way towards Soho.

  Few are there who escape these
    visitings, —
Perhaps one or two whose lives have patent
  wings,
And thro' whose curtains peeps no hellish
  nose,
No wild-boar tushes, and no Mermaid's toes;

But flowers bursting out with lusty pride,
And young Æolian harps personified;
Some Titian colours touch'd into real life, —
The sacrifice goes on; the pontiff knife
Gleams in the Sun, the milk-white heifer
    lows,
The pipes go shrilly, the libation flows:
A white sail shows above the green-head cliff,
Moves round the point, and throws her
    anchor stiff;
The mariners join hymn with those on land.

   You know the Enchanted Castle, — it doth
      stand
Upon a rock, on the border of a Lake,
Nested in trees, which all do seem to shake
From some old magic-like Urganda's Sword.
O Phœbus! that I had thy sacred word
To show this Castle, in fair dreaming wise,
Unto my friend, while sick and ill he lies!

   You know it well enough, where it doth
      seem
A mossy place, a Merlin's Hall, a dream;
You know the clear Lake, and the little Isles,
The mountains blue, and cold near neigh-
    bour rills.
All which elsewhere are but half animate;
There do they look alive to love and hate,
To smiles and frowns; they seem a lifted
    mound
Above some giant, pulsing underground.

Part of the Building was a chosen See,
Built by a banish'd Santon of Chaldee;
The other part, two thousand years from him,
Was built by Cuthbert de Saint Aldebrim;
Then there's a little wing, far from the Sun,
Built by a Lapland Witch turn'd maudlin
    Nun:
And many other juts of aged stone
Founded with many a mason-devil's groan.

The doors all look as if they op'd them-
    selves,
The windows as if latch'd by Fays and Elves,
And from them comes a silver flash of light,
As from the westward of a Summer's night;
Or like a beauteous woman's large blue eyes
Gone mad thro' olden songs and poesies.

See! what is coming from the distance dim!
A golden Galley all in silken trim!
Three rows of oars are lightening, moment
    whiles,
Into the verd'rous bosoms of those isles;
Towards the shade, under the Castle wall,
It comes in silence, — now 'tis hidden all.
The Clarion sounds, and from a Postern-
    gate
An echo of sweet music doth create
A fear in the poor Herdsman, who doth bring
His beasts to trouble the enchanted
    spring, —
He tells of the sweet music, and the spot,

To all his friends, and they believe him not.

O that our dreamings all, of sleep or wake,
Would all their colours from the sunset take:
From something of material sublime,
Rather than shadow our own soul's day-time
In the dark void of night. For in the world
We jostle, — but my flag is not unfurl'd
On the Admiral-staff, — and so philosophize
I dare not yet! Oh, never will the prize,
High reason, and the love of good and ill,
Be my award! Things cannot to the will
Be settled, but they tease us out of thought;
Or is it that imagination brought
Beyond its proper bound, yet still confin'd,
Lost in a sort of Purgatory blind,
Cannot refer to any standard law
Of either earth or heaven? It is a flaw
In happiness, to see beyond our bourn, —
It forces us in summer skies to mourn,
It spoils the singing of the Nightingale.

Dear Reynolds! I have a mysterious tale,
And cannot speak it: the first page I read
Upon a Lampit rock of green sea-weed
Among the breakers; 'twas a quiet eve,
The rocks were silent, the wide sea did weave
An untumultuous fringe of silver foam
Along the flat brown sand; I was at home
And should have been most happy, — but I
    saw
Too far into the sea, where every maw

433

The greater on the less feeds evermore. —
But I saw too distinct into the core
Of an eternal fierce destruction,
And so from happiness I far was gone.
Still am I sick of it, and tho', to-day,
I've gather'd young spring-leaves, and flow-
    ers gay
Of periwinkle and wild strawberry,
Still do I that most fierce destruction see, —
The Shark at savage prey, — the Hawk at
    pounce, —
The gentle Robin, like a Pard or Ounce,
Ravening a worm. — Away, ye horrid moods!
Moods of one's mind! You know I hate them
    well,
You know I'd sooner be a clapping bell
To some Kamchatkan missionary church,
Than with these horrid moods be left in
    lurch.
Do you get health — and Tom the same —
    I'll dance,
And from detested moods in new romance
Take refuge. Of bad lines a centaine dose
Is sure enough — and so 'here follows
    prose' . . .

'Over the hill and over the dale'

Over the hill and over the dale,
And over the bourn to Dawlish —
Where Gingerbread Wives have a scanty sale
And gingerbread nuts are smallish.

Rantipole Betty she ran down a hill
And kicked up her petticoats fairly.
Says I I'll be Jack if you will be Jill.
So she sat on the grass debonairly.

Here's somebody coming, here's somebody
   coming!
Says I, 'Tis the wind at a parley.
So without any fuss, any hawing and hum-
   ming,
She lay on the grass debonairly.

Here's somebody here, and here's somebody
   there!
Says I, Hold your tongue, you young gipsy.
So she held her tongue and lay plump and
   fair,
And dead as a Venus tipsy.

O who wouldn't hie to Dawlish fair,
O who wouldn't stop in a meadow?
O who would not rumple the daisies there,
And make the wild fern for a bed do?

To J. R.

O that a week could be an age, and we
   Felt parting and warm meeting every week,
Then one poor year a thousand years would
   be,
   The flush of welcome ever on the cheek:
So could we live long life in little space,
   So time itself would be annihilate,

So a day's journey in oblivious haze
　　To serve our joys would lengthen and dilate.
O to arrive each Monday morn from Ind!
　　To land each Tuesday from the rich Levant!
In little time a host of joys to bind,
　　And keep our souls in one eternal pant!
This morn, my friend, and yester-evening
　　taught
Me how to harbour such a happy thought.

Fragment of an Ode to Maia

Mother of Hermes! and still youthful Maia!
　　　May I sing to thee
As thou wast hymned on the shores of Baiæ?
　　　Or may I woo thee
In earlier Sicilian? or thy smiles
Seek as they once were sought, in Grecian
　　isles,
By bards who died content on pleasant
　　sward,
　　Leaving great verse unto a little clan?
O, give me their old vigour, and unheard
　　Save of the quiet Primrose, and the span
　　　Of heaven and few ears,
Rounded by thee, my song should die away
　　　Content as theirs,
Rich in the simple worship of a day.

'Sweet, sweet is the greeting of eyes'

Sweet, sweet is the greeting of eyes,
And sweet is the voice in its greeting,

When adieus have grown old and goodbyes
Fade away where old Time is retreating.

Warm the nerve of a welcoming hand,
And earnest a kiss on the brow,
When we meet over sea and o'er land
Where furrows are new to the plough.

Acrostic

Give me your patience, sister, while I frame
Exact in capitals your golden name,
Or sue the fair Apollo, and he will
Rouse from his heavy slumber and instill
Great love in me for thee and Poesy.
Imagine not that greatest mastery
And kingdom over all the realms of verse
Nears more to Heaven in aught than when
    we nurse,
And surety give, to love and brotherhood.

Anthropophagi in Othello's mood,
Ulysses stormed, and his enchanted belt
Glow with the Muse, but they are never felt
Unbosomed so and so eternal made,
Such tender incense in their laurel shade,
To all the regent sisters of the Nine,
As this poor offering to you, sister mine.

Kind sister! ay, this third name says you are.
Enchanted has it been the Lord knows where.
And may it taste to you like good old wine,
Take you to real happiness and give

Sons, daughters and a home like honeyed
  hive.

On visiting the Tomb of Burns

The town, the churchyard, and the setting
  sun,
  The clouds, the trees, the rounded hills all
  seem
  Though beautiful, cold — strange — as in
  a dream
I dreamed long ago. Now new begun,
The short-lived, paly summer is but won
  From winter's ague for one hour's gleam;
  Though sapphire warm their stars do never
  beam;
All is cold beauty; pain is never done
For who has mind to relish, Minos-wise,
  The real of beauty, free from that dead hue
  Fickly imagination and sick pride
  Cast wan upon it! Burns! with honour due
  I have oft honoured thee. Great shadow,
  hide
Thy face, I sin against thy native skies.

A Song about Myself

I

There was a naughty boy,
  A naughty boy was he,
He would not stop at home,
  He could not quiet be —
  He took

438

In his knapsack
A book
Full of vowels
And a shirt
With some towels —
A slight cap
For night-cap —
A hair brush,
Comb ditto,
New stockings,
For old ones
Would split O!
This knapsack
Tight at's back
He rivetted close
And followed his nose
   To the North,
   To the North,
And followed his nose
   To the North.

II

There was a naughty boy
   And a naughty boy was he,
For nothing would he do
   But scribble poetry —
      He took
      An inkstand
      In his hand
      And a pen
      Big as ten
      In the other

And away
In a pother
He ran
To the mountains
And fountains
And ghostès
And postès
And witches
And ditches,
And wrote
In his coat
When the weather
Was cool —
Fear of gout —
And without
When the weather
Was warm.
Och, the charm
When we choose
To follow one's nose
To the North,
To the North,
To follow one's nose
To the North!

III

There was a naughty boy
  And a naughty boy was he,
He kept little fishes
  In washing tubs three
    In spite
    Of the might

Of the maid,
Nor afraid
Of his granny-good,
He often would
Hurly burly
Get up early
And go,
By hook or crook,
To the brook
And bring home
Miller's thumb,
Tittlebat
Not over fat,
Minnows small
As the stall
Of a glove,
Not above
The size
Of a nice
Little baby's
Little finger —
O he made
('Twas his trade)
Of fish a pretty kettle,
A kettle —
A kettle,
Of fish a pretty kettle;
A kettle!

IV

There was a naughty boy,
And a naughty boy was he,

He ran away to Scotland
  The people for to see —
    There he found
    That the ground
    Was as hard,
    That a yard
    Was as long,
    That a song
    Was as merry,
    That a cherry
    Was as red,
    That lead
    Was as weighty,
    That fourscore
    Was as eighty,
    That a door
    Was as wooden
    As in England —
So he stood in his shoes
  And he wondered,
    He wondered,
He stood in his
  Shoes and he wondered.

To Ailsa Rock

Hearken, thou craggy ocean pyramid!
  Give answer by thy voice, the sea-fowls'
    screams!
  When were thy shoulders mantled in huge
    streams?
When from the sun was thy broad forehead
  hid?

How long is't since the mighty power bid
　　Thee heave to airy sleep from fathom
　　　dreams?
　　Sleep in the lap of thunder or sunbeams,
Or when grey clouds are thy cold coverlid?
Thou answer'st not; for thou art dead asleep.
　　Thy life is but two dead eternities —
The last in air, the former in the deep,
　　First with the whales, last with the eagle-
　　　skies.
Drowned wast thou till an earthquake made
　　thee steep,
　　Another cannot wake thy giant size!

Meg Merrilies

Old Meg she was a gipsy;
　　And lived upon the moors:
Her bed it was the brown heath turf,
　　And her house was out of doors.

Her apples were swart blackberries,
　　Her currants pods o' broom;
Her wine was dew of the wild white rose
　　Her book a churchyard tomb.

Her brothers were the craggy hills,
　　Her sisters larchen trees;
Alone with her great family
　　She lived as she did please.

No breakfast had she many a morn,
　　No dinner many a noon,

And 'stead of supper she would stare
  Full hard against the moon.

But every morn of woodbine fresh
  She made her garlanding,
And every night the dark glen yew
  She wove, and she would sing.

And with her fingers old and brown
  She plaited mats o' rushes,
And gave them to the cottagers
  She met among the bushes.

Old Meg was brave as Margaret Queen,
  And tall as Amazon;
An old red blanket cloak she wore,
  A chip hat had she on.
God rest her aged bones somewhere;
  She died full long agone!

'Ah! ken ye what I met the day'

Ah! ken ye what I met the day
  Out oure the mountains,
A-coming down by craggis grey
  An mossie fountains?
Ah! goud-haired Marie yeve I pray
  Ane minute's guessing,
For that I met upon the way
  Is past expressing.
As I stood where a rocky brig
  A torrent crosses,
I spied upon a misty rig

A troup o' horses —
And as they trotted down the glen
  I sped to meet them
To see if I might know the men
  To stop and greet them.
First Willie on his sleek mare came
  At canting gallop —
His long hair rustled like a flame
  On board a shallop.
Then came his brother Rab and then
  Young Peggy's mither
And Peggy too — adown the glen
  They went togither.
I saw her wrappit in her hood
  Fra wind and raining —
Her cheek was flush wi' timid blood
  Twixt growth and waning.
She turn'd her dazèd head full oft
  For thence her brithers
Came riding with her bridegroom soft
  An mony ithers.
Young Tam came up an' eyed me quick
  With reddened cheek.
Braw Tam was daffèd like a chick —
  He could na speak.
Ah! Marie they are all gane hame
  Through blustering weather,
An' every heart is full on flame
  An' light as feather.
Ah! Marie they are all gone hame
  Fra happy wedding,

Whilst I — Ah! is it not a shame? —
  Sad tears am shedding.

'All gentle folks who owe a grudge'

All gentle folks who owe a grudge
  To any living thing,
Open your ears and stay your trudge
  Whilst I in dudgeon sing.

The gad-fly he hath stung me sore —
  O may he ne'er sting you!
But we have many a horrid bore
  He may sting black and blue.

Has any here an old grey mare
  With three legs all her store?
O put it to her buttocks bare
  And straight she'll run on four.

Has any here a lawyer suit
  Of 1743?
Take lawyer's nose and put it to 't
  And you the end will see.

Is there a man in Parliament
  Dumbfoundered in his speech?
O let his neighbour make a rent
  And put one in his breech.

O Lowther, how much better thou
  Hadst figured t'other day,

When to the folks thou mad'st a bow
  And hadst no more to say,

If lucky gad-fly had but ta'en
  His seat upon thine arse,
And put thee to a little pain
  To save thee from a worse.

Better than Southey it had been,
  Better than Mr D — ,
Better than Wordsworth too, I ween,
  Better than Mr V — .

Forgive me pray, good people all,
  For deviating so.
In spirit sure I had a call —
  And now I on will go.

Has any here a daughter fair
  Too fond of reading novels,
Too apt to fall in love with care
  And charming Mister Lovels?

O put a gad-fly to that thing
  She keeps so white and pert —
I mean the finger for the ring,
  And it will breed a Wert.

Has any here a pious spouse
  Who seven times a day
Scolds as King David prayed, to chouse
  And have her holy way?

O let a gad-fly's little sting
   Persuade her sacred tongue
That noises are a common thing,
   But that her bell has rung.

And as this is the *summum bo-*
   num of all conquering,
I leave withouten wordès mo
   The gad-fly's little sting.

'Of late two dainties were before me plac'd'

Of late two dainties were before me plac'd
   Sweet, holy, pure, sacred and innocent,
   From the ninth sphere to me benignly sent
That Gods might know my own particular
   taste:
First the soft Bag-pipe mourn'd with zealous
   haste,
   The Stranger next with head on bosom
   bent
   Sigh'd; rueful again the piteous Bag-pipe
   went,
Again the Stranger sighings fresh did waste.
O Bag-pipe thou didst steal my heart
   away —
   O Stranger thou my nerves from Pipe didst
   charm —
O Bagpipe thou didst re-assert thy sway —
   Again thou Stranger gav'st me fresh
   alarm —
Alas! I could not choose. Ah! my poor heart.

Mumchance art thou with both oblig'd to
  part.

*Sonnet written in the Cottage where Burns was
  born*

This mortal body of a thousand days
Now fills, O Burns, a space in thine own
  room,
Where thou didst dream alone on budded
  bays,
Happy and thoughtless of thy day of doom!
My pulse is warm with thine own Barley-
  bree,
My head is light with pledging a great soul,
My eyes are wandering, and I cannot see,
Fancy is dead, and drunken at its goal;
Yet can I stamp my foot upon thy floor,
Yet can I ope thy window-sash to find
The meadow thou hast trampèd o'er and
  o'er, —
Yet can I think of thee till thought is
  blind, —
Yet can I gulp a bumper to thy name, —
O smile among the shades, for this is fame!

*Lines written in the Highlands after visiting the
  Burns Country*

There is a charm in footing slow across a
  silent plain,
Where patriot battle has been fought, where
  glory had the gain;
There is a pleasure on the heath, where
449

Druids old have been,
Where mantles grey have rustled by, and
 swept the nettled green;
There is a joy in every spot made known in
 times of old,
New to the feet although each tale a hundred
 times be told;
There is a deeper joy than all, more solemn
 in the heart,
More parching to the tongue than all, of
 more divine a smart,
When weary steps forget themselves upon a
 pleasant turf,
Upon hot sand, or flinty road, or sea-shore
 iron scurf,
Toward the castle or the cot, where long ago
 was born
One who was great through mortal days, and
 died of fame unshorn.

Light heather-bells may tremble then, but
 they are far away;
Wood-lark may sing from sandy fern, — the
 Sun may hear his lay;
Runnels may kiss the grass on shelves and
 shallows clear, —
But their low voices are not heard, tho'; come
 on travels drear;
Blood-red the sun may set behind black
 mountain peaks,
Blue tides may sluice and drench their time
 in caves and weedy creeks,

Eagles may seem to sleep wing-wide upon
the air,
Ring-doves may fly convulsed across to some
high cedared lair, —
But the forgotten eye is still fast lidded to the
ground,
As Palmer's that with weariness mid-desert
shrine hath found.

At such a time the soul's a child, in childhood is the brain,
Forgotten is the worldly heart, — alone, it
beats in vain.
Ay, if a madman could have leave to pass a
healthful day,
To tell his forehead's swoon and faint, when
first began decay,
He might make tremble many a one, whose
spirit had gone forth
To find a Bard's low cradle-place about the
silent north!
Scanty the hour, and few the steps, beyond
the bourn of care,
Beyond the sweet and bitter world, — beyond
it unaware!
Scanty the hour, and few the steps, —
because a longer stay
Would bar return and make a man forget his
mortal way:
O horrible! to lose the sight of well-
remember'd face,
Of Brother's eyes, of Sister's brow, — con-

stant to every place,
Filling the air as on we move with portraiture
intense,
More warm than those heroic tints that pain
a painter's sense,
When shapes of old come striding by, and
visages of old,
Locks shining black, hair scanty grey, and
passions manifold.

No, no, — that horror cannot be! for at the
cable's length
Man feels the gentle anchor pull, and gladdens in its strength:
One hour, half idiot, he stands by mossy
waterfall,
But in the very next he reads his soul's
memorial;
He reads it on the mountain's height, where
chance he may sit down,
Upon rough marble diadem, that hill's
eternal crown.
Yet be his anchor e'er so fast, room is there
for a prayer,
That man may never lose his mind in mountains black and bare;
That he may stray, league after league, some
great birthplace to find,
And keep his vision clear from speck, his
inward sight unblind.

Staffa

Not Aladdin magian
Ever such a work began;
Not the wizard of the Dee
Ever such a dream could see;
Not St. John, in Patmos' Isle,
In the passion of his toil,
When he saw the churches seven,
Golden-aisled, built up in heaven,
Gazed at such a rugged wonder,
As I stood its roofing under.
Lo! I saw one sleeping there,
On the marble cold and bare;
While the surges wash'd his feet,
And his garments white did beat
Drench'd about the sombre rocks;
On his neck his well-grown locks,
Lifted dry above the main,
Were upon the curl again.
'What is this? and what art thou?'
Whisper'd I, and touch'd his brow;
'What art thou? and what is this?'
Whisper'd I, and strove to kiss
The spirit's hand, to wake his eyes;
Up he started in a trice:
'I am Lycidas,' said he,
'Fam'd in funeral minstrelsy!
This was architectured thus
By the great Oceanus! —
Here his mighty waters play
Hollow organs all the day;

Here, by turns, his dolphins all,
Finny palmers, great and small,
Come to pay devotion due, —
Each a mouth of pearls must strew!
Many a mortal of these days,
Dares to pass our sacred ways;
Dares to touch, audaciously,
This cathedral of the sea!
I have been the pontiff-priest,
Where the waters never rest,
Where a fledgy sea-bird choir
Soars for ever; holy fire
I have hid from mortal man;
Proteus is my Sacristan!
But the dullèd eye of mortal
Hath pass'd beyond the rocky portal:
So for ever will I leave
Such a taint, and soon unweave
All the magic of the place.'
So saying, with a Spirit's glance
He dived!

'Read me a lesson, Muse, and speak it loud'

Read me a lesson, Muse, and speak it loud
  Upon the top of Nevis, blind in mist!
I look into the chasms, and a shroud
  Vapourous doth hide them; just so much I
    wist
Mankind do know of Hell. I look o'erhead,
  And there is sullen mist; even so much
Mankind can tell of Heaven. Mist is spread
  Before the earth, beneath me — even such,

Even so vague is man's sight of himself.
  Here are the craggy stones beneath my
    feet —
Thus much I know, that, a poor witless elf,
  I tread on them, that all my eye doth meet
Is mist and crag, not only on this height,
  But in the world of thought and mental
    might.

Ben Nevis: a Dialogue

Mrs. C.

Upon my life Sir Nevis I am piqued
That I have so far panted tugg'd and reek'd
To do an honour to your old bald pate
And now am sitting on you just to bait,
Without your paying me one compliment.
Alas 'tis so with all, when our intent
Is plain, and in the eye of all Mankind
We fair ones show a preference, too blind,
You Gentle men immediately turn tail —
O let me then my hapless fate bewail!
Ungrateful Baldpate have I not disdain'd
The pleasant Valleys — have I not
    madbrain'd
Deserted all my Pickles and preserves.
My China closet too — with wretched Nerves
To boot — say wretched ingrate have I not
Le[f]t my soft cushion chair and caudle pot?
'Tis true I had no corns — no! thank the
    fates,
My Shoemaker was always Mr. Bates.

And if not Mr. Bates why I'm not old!
Still dumb, ungrateful Nevis — still so cold!

Here the Lady took some more wiskey and was
putting even more to her lips when she dashed
[it] to the Ground for the Mountain began to
grumble — which continued for a few minutes
before he thus began:

BEN NEVIS

What whining bit of tongue and Mouth thus
    dares
Disturb my slumber of a thousand years?
Even so long my sleep has been secure —
And to be so awaked I'll not endure.
Oh pain — for since the Eagle's earliest
    scream
I've had a dam[n]'d confounded ugly dream,
A Nightmare sure. What Madam was it you?
It cannot be! My old eyes are not true!
Red-Crag, my Spectacles! Now let me see!
Good Heavens Lady, how the gemini
Did you get here? O I shall split my sides!
I shall earthquake —

MRS. C.

Sweet Nevis, do not quake, for though I love
You[r] honest Countenance all things above,
Truly I should not like to be convey'd
So far into your Bosom — gentle Maid
Loves not too rough a treatment gentle
    Sir —

Pray thee be calm and do not quake nor stir
No not a Stone or I shall go in fits —

BEN NEVIS

I must — I shall — I meet not such tit
   bits —
I meet not such sweet creatures every day —
By my old night cap night cap night and day,
I must have one sweet Buss — I must and
   shall!
Red-Crag! — What Madam can you then
   repent
Of all the toil and vigour you have spent
To see Ben Nevis and to touch his nose?
Red-Crag, I say! O I must have them close!
Red-Crag, there lies beneath my farthest toe
A vein of Sulphur — go dear Red-Crag,
   go —
And rub your flinty back against it — budge!
Dear Madam I must kiss you faith I must!
I must Embrace you with my dearest gust!
Block-head, d'ye hear — Block-head I'll
   make her feel
There lies beneath my east leg's northern
   heel
A cave of young earth dragons — well my
   boy
Go thither quick and so complete my joy;
Take you a bundle of the largest pines
And when the sun on fiercest Phosphor
   shines

Fire them and ram them in the Dragon's
   nest,
Then will the dragons fry and fizz their best
Until ten thousand now no bigger than
Poor Al[l]igators — poor things of one
   span —
Will each one swell to twice ten times the
   size
Of northern whale — then for the tender
   prize —
The moment then — for then will Red-Crag
   rub
His flinty back — and I shall kiss and snub
And press my dainty morsel to my breast.
Block-head make haste!
                    O Muses weep the rest —
The Lady fainted and he thought her dead
So pulled the clouds again about his head
And went to sleep again — soon she was
   rous'd
By her affrighted servants — next day hous'd
Safe on the lowly ground she bless'd her fate
That fainting fit was not delayed too late.

Song

I

Spirit here that reignest!
Spirit here that painest!
Spirit here that burnest!
Spirit here that mournest!
   Spirit, I bow

My forehead low,
Enshaded with thy pinions.
   Spirit, I look
   All passion-struck
Into thy pale dominions.

II

Spirit here that laughest!
Spirit here that quaffest!
Spirit here that dancest!
Noble soul that prancest!
   Spirit, with thee
   I join in the glee
A-nudging the elbow of Momus.
   Spirit, I flush
   With a Bacchanal blush
Just fresh from the Banquet of Comus.

To his Brother George in America

'Tis the witching time of night,
Orbèd is the moon and bright,
And the stars they glisten, glisten,
Seeming with bright eyes to listen —
   For what listen they?
For a song and for a charm.
See they glisten in alarm,
And the moon is waxing warm
   To hear what I shall say.
Moon! keep wide thy golden ears —
Hearken, stars! and hearken, spheres! —
Hearken, thou eternal sky!
I sing an Infant's lullaby,

A pretty lullaby.
Listen, listen, listen, listen,
Glisten, glisten, glisten, glisten,
    And hear my lullaby!
Though the rushes that will make
Its cradle still are in the lake —
Though the linen that will be
Its swathe, is on the cotton tree —
Though the woollen that will keep
It warm, is on the silly sheep —
Listen, starlight, listen, listen,
Glisten, glisten, glisten, glisten,
    And hear my lullaby:
Child, I see thee! Child, I've found thee
Midst of the quiet all around thee!
Child, I see thee! Child, I spy thee!
And thy mother sweet is nigh thee!
Child, I know thee! Child no more,
But a Poet evermore!
See, see, the lyre, the lyre,
In a flame of fire,
Upon the little cradle's top
Flaring, flaring, flaring,
Past the eyesight's bearing.
Awake it from its sleep,
And see if it can keep
Its eyes upon the blaze —
    Amaze, amaze!
It stares, it stares, it stares,
It dares what no one dares!
It lifts its little hand into the flame
Unharm'd, and on the strings

Paddles a little tune, and sings,
With dumb endeavour sweetly —
Bard art thou completely!
  Little child
  O' th' western wild,
Bard art thou completely!
Sweetly with dumb endeavour
A Poet now or never,
  Little child
  O' th' western wild,
A Poet now or never!

'Where's the Poet?'

Where's the Poet? show him, show him,
Muses nine, that I may know him!
'Tis the man who with a man
Is an equal, be he King,
Or poorest of the beggar-clan,
Or any other wondrous thing
A man may be 'twixt ape and Plato;
'Tis the man who with a bird,
Wren or Eagle, finds his way to
All its instincts; he hath heard
The Lion's roaring, and can tell
What his horny throat expresseth,
And to him the Tiger's yell
Comes articulate and presseth
On his ear like mother-tongue.

Modern Love

And what is love? It is a doll dress'd up
For idleness to cosset, nurse, and dandle;

461

A thing of soft misnomers, so divine
That silly youth doth think to make itself
Divine by loving, and so goes on
Yawning and doting a whole summer long,
Till Miss's comb is made a pearl tiara,
And common Wellingtons turn Romeo boots;
Then Cleopatra lives at number seven,
And Antony resides in Brunswick Square.
Fools! if some passions high have warm'd
    the world,
If Queens and Soldiers have play'd deep for
    hearts,
It is no reason why such agonies
Should be more common than the growth of
    weeds.
Fools! make me whole again that weighty
    pearl
The Queen of Egypt melted, and I'll say
That ye may love in spite of beaver hats.

The Castle Builder
Fragments of a Dialogue

CASTLE BUILDER

. . . In short, convince you that however wise
You may have grown from Convent libraries,
I have, by many yards at least, been carding
A longer skein of wit in Convent garden.

BERNADINE

A very Eden that same place must be!

Pray what demesne? Whose Lordship's
    legacy?
What, have you convents in that Gothic Isle?
Pray pardon me, I cannot help but smile.

CASTLE BUILDER

Sir, Convent Garden is a monstrous beast.
From morning, four o'clock, to twelve at
    noon,
It swallows cabbages without a spoon,
And then, from twelve till two, this Eden
    made is
A promenade for cooks and ancient ladies;
And then for supper, 'stead of soup and
    poaches,
It swallows chairmen, damns, and Hackney
    coaches.
In short, Sir, 'tis a very place for monks,
For it containeth twenty thousand punks,
Which any man may number for his sport,
By following fat elbows up a court.

In suchlike nonsense would I pass an hour
With random Friar, or Rake upon his tour,
Or one or few of that imperial host
Who came unmaimèd from the Russian frost.

To-night I'll have my friar — let me think
About my room, — I'll have it in the pink;
It should be rich and sombre, and the moon,
Just in its mid-life in the midst of June,

Should look thro' four large windows and
  display
Clear, but for gold-fish vases in the way,
Their glassy diamonding on Turkish floor;
The tapers keep aside, an hour or more,
To see what else the moon alone can show;
While the night-breeze doth softly let us
  know
My terrace is well-bower'd with oranges.
Upon the floor the dullest spirit sees
A guitar-ribband and a lady's glove
Beside a crumple-leavèd tale of love;
A tambour-frame, with Venus sleeping there,
All finish'd but some ringlets of her hair;
A viol-bow, strings torn, cross-wise upon
A glorious folio of Anacreon;
A skull upon a mat of roses lying,
Ink'd purple with a song concerning dying;
An hour-glass on the turn, amid the trails
Of passion-flower; — just in time there sails
A cloud across the moon, — the lights bring
  in,
And see what more my phantasy can win.
It is a gorgeous room, but somewhat sad;
The draperies are so, as tho'; they had
Been made for Cleopatra's winding-sheet:
And opposite the stedfast eye doth meet
A spacious looking-glass, upon whose face,
In letters raven-sombre, you may trace
Old 'Mene, Mene, Tekel, Upharsin.'
Greek busts and statuary have ever been
Held, by the finest spirits, fitter far

Than vase grotesque and Siamesian jar;
Therefore 'tis sure a want of Attic taste
That I should rather love a Gothic waste
Of eyesight on cinque-coloured potter's clay,
Than on the marble fairness of old Greece.
My table-coverlets of Jason's fleece
And black Numidian sheep-wool should be
   wrought,
Gold, black, and heavy, from the Lama
   brought.
My ebon sofas should delicious be
With down from Leda's cygnet progeny.
My pictures all Salvator's, save a few
Of Titian's portraiture, and one, though new,
Of Haydon's in its fresh magnificence.
My wine — O good! 'tis here at my desire,
And I must sit to supper with my friar.

'Welcome Joy, and Welcome Sorrow'

                'Under the flag
Of each his faction, they to battle bring
Their embryo atoms.'
                    — MILTON.

Welcome joy, and welcome sorrow,
  Lethe's weed and Hermes' feather;
Come to-day and come to-morrow,
  I do love you both together!
  I love to mark sad faces in fair weather;
And hear a merry laugh amid the thunder;
  Fair and foul I love together:

Meadows sweet where flames are under,
And a giggle at a wonder;
Visage sage at pantomime;
Funeral, and steeple-chime;
Infant playing with a skull;
Morning fair, and shipwreck'd hull;
Nightshade with the woodbine kissing;
Serpents in red roses hissing;
Cleopatra regal-dress'd
With the aspic at her breast;
Dancing music, music sad,
Both together, sane and mad;
Muses bright and muses pale;
Sombre Saturn, Momus hale; —
Laugh and sigh, and laugh again;
Oh! the sweetness of the pain!
Muses bright and muses pale,
Bare your faces of the veil;
Let me see; and let me write
Of the day and of the night —
Both together: — let me slake
All my thirst for sweet heart-ache;
Let my bower be of yew,
Interwreath'd with myrtles new;
Pines and lime-trees full in bloom
And my couch a low grass-tomb.

'Hush, hush! Tread softly! hush, hush, my dear!'

Hush, hush! Tread softly! hush, hush, my
dear!
All the house is asleep, but we know very
well

466

That the jealous, the jealous old bald-pate
    may hear,
      Tho' you've padded his nightcap — O
      sweet Isabel!
        Tho' your feet are more light than a
        Faery's feet,
        Who dances on bubbles where brooklets
        meet, —
Hush, hush! soft tiptoe! hush, hush, my dear!
For less than a nothing the jealous can hear.

No leaf doth tremble, no ripple is there
    On the river, — all's still, and the night's
    sleepy eye
Closes up, and forgets all its Lethean care,
    Charm'd to death by the drone of the hum-
    ming May-fly;
      And the moon, whether prudish or com-
      plaisant,
      Has fled to her bower, well knowing I
      want
No light in the dusk, no torch in the gloom,
But my Isabel's eyes and her lips pulp'd with
    bloom.

Lift the latch! ah gently! ah tenderly — sweet!
    We are dead if that latchet gives one little
    clink.
Well done! — now those lips, and a flowery
    seat —
    The old man may sleep, and the planets
    may wink;

The shut rose shall dream of our loves
and awake
Full-blown, and such warmth for the
morning take,
The stock-dove shall hatch his soft brace and
shall coo,
While I kiss to the melody, aching all
through!

The Dove

I had a dove, and the sweet dove died;
    And I have thought it died of grieving;
O, what could it grieve for? its feet were tied
    With a silken thread of my own hand's
    weaving;

Sweet little red feet, why should you die?
Why should you leave me, sweet bird, why?
You lived alone in the forest tree,
Why, pretty thing! would you not live with
    me?
I kissed you oft and gave you white peas;
Why not live sweetly, as in the green trees?

Extracts from an Opera

I

O! were I one of the Olympian twelve,
Their godships should pass this into a law —
That when a man doth set himself in toil
After some beauty veilèd far away,

Each step he took should make his lady's
    hand
More soft, more white, and her fair cheek
    more fair;
And for each briar-berry he might eat,
A kiss should bud upon the tree of love,
And pulp and ripen richer every hour,
To melt away upon the traveller's lips.

II DAISY'S SONG

1

The sun, with his great eye,
Sees not so much as I;
And the moon, all silver-proud,
Might as well be in a cloud.

2

And O the spring — the spring!
I lead the life of a king!
Couched in the teeming grass,
I spy each pretty lass.

3

I look where no one dares,
And I stare where no one stares,
And when the night is nigh,
Lambs bleat my lullaby.

When wedding fiddles are a-playing,
    Huzza for folly O!
And when maidens go a-maying,
    Huzza, etc.
When a milk-pail is upset,
    Huzza, etc.
And the clothes left in the wet,
    Huzza, etc.

When the barrel's set abroach,
    Huzza, etc.
When Kate Eyebrow keeps a coach,
    Huzza, etc.
When the pig is over-roasted,
    Huzza, etc.
And the cheese is over-toasted,
    Huzza, etc.
When Sir Snap is with his lawyer,
    Huzza, etc.
And Miss Chip has kissed the sawyer,
    Huzza, etc.

IV

O, I am frightened with most hateful
  thoughts!
Perhaps her voice is not a nightingale's,
Perhaps her teeth are not the fairest pearl;
Her eye-lashes may be, for aught I know,
Not longer than the may-fly's small fan-
  horns;

There may not be one dimple on her
    hand —
And freckles many. Ah! a careless nurse,
In haste to teach the little thing to walk,
May have crumped up a pair of Dian's legs
And warped the ivory of a Juno's neck.

V SONG

1

The stranger lighted from his steed,
    And ere he spake a word,
He seized my lady's lily hand,
    And kissed it all unheard.

2

The stranger walked into the hall,
    And ere he spake a word,
He kissed my lady's cherry lips,
    And kissed 'em all unheard.

3

The stranger walked into the bower —
    But my lady first did go:
Ay, hand in hand into the bower,
    Where my lord's roses blow.

4

My lady's maid had a silken scarf,
    And a golden ring had she,

And a kiss from the stranger, as off he went
  Again on his fair palfrey.

The Eve of Saint Mark

Upon a Sabbath-day it fell;
Twice holy was the Sabbath-bell,
That call'd the folk to evening prayer;
The city streets were clean and fair
From wholesome drench of April rains;
And, on the western window panes,
The chilly sunset faintly told
Of unmatured green valleys cold,
Of the green thorny bloomless hedge,
Of rivers new with spring-tide sedge,
Of primroses by shelter'd rills,
And daisies on the aguish hills.
Twice holy was the Sabbath-bell:
The silent streets were crowded well
With staid and pious companies,
Warm from their fire-side orat'ries;
And moving, with demurest air,
To even-song, and vesper prayer,
Each archèd porch, and entry low,
Was fill'd with patient folk and slow,
With whispers hush, and shuffling feet,
While play'd the organ loud and sweet.

The bells had ceased, the prayers begun,
And Bertha had not yet half done
A curious volume, patch'd and torn,
That all day long, from earliest morn,
Had taken captive her two eyes,

472

Among its golden broideries;
Perplex'd her with a thousand things, —
The stars of heaven, and angels' wings,
Martyrs in a fiery blaze,
Azure saints in silver rays,
Moses' breastplate, and the seven
Candlesticks John saw in heaven,
The wingèd Lion of Saint Mark,
And the Covenantal Ark,
With its many mysteries
Cherubim and golden mice.

Bertha was a maiden fair,
Dwelling in th' old Minster-square;
From her fire-side she could see,
Sidelong, its rich antiquity,
Far as the Bishop's garden-wall;
Where sycamores and elm-trees tall,
Full-leaved, the forest had outstript,
By no sharp north-wind ever nipt,
So shelter'd by the mighty pile.
Bertha arose, and read awhile,
With forehead 'gainst the window-pane.
Again she tried, and then again,
Until the dusk eve left her dark
Upon the legend of St. Mark.
From plaited lawn-frill, fine and thin,
She lifted up her soft warm chin,
With aching neck and swimming eyes,
And dazed with saintly imageries.

All was gloom, and silent all,

Save now and then the still foot-fall
Of one returning homewards late,
Past the echoing minster-gate.
The clamorous daws, that all the day
Above tree-tops and towers play,
Pair by pair had gone to rest,
Each in its ancient belfry-nest,
Where asleep they fall betimes,
To music and the drowsy chimes.

All was silent, all was gloom,
Abroad and in the homely room:
Down she sat, poor cheated soul!
And struck a lamp from the dismal coal;
Lean'd forward, with bright drooping hair
And slant book, full against the glare.
Her shadow, in uneasy guise,
Hover'd about, a giant size,
On ceiling-beam and old oak chair,
The parrot's cage, and panel square;
And the warm angled winter screen,
On which were many monsters seen,
Call'd doves of Siam, Lima mice,
And legless birds of Paradise,
Macaw, and tender Avadavat,
And silken-furr'd Angora cat.
Untired she read, her shadow still
Glower'd about, as it would fill
The room with wildest forms and shades,
As though some ghostly queen of spades
Had come to mock behind her back,
And dance, and ruffle her garments black.

Untired she read the legend page,
Of holy Mark, from youth to age,
On land, on sea, in pagan chains,
Rejoicing for his many pains.
Sometimes the learned eremite,
With golden star, or dagger bright,
Referr'd to pious poesies
Written in smallest crow-quill size
Beneath the text; and thus the rhyme
Was parcell'd out from time to time:
— 'Als writith he of swevenis,
Men han beforne they wake in bliss,
Whanne that hir friendes thinke hem bound
In crimpèd shroude farre under grounde;
And how a litling child mote be
A saint er its nativitie,
Gif that the modre (God her blesse!)
Kepen in solitarinesse,
And kissen devoute the holy croce.
Of Goddes love, and Sathan's force, —
He writith; and thinges many mo:
Of swiche thinges I may not shew.
Bot I must tellen verilie
Somdel of Sainte Cicilie,
And chieflie what he auctorethe
Of Sainte Markis life and dethe':

At length her constant eyelids come
Upon the fervent martyrdom;
Then lastly to his holy shrine,
Exalt amid the tapers' shine
At Venice, —

To Sleep

O soft embalmer of the still midnight!
  Shutting, with careful fingers and benign,
Our gloom-pleased eyes, embower'd from
    the light,
  Enshaded in forgetfulness divine;
O soothest Sleep! if so it please thee, close,
  In midst of this thine hymn, my willing
    eyes,
Or wait the amen, ere thy poppy throws
  Around my bed its lulling charities;
  Then save me, or the passèd day will shine
Upon my pillow, breeding many woes;
  Save me from curious conscience, that still
    lords
Its strength in darkness, burrowing like a
    mole;
  Turn the key deftly in the oilèd wards,
And seal the hushèd casket of my soul.

'Why did I laugh to-night?'

Why did I laugh to-night? No voice will tell:
  No God, no Demon of severe response,
Deigns to reply from Heaven or from Hell.
  Then to my human heart I turn at once.
Heart! Thou and I are here, sad and alone;
  Say, wherefore did I laugh? O mortal pain!
O Darkness! Darkness! ever must I moan,
  To question Heaven and Hell and Heart in
    vain.
Why did I laugh? I know this Being's lease,

My fancy to its utmost blisses spreads;
Yet would I on this very midnight cease,
    And the world's gaudy ensigns see in
    shreds;
Verse, Fame, and Beauty are intense indeed,
But Death intenser — Death is Life's high
    meed.

On a Dream after reading of Paolo and Francesca in Dante's 'Inferno'

As Hermes once took to his feathers light,
    When lullèd Argus, baffled, swoon'd and
    slept,
So on a Delphic reed, my idle spright,
    So play'd, so charm'd, so conquer'd, so
    bereft
The dragon-world of all its hundred eyes,
    And seeing it asleep, so fled away,
Not to pure Ida with its snow-cold skies,
    Nor unto Tempe, where Jove grieved a day;
But to that second circle of sad Hell,
    Where in the gust, the whirlwind, and the
    flaw
Of rain and hail-stones, lovers need not tell
    Their sorrows, — pale were the sweet lips I
    saw,
Pale were the lips I kiss'd, and fair the form
I floated with, about that melancholy storm.

'The House of Mourning written by Mr. Scott'

The House of Mourning written by Mr.
    Scott,

A sermon at the Magdalen, a tear
Dropped on a greasy novel, want of cheer
  After a walk uphill to a friend's cot,
Tea with a maiden lady, a cursed lot
  Of worthy poems with the author near,
  A patron lord, a drunkenness from beer,
Haydon's great picture, a cold coffee pot
At midnight when the Muse is ripe for la-
    bour,
  The voice of Mr. Coleridge, a French bon-
    net
Before you in the pit, a pipe and tabour,
A damned inseparable flute and
    neighbour —
  All these are vile, but viler Wordsworth's
    sonnet
On Dover. Dover! — who *could* write upon
    it?

'Fame, like a wayward girl'

Fame, like a wayward girl, will still be coy
  To those who woo her with too slavish
    knees,
But makes surrender to some thoughtless
    boy,
  And dotes the more upon a heart at ease;
She is a Gipsy will not speak to those
  Who have not learnt to be content without
    her;
A Jilt, whose ear was never whisper'd close,
  Who thinks they scandal her who talk
    about her;

A very Gipsy is she, Nilus-born,
  Sister-in-law to jealous Potiphar;
Ye love-sick Bards! repay her scorn for scorn;
  Ye Artists lovelorn! madmen that ye are!
Make your best bow to her and bid adieu,
Then, if she likes it, she will follow you.

Song of Four Fairies

Fire, Air, Earth, and Water, Salamander,
  Zephyr, Dusketha, and Breama.

Sal. Happy, happy, glowing fire!
Zeph. Fragrant air! delicious light!
Dus. Let me to my glooms retire!
Bre. I to green-weed rivers bright!
Sal. Happy, happy glowing fire!
Dazzling bowers of soft retire,
Ever let my nourish'd wing,
Like a bat's, still wandering,
Faintless fan your fiery spaces,
Spirit sole in deadly places.
In unhaunted roar and blaze,
Open eyes that never daze,
Let me see the myriad shapes
Of men, and beasts, and fish, and apes,
Portray'd in many a fiery den,
And wrought by spumy bitumen
On the deep intenser roof,
Archèd every way aloof.
Let me breathe upon their skies,
And anger their live tapestries;

Free from cold, and every care
Of chilly rain and shivering air.
    Zeph. Spirit of Fire! away! away!
Or your very roundelay
Will sear my plumage newly budded
From its quillèd sheath, all studded
With the self-same dews that fell
On the May-grown Asphodel.
Spirit of Fire — away! away!
    Bre. Spirit of Fire — away! away!
Zephyr, blue-eyed fairy, turn,
And see my cool sedge-buried urn,
Where it rests its mossy brim
'Mid water-mint and cresses dim;
And the flowers, in sweet troubles,
Lift their eyes above the bubbles,
Like our Queen, when she would please
To sleep and Oberon *will* tease —
Love me, blue-eyed Fairy! true.
Soothly I am sick for you.
    Zeph. Gentle Breama! by the first
Violet young nature nurst,
I will bathe myself with thee,
So you sometimes follow me
To my home, far, far in west,
Beyond the nimble-wheelèd quest
Of the golden-browèd sun.
Come with me, o'er tops of trees,
To my fragrant palaces,
Where they ever floating are
Beneath the cherish of a star

Call'd Vesper, who with silver veil
Ever hides his brilliance pale,
Ever gently-drowsed doth keep
Twilight for the Fayes to sleep.
Fear not that your watery hair
Will thirst in drouthy ringlets there;
Clouds of storèd summer rains
Thou shalt taste, before the stains
Of the mountain soil they take,
And too unlucent for thee make.
I love thee, crystal Fairy, true!
Sooth I am as sick for you!

   Sal. Out, ye aguish Fairies, out!
Chilly lovers, what a rout
Keep ye with your frozen breath,
Colder than the mortal death!
Adder-eyed Dusketha, speak!
Shall we leave these, and go seek
In the earth's wide entrails old
Couches warm as theirs are cold?
O for a fiery gloom and thee,
Dusketha, so enchantingly
Freckle-wing'd and lizard-sided!

   Dus. By thee, Sprite, will I be guided!
I care not for cold or heat:
Frost and flame, or sparks, or sleet,
To my essence are the same; —
But I honour more the flame.
Sprite of Fire, I follow thee
Wheresoever it may be, —
To the torrid spouts and fountains,

Underneath earth-quakèd mountains;
Or, at thy supreme desire,
Touch the very pulse of fire
With my bare unlidded eyes.
  Sal. Sweet Dusketha! paradise!
Off, ye icy Spirits, fly!
Frosty creatures of the sky.
  Dus. Breathe upon them, fiery sprite!

Zeph.}
       Away! away to our delight!
  Bre.}

  Sal. Go, feed on icicles, while we
Bedded in tongue-flames will be.
  Dus. Lead me to those feverous glooms,
Sprite of Fire!
  Bre.   Me to the blooms,
Blue-eyed Zephyr, of those flowers
Far in the west where the May-cloud lowers;
And the beams of still Vesper, when winds
       are all wist,
Are shed through the rain and the milder
  mist,
And twilight your floating bowers.

La Belle Dame sans Mercy
[*Indicator* Version]

Ah, what can ail thee, wretched wight,
  Alone and palely loitering;
The sedge is wither'd from the lake,
   And no birds sing.

Ah, what can ail thee, wretched wight,
  So haggard and so woe-begone?
The squirrel's granary is full,
   And the harvest's done.

I see a lily on thy brow,
  With anguish moist and fever dew;
And on thy cheek a fading rose
   Fast withereth too.

I met a Lady in the meads
  Full beautiful, a fairy's child;
Her hair was long, her foot was light,
   And her eyes were wild.

I set her on my pacing steed,
  And nothing else saw all day long;
For sideways would she lean, and sing
   A fairy's song.

I made a garland for her head,
  And bracelets too, and fragrant zone:
She look'd at me as she did love,
   And made sweet moan.

She found me roots of relish sweet,
  And honey wild, and manna dew;
And sure in language strange she said,
  I love thee true.

She took me to her elfin grot,
  And there she gaz'd and sighed deep,
And there I shut her wild sad eyes —
  So kiss'd to sleep.

And there we slumber'd on the moss,
  And there I dream'd, ah woe betide,
The latest dream I ever dream'd
  On the cold hill side.

I saw pale kings, and princes too,
  Pale warriors, death-pale were they all;
Who cried, 'La belle Dame sans mercy
  Hath thee in thrall!'

I saw their starv'd lips in the gloom
  With horrid warning gaped wide,
And I awoke, and found me here
  On the cold hill side.

And this is why I sojourn here
  Alone and palely loitering,
Though the sedge is wither'd from the lake,
  And no birds sing.

                                        CAVIARE

La belle dame sans merci

O what can ail thee knight at arms,
  Alone and palely loitering?
The sedge has withered from the lake
  And no birds sing!

O what can ail thee knight at arms,
  So haggard and so woe begone?
The squirrel's granary is full
  And the harvest's done.

I see a lilly on thy brow
  With anguish moist and fever dew,
And on thy cheeks a fading rose
  Fast Withereth too —

I met a Lady in the Meads
  Full beautiful, a faery's child;
Her hair was long, her foot was light
  And her eyes were wild —

I made a Garland for her head,
  And bracelets too, and fragrant Zone
She look'd at me as she did love
  And made sweet moan —

I set her on my pacing steed
  And nothing else saw all day long,
For sidelong would she bend, and sing
  A faery's song —

She found me roots of relish sweet
  And honey wild and manna dew,
And sure in language strange she said
  I love thee true —

She took me to her elfin grot
  And there she wept and sigh'd full sore,
And there I shut her wild wild eyes
  With kisses four.

And there she lulled me asleep
  And there I dream'd — Ah! Woe betide!
The latest dream I ever dreamt
  On the cold hill side.

I saw pale kings and Princes too,
  Pale warriors, death pale were they all;
They cried 'La belle dame sans merci
  Thee hath in thrall.'

I saw their starv'd lips in the gloam
  With horrid warning gaped wide,
And I awoke and found me here
  On the cold hill's side.

And this is why I sojourn here
  Alone and palely loitering;
Though the sedge is wither'd from the Lake
  And no birds sing.

'How fever'd is the man, who cannot look'

'You cannot eat your cake and have it too.' —
Proverb

How fever'd is the man, who cannot look
  Upon his mortal days with temperate
  blood,
Who vexes all the leaves of his life's book,
  And robs his fair name of its maidenhood;
It is as if the rose should pluck herself,
  Or the ripe plum finger its misty bloom,
As if a Naiad, like a meddling elf,
  Should darken her pure grot with muddy
  gloom,
But the rose leaves herself upon the briar,
  For winds to kiss and grateful bees to feed,
And the ripe plum still wears its dim attire,
  The undisturbed lake has crystal space,
  Why then should man, teasing the world
  for grace,
Spoil his salvation for a fierce miscreed?

'If by dull rhymes our English must be chain'd'

If by dull rhymes our English must be
  chain'd,
And, like Andromeda, the Sonnet sweet
Fetter'd, in spite of pained loveliness,
Let us find out, if we must be constrain'd,
Sandals more interwoven and complete
To fit the naked foot of Poesy:
Let us inspect the Lyre, and weigh the stress

Of every chord, and see what may be gain'd
By ear industrious, and attention meet;
Misers of sound and syllable, no less
Than Midas of his coinage, let us be
Jealous of dead leaves in the bay wreath
    crown;
So, if we may not let the Muse be free,
She will be bound with garlands of her own.

Faery Songs

1

Shed no tear! oh shed no tear!
The flower will bloom another year.
Weep no more! oh weep no more!
Young buds sleep in the root's white core.
Dry your eyes! oh dry your eyes!
For I was taught in Paradise
To ease my breast of melodies —
                         Shed no tear.

Overhead! look overhead!
'Mong the blossoms white and red —
Look up, look up. I flutter now
On this flush pomegranate bough.
See me! 'tis this silvery bill
Ever cures the good man's ill.
Shed no tear! Oh shed no tear!
The flower will bloom another year.
Adieu, adieu! — I fly, adieu!
I vanish in the heaven's blue —
                       Adieu! Adieu!

2

Ah! woe is me! poor Silver-wing!
  That I must chant thy lady's dirge,
And death to this fair haunt of spring,
Of melody, and streams of flowery verge, —
    Poor Silver-wing! ah! woe is me!
      That I must see
These blossoms snow upon thy lady's pall!
  Go, pretty page, and in her ear
  Whisper that the hour is near.
  Softly tell her not to fear
Such calm favonian burial!
  Go, pretty page! and soothly tell, —
  The blossoms hang by a melting spell,
And fall they must ere a star wink thrice
    Upon her closèd eyes,
That now in vain are weeping their last tears
  At sweet life leaving, and these arbours
    green, —
Rich dowry from the Spirit of the
    Spheres, —
      Alas! poor Queen!

Spenserian Stanzas on Charles Armitage Brown

I

He is to weet a melancholy carle:
Thin in the waist, with bushy head of hair,
As hath the seeded thistle when in parle
It holds the Zephyr, ere it sendeth fair
Its light balloons into the summer air;
Therto his beard had not begun to bloom,

489

No brush had touch'd his chin or razor
  sheer;
No care had touch'd his cheek with mortal
  doom,
But new he was and bright as scarf from
  Persian loom.

II

Ne cared he for wine, or half-and-half
Ne cared he for fish or flesh or fowl,
And sauces held he worthless as the chaff;
He's deigned the swine-head at the wassail-
  bowl;
Ne with lewd ribbalds sat he cheek by jowl;
Ne with sly Lemans in the scorner's chair;
But after water-brooks this Pilgrim's soul
Panted, and all his food was woodland air
Though he would oft-times feast on gilliflow-
  ers rare.

III

The slang of cities in no wise he knew,
Tipping the wink to him was heathen Greek;
He sipp'd no olden Tom or ruin blue,
Or nantz or cherry-brandy drank full meek
By many a damsel hoarse and rouge of
  cheek;
Nor did he know each aged watchman's
  beat,
Nor in obscured purlieus would he seek
For curled Jewesses, with ankles neat,

Who as they walk abroad make tinkling with
  their feet.

Ode on Indolence

'They toil not, neither do they spin.'

One morn before me were three figures seen,
  With bowèd necks, and joinèd hands, side-
    faced;
And one behind the other stepp'd serene,
  In placid sandals, and in white robes
    graced;
    They pass'd, like figures on a marble urn,
  When shifted round to see the other side;
They came again; as when the urn once more
    Is shifted round, the first seen shades
      return;
  And they were strange to me, as may betide
With vases, to one deep in Phidian lore.

How is it, Shadows! that I knew ye not?
  How came ye muffled in so hush a mask?
Was it a silent deep-disguisèd plot
  To steal away, and leave without a task
    My idle days? Ripe was the drowsy hour;
  The blissful cloud of summer-indolence
Benumb'd my eyes; my pulse grew less and
    less;
    Pain had no sting, and pleasure's wreath
      no flower:
  O, why did ye not melt, and leave my sense
Unhaunted quite of all but — nothingness?

A third time pass'd they by, and, passing,
    turn'd
  Each one the face a moment whiles to me;
Then faded, and to follow them I burn'd
  And ached for wings, because I knew the
    three;
    The first was a fair Maid, and Love her
      name;
  The second was Ambition, pale of cheek,
And ever watchful with fatiguèd eye;
    The last, whom I love more, the more of
      blame
  Is heap'd upon her, maiden most
    unmeek, —
I knew to be my demon Poesy.

They faded, and, forsooth! I wanted wings:
  O folly! What is Love? and where is it?
And for that poor Ambition! it springs
  From a man's little heart's short fever-fit;
    For Poesy! — no, — she has not a joy, —
At least for me, — so sweet as drowsy
    noons,
And evenings steep'd in honey'd indolence;
    O, for an age so shelter'd from annoy,
  That I may never know how change the
    moons,
Or hear the voice of busy common-sense!

And once more came they by; — alas! where-
    fore?

My sleep had been embroider'd with dim
    dreams;
My soul had been a lawn besprinkled o'er
    With flowers, and stirring shades; and
    baffled beams:
      The morn was clouded, but no shower
      fell,
    Tho' in her lids hung the sweet tears of
    May;
The open casement press'd a new-leaved
    vine,
    Let in the budding warmth and throstle's
    lay;
      O Shadows! 'twas a time to bid farewell!
Upon your skirts had fallen no tears of mine.

So, ye three Ghosts, adieu! Ye cannot raise
    My head cool-bedded in the flowery grass;
For I would not be dieted with praise,
    A pet-lamb in a sentimental farce!
      Fade softly from my eyes, and be once
      more
    In masque-like figures on the dreamy urn;
Farewell! I yet have visions for the night,
    And for the day faint visions there is store;
Vanish, ye Phantoms! from my idle spright,
    Into the clouds, and never more return!

A Party of Lovers

Pensive they sit, and roll their languid eyes,
Nibble their toast and cool their tea with
    sighs;

Or else forget the purpose of the night,
Forget their tea, forget their appetite.
See, with cross'd arms they sit — Ah! happy
    crew,
The fire is going out and no one rings
For coals, and therefore no coals Betty
    brings.
A fly is in the milk-pot. Must he die
Circled by a humane society?
No, no; there, Mr. Werter takes his spoon,
Inserts it, dips the handle, and lo! soon
The little straggler, sav'd from perils dark,
Across the teaboard draws a long wet mark.

Romeo! Arise, take snuffers by the handle,
There's a large cauliflower in each candle.
A winding sheet — ah, me! I must away
To No. 7, just beyond the circus gay.
Alas, my friend, your coat sits very well;
Where may your Tailor live? I may not tell.
O pardon me. I'm absent now and then.
Where *might* my Tailor live? I say again
I cannot tell, let me no more be teased;
He lives in Wapping, might live where he
    pleased.

'The day is gone'

The day is gone, and all its sweets are gone!
  Sweet voice, sweet lips, soft hand, and
    softer breast,
Warm breath, light whisper, tender semi-
    tone,

Bright eyes, accomplish'd shape, and
　　lang'rous waist!
Faded the flower and all its budded charms,
　　Faded the sight of beauty from my eyes,
Faded the shape of beauty from my arms,
　　Faded the voice, warmth, whiteness, para-
　　　dise —
Vanish'd unseasonably at shut of eve,
　　When the dusk holiday — or holinight
Of fragrant-curtain'd love begins to weave
　　The woof of darkness thick, for hid delight;
But, as I've read love's missal through to-
　　day,
He'll let me sleep, seeing I fast and pray.

Lines to Fanny

What can I do to drive away
Remembrance from my eyes? for they have
　　seen,
Ay, an hour ago, my brilliant Queen!
Touch has a memory. O say, love, say,
What can I do to kill it and be free
In my old liberty?
When every fair one that I saw was fair
Enough to catch me in but half a snare,
Not keep me there:
When, howe'er poor or particolour'd things,
My muse had wings,
And ever ready was to take her course
Whither I bent her force,
Unintellectual, yet divine to me; —
Divine, I say! — What sea-bird o'er the sea

Is a philosopher the while he goes
Winging along where the great water throes?
How shall I do
To get anew
Those moulted feathers, and so mount once
    more
Above, above
The reach of fluttering Love,
And make him cower lowly while I soar?
Shall I gulp wine? No, that is vulgarism,
A heresy and schism,
Foisted into the canon-law of love; —
No, — wine is only sweet to happy men;
More dismal cares
Seize on me unawares, —
Where shall I learn to get my peace again?
To banish thoughts of that most hateful land,
Dungeoner of my friends, that wicked strand
Where they were wreck'd and live a wreckèd
    life;
That monstrous region, whose dull rivers
    pour,
Ever from their sordid urns unto the shore,
Unown'd of any weedy-hairèd gods;
Whose winds, all zephyrless, hold scourging
    rods,
Iced in the great lakes, to afflict mankind;
Whose rank-grown forests, frosted, black,
    and blind,
Would fright a Dryad; whose harsh herbaged
    meads

Make lean and lank the starv'd ox while he
    feeds;
There bad flowers have no scent, birds no
    sweet song,
And great unerring Nature once seems
    wrong.

O, for some sunny spell
To dissipate the shadows of this hell!
Say they are gone, — with the new dawning
    light
Steps forth my lady bright!
O, let me once more rest
My soul upon that dazzling breast!
Let once again these aching arms be placed,
The tender gaolers of thy waist!
And let me feel that warm breath here and
    there
To spread a rapture in my very hair, —
O, the sweetness of the pain!
Give me those lips again!
Enough! Enough! it is enough for me
To dream of thee!

To Fanny

Physician Nature! let my spirit blood!
O ease my heart of verse and let me rest:
Throw me upon thy Tripod, till the flood
Of stifling numbers ebbs from my full breast.
A theme! a theme! great nature! give a theme;
        Let me begin my dream.
I come — I see thee, as thou standest there,

497

Beckon me not into the wintry air.

Ah! dearest love, sweet home of all my fears,
And hopes, and joys, and panting
    miseries, —
To-night, if I may guess, thy beauty wears
        A smile of such delight,
        As brilliant and as bright,
As when with ravish'd, aching, vassal eyes,
        Lost in soft amaze,
          I gaze, I gaze!

Who now, with greedy looks, eats up my
    feast?
What stare outfaces now my silver moon?
Ah! keep that hand unravish'd at the least;
        Let, let, the amorous burn —
        But, pr'ythee, do not turn
The current of your heart from me so soon.
        O! save, in charity,
        The quickest pulse for me.

Save it for me, sweet love! though music
    breathe
Voluptuous visions into the warm air,
Though swimming through the dance's
    dangerous wreath:
        Be like an April day,
        Smiling and cold and gay,
A temperate lily, temperate as fair;
        Then, Heaven! there will be
        A warmer June for me.

Why, this — you'll say, my Fanny! is not true:
Put your soft hand upon your snowy side,
Where the heart beats: confess — 'tis noth-
  ing new —
        Must not a woman be
        A feather on the sea,
Sway'd to and fro by every wind and tide?
        Of as uncertain speed
        As blow-ball from the mead?

I know it — and to know it is despair
To one who loves you as I love, sweet Fanny!
Whose heart goes flutt'ring for you every-
  where,
        Nor, when away you roam,
        Dare keep its wretched home,
Love, love alone, his pains severe and many:
        Then, loveliest! keep me free,
        From torturing jealousy.

Ah! if you prize my subdued soul above
The poor, the fading, brief pride of an hour;
Let none profane my Holy See of love,
        Or with a rude hand break
        The sacramental cake:
Let none else touch the just new-budded
  flower.
        If not — may my eyes close,
        Love! on their last repose.

To Fanny

I cry your mercy — pity — love! — ay, love!

499

Merciful love that tantalises not
One-thoughted, never-wandering, guileless
    love,
  Unmask'd, and being seen — without a
  blot!
O! let me have thee whole, — all — all — be
  mine!
  That shape, that fairness, that sweet minor
  zest
Of love, your kiss, — those hands, those eyes
  divine,
  That warm, white, lucent, million-pleasured
  breast, —
Yourself — your soul — in pity give me all,
  Withhold no atom's atom or I die,
Or living on, perhaps, your wretched thrall,
  Forget, in the mist of idle misery,
Life's purposes, — the palate of my mind
Losing its gust, and my ambition blind!

  'This living hand, now warm and capable'
This living hand, now warm and capable
Of earnest grasping, would, if it were cold
And in the icy silence of the tomb,
So haunt thy days and chill thy dreaming
  nights
That thou would[st] wish thine own heart
  dry of blood
So in my veins red life might stream again,
And thou be conscience-calm'd — see here
  it is —
I hold it towards you.

'Bright Star, would I were stedfast as thou art'

Bright Star, would I were stedfast as thou
    art —
  Not in lone splendor hung aloft the night
And watching, with eternal lids apart,
  Like nature's patient, sleepless Eremite,
The moving waters at their priestlike task
    Of pure ablution round earth's human
    shores,
Or gazing on the new soft-fallen masque
    Of snow upon the mountains and the
    moors.
No — yet still stedfast, still unchangeable,
    Pillow'd upon my fair love's ripening
    breast,
To feel for ever its soft swell and fall,
  Awake for ever in a sweet unrest,
Still, still to hear her tender-taken breath,
And so live ever — or else swoon to death.

Two or three Posies
From a Letter to His Sister

Two or three Posies
With two or three simples —
Two or three Noses
With two or three pimples —
Two or three wise men
And two or three ninny's —
Two or three purses
And two or three guineas —
Two or three raps

At two or three doors —
Two or three naps
Of two or three hours —
Two or three Cats
And two or three mice —
Two or three sprats
At a very great price —
Two or three sandies
And two or three tabbies —
Two or three dandies
And two Mrs. — — mum!
Two or three Smiles
And two or three frowns —
Two or three Miles
To two or three towns —
Two or three pegs
For two or three bonnets —
Two or three dove eggs
To hatch into sonnets.

'When they were come unto the Faery's Court'

When they were come unto the Faery's Court
They rang — no one at home; all gone to
 sport
And dance and kiss and love as faeries do,
For faeries be, as humans, lovers true.
Amid the woods they were, so lone and wild,
Where even the robin feels himself exiled,
And where the very brooks as if afraid
Hurry along to some less magic shade.
'No one at home!' the fretful princess cried,
'And all for nothing such a dre[a]ry ride,

And all for nothing my new diamond cross,
No one to see my Persian feathers toss,
No one to see my Ape, my Dwarf, my Fool,
Or how I pace my Otaheitan mule.
Ape, Dwarf and Fool, why stand you gaping
    there?
Burst the door open, quick — or I declare
I'll switch you soundly and in pieces tear.'
The Dwarf began to tremble and the Ape
Star'd at the Fool, the Fool was all agape,
The Princess grasp'd her switch, but just in
    time
The dwarf with piteous face began to rhyme.
'O mighty Princess did you ne'er hear tell
What your poor servants know but too too
    well?
Know you the three great crimes in faery
    land?
The first, alas! poor Dwarf, I understand —
I made a whipstock of a faery's wand —
The next is snoring in their company —
The next, the last, the direst of the three
Is making free when they are not at home.
I was a Prince — a baby prince — my doom
You see, I made a whipstock of a wand —
My top has henceforth slept in faery land.
He was a Prince, the Fool, a grown up Prince,
But he has never been a King's son since
He fell a-snoring at a faery Ball —
Your poor Ape was a prince and he, poor
    thing,
Picklock'd a faery's boudoir — now no king,

But ape — so pray your highness stay awhile;
'Tis sooth indeed, we know it to our
    sorrow —
Persist and *you* may be an ape tomorrow —'
While the Dwarf spake the Princess all for
    spite
Peel'd the brown hazel twig to lily white,
Clench'd her small teeth, and held her lips
    apart,
Try'd to look unconcern'd with beating
    heart.
They saw her highness had made up her
    mind
And quaver'd like the reeds before the wind,
And they had had it, but, O happy chance!
The Ape for very fear began to dance
And grinn'd as all his ugliness did ache —
She staid her vixen fingers for his sake,
He was so very ugly: then she took
Her pocket glass mirror and began to look
First at herself and [then] at him and then
She smil'd at her own beauteous face again.
Yet for all this — for all her pretty face
She took it in her head to see the place.
Women gain little from experience
Either in Lovers, husbands or expense.
The more the beauty, the more fortune too,
Beauty before the wide world never knew.
So each fair reasons — tho'; it oft miscarries.
She thought *her* pretty face would please the
    fa[e]ries.
'My darling Ape I won't whip you today —

Give me the Picklock, sirrah, and go play.'
They all three wept — but counsel was as
    vain
As crying cup biddy to drops of rain.
Yet lingeringly did the sad Ape forth draw
The Picklock from the Pocket in his Jaw.
The Princess took it and dismounting
    straight
Trip'd in blue silver'd slippers to the gate
And touch'd the wards, the Door full
    cou[r]teou[s]ly
Opened — she enter'd with her servants
    three.
Again it clos'd and there was nothing seen
But the Mule grazing on the herbage green.

End of Canto xii

Canto the XIII

The Mule no sooner saw himself alone
Than he prick'd up his Ears — and said 'well
    done!
At least, unhappy Prince, I may be free —
No more a Princess shall side-saddle me.
O King of Othaietè — tho'; a Mule
"Aye every inch a King" — tho' "Fortune's
    fool" —
Well done — for by what Mr. Dwarfy said
I would not give a sixpence for her head.'
Even as he spake he trotted in high glee
To the knotty side of an old Pollard tree
Aud rub['d] his sides against the mossed bark

505